Fight Against Idols

Svante Lundgren

Fight
Against
Idols

Erich Fromm on Religion, Judaism and the Bible

PETER LANG

Frankfurt am Main · Berlin · Bern · New York · Paris · Wien

Die Deutsche Bibliothek - CIP-Einheitsaufnahme

Lundgren, Svante:

Fight against idols : Erich Fromm on religion, judaism and the
bible / Svante Lundgren. - Frankfurt am Main ; Berlin ; Bern ;
New York ; Paris ; Wien : Lang, 1998
   ISBN 3-631-32757-9

ISBN 3-631-32757-9
US-ISBN 0-8204-3557-0

© Peter Lang GmbH
Europäischer Verlag der Wissenschaften
Frankfurt am Main 1998
All rights reserved.

Printed in Germany 1 2   4 5 6 7

To Frank and Jolanta

Be brave, and let us be brave together.
The Talmud

Author's Foreword

Living with Erich Fromm for one year has been an interesting and rewarding experience. I feel sorry for not ever having met him when he was alive.

Two persons have been of extreme importance for the writing of this book. My *Doktorvater* Professor Karl-Johan Illman suggested that I should do research on Fromm. It was an excellent suggestion which I did not hesitate to follow. Professor Illman has always been ready to discuss my work with me and to help me with useful advice.

Dr. Rainer Funk at the Erich Fromm Archives in Tübingen guided me to the essential material and always answered my many questions. I wish to express my gratitude to these two men, who both are not only eminent scholars but also true gentlemen.

I also want to thank other persons who have helped me. Susan Sinisalo has corrected my English manuscript. Many friends have encouraged me during my work. I dare not name any of these because of the risk that someone will be forgotten. They, and not least my wife and my children, have demonstrated to me the truth of Erich Fromm's claim that the only solution to man's existential dilemma is love.

Pargas, September 1997
Svante Lundgren

Contents

1. Introduction

Erich Fromm was "one of the world's outstanding thinkers and writers".[1] He wrote books that "were eagerly bought not only in bookstores but from the racks of drugstores and airport newsstands".[2] It has been claimed that Fromm's "impact and relevance to the humanities and social sciences in the 1950's, 1960's, and 1970's is second to none".[3]

But Fromm was also an intellectual outsider. In the psychoanalytical movement he was a dissident who always went his own way. As a humanist Marxist he had many allies but the so called Marxist orthodoxy condemned him with the intensity it turned on anyone expressing the obvious fact that Soviet communism was as far from the ideals of Marx as the church of the Inquisition was from the gospel of Christ. In academic circles Fromm was the object of suspicion because he wrote books that could also be understood the reading public at large.

Erich Fromm was born in Frankfurt on 23 March 1900 into an orthodox Jewish family. In 1922 he got his doctorate in sociology from the University of Heidelberg. During the 1920's he received psychoanalytical training in Munich and Berlin. In 1930 he started to work at the Institut für Sozialforschung in Frankfurt (the Frankfurter School), from 1934 in New York. In 1938 he left the Institute and three years later published his first, and perhaps most famous book, *Escape from Freedom.* He saw patients, wrote and lectured at several universities in the USA. In 1949 he moved to Mexico City, where he became professor at the National University and founded a Psychoanalytical Institute. For 25 years he divided his time between Mexico and the USA, where he lectured and participated in the public debate, in politics and in the peace movement. He was a democratic socialist opposed to Soviet communism and very critical of the materialist Western society that made man into a machine and a commodity on the market. In 1974 he moved to live permanently in Locarno in Switzerland, where he had earlier spent several summers. *To have or to be?* that appeared in 1976 became a bestseller and made Fromm well-known in the part of the world

---

[1]Rubins: *Karen Horney,* 121.
[2]Coser: *Refugee Scholars in America,* 74. A theologian has complained that Fromm's best seller *The Art of Loving* was more often found on the desks and bedside tables of students of theology than the Old or New Testament. (Stählin: "Die Kunst des Liebens und der christliche Glaube. Gespräch und Auseinandersetzung mit Erich Fromm" *WuD* 18 (1985), 255)
[3]Burston: "A Profile of Erich Fromm" *Social Science and Modern Society* 28 (No.4, 1991), 85.

he had left as a young man but to which he had now returned. He died at his home on 18 March 1980, five days before his 80th birthday.[4]

Fromm is best known for his popular writings, which in addition to *Escape from Freedom* and *To have or to be?*, include *The Sane Society*, his all-time best seller *The Art of Loving*, and many others. But Fromm was not only a popular writer, for he made significant contributions to social psychology and characterology. He was one of the first to combine psychoanalysis and Marxism, and his empirical study of *Social Character in a Mexican Village* (together with Michael Maccoby) was a historic work.

1.1. The aim and structure of the study

To establish the aim of this study we will begin by stating what the aim is not. The aim of this study is not to describe and analyze the religious belief of Erich Fromm. This has been admirably done by Rainer Funk.[5] The aim is to analyze not Fromm's religious thought but Fromm's thoughts about religion.

This is not only a study about what Fromm thought of Protestantism or mysticism, about his writings on Buddhism or new religious movements, about his attitude to his own Jewish tradition or his interpretation of the Bible. It is all this and more. The aim of the study is to give an overall picture of Fromm's attitude to religion, Judaism and the Bible.

This means that for considerations of space not every theme can be explored in all its details. The reader especially interested in certain themes or aspects of this study will find references to special studies on specific subjects.

This introductory chapter will be followed by a chapter on Fromm's view of religion: his definition of religion, his broad notion of religious experience and his utterances about established religions with the exception of Judaism, which will be reserved for the next chapter. Buddhism, Christianity and mysticism are the focal points of this chapter.

---

[4]There is no big detailed biography of Fromm, although several books have biographical chapters. For the best information about Fromm's life one should consult Rainer Funk's small biography, *Erich Fromm*, of 1983.
[5]Funk: *Mut zum Menschen*. The subtitle of this book is *Erich Fromms Denken und Werk, seine humanistische Religion und Ethik.*

The chapter on Judaism begins with a biographical description. It describes the young Fromm's career as a believing Jew and his development away from Jewish praxis. Then follows an analysis of his statements on the most important Jewish issues, including his doctoral dissertation of 1922 and his political activity in the Near Eastern conflict.

The chapter on Fromm's interpretation of the Bible shows the massive impact og the Books of the Prophets on his thinking. In the last chapter we will sum up the conclusions of the study.

1.2. Material and method

The prime material for this study consists of the complete statements of Erich Fromm, be they in published works, unpublished manuscripts, personal letters, lectures or interviews. Finding this material is nowadays very easy thanks to Rainer Funk, the Executor of Fromm's literary estate. Funk has established The Erich Fromm Archives in Tübingen where everything written by and almost everything written about Fromm is preserved.

Rainer Funk has also edited the German *Gesamtausgabe (GA)* of Fromm's writings in ten volumes. It is not a true *Gesamtausgabe* because it does not contain everything Fromm published, but it does include all the major works. The tenth volume contains an extensive index and a register of all his published works, both indispensable for any serious Frommscholar. Funk has also published eight volumes of the unpublished material that Fromm left for posterity, *Schriften aus dem Nachlass*. Four of these volumes have also been published in English.

I have tried always to read and quote a work in its original language. Sometimes this has not been possible. Three of the Nachlass-volumes are German translations of manuscripts I have not bothered to study in the original at the Archives, because they are not of any great importance to my subject. On three occasions I have decided to stick to an English translation of works originally published in another language. I have read *Die Entwicklung der Christusdogma* in English translation as *The Dogma of Christ*, because the translation was revised and thus sanctioned by Fromm.[6] And Fromm's essay "Humanismo y Psicoanálisis" originally in Spanish I have read in English translation, as "Humanism and Psychoanalysis", because the translation was made by Fromm himself. The reason why I have read *For the Love of Life* in English translation

---

[6]See Fromm's preface in *The Dogma of Christ*, viif.

and not in the original German (some of the essays I have read in the original in the *Gesamtausgabe*) is pure convenience.

The quotaton in this work are always given exactly as they are to be found in the source quoted, though the German "ß" is rendered with "ss". Some of the quotations from letters contain misprints, misspellings and linguistic errors. I have pointed out the misprints and misspellings with [sic] and corrected some of the linguistic errors by, e.g., inserting a missing word. Anything not in the original is always given within [square brackets]. On the few occasions I have quoted transcripts of lectures given by Fromm I have made a few corrections when it is clear that the person making the transcript has made a mistake, e.g. by writing "God" instead of "god".

The method used in this study is basically descriptive. I want to describe how Fromm expressed his thoughts on matters dealing with religion in general and Judaism in specific. The description is also genetic in that I want to show the development and the changes that occurred in Fromm's opinions during his quite long lifetime. Some of the issues involved did not call for much comment from him and it is impossible to compare, e.g., the Fromm of the 1950's with the old Fromm. But on some issues it is easy to follow the evolution in his opinions.

Sometimes I compare Fromm's statements with those of others, establish his possible influences. On other occasions, as in the case of some of his exegetical statements, I want to see how his theories are viewed by experts in the field in question. Because Fromm was the object of widespread critique, I often describe this critique and evaluate its tenability.

1.3. Review of research

Erich Fromm is a famous person and has been the object of many studies. A bibliography of the literature about him published in early 1996 comprises about 3,250 titles, from short newspaper items to large monographis.[7]

Fromm has also aroused considerable interest among Christian theologians. There are many studies about his critique of traditional religions, many of them apologetical, i.e. they defend Christianity against Fromm's critique. Other studies compare Fromm's thoughts with those of different theologians, like Tillich and

---

[7]Funk: *Bibliography of the Literature about Erich Fromm.*

Niebuhr. The studies about his relation to Judaism are not numerous, but there are a few.

So far as I know, there is only one book that comes very close to mine in topic and perspective: Jürgen Hardeck's *Vernunft und Liebe. Religion im Werk von Erich Fromm* giving an overall description of Fromm's utterances on the subject of religion. But there are several differences between Hardeck's work and mine. Hardeck's is not as detailed, and he does not at all deal with the minor themes, the statements about different religious topics that are not so frequent or important. In this sense my study is more total in its approach. The second difference is that Hardeck's material is the published works of Fromm (in German translation). He has not studied the unpublished material, such as the letters.

Although much has been written about Fromm, there is still room for a book such as this aiming to describe the attitude in all its variety of Erich Fromm to the multiple matter of religion.

2. View of Religion

2.1. What is religion?

Fromm was extremely interested in religion. He wrote several books on different religious topics, and in his other works he touched on religion very frequently. For him religion was something broader than is often meant by the term.[1] He rejected the normal definitions of religion in which "higher powers" play a central part as being too narrow, describing only the authoritarian type of religion.[2] Fromm's definition of religion is "any group-shared system of thought and action that offers the individual a frame of orientation and an object of devotion".[3]

On examining his view of religion one has to distinguish between the young and the mature Fromm. In *Die Entwicklung der Christusdogma* of 1930 he treats religion in a very Freudian way, which is not surprising because it was written during the short period when he was an orthodox Freudian. Here he sees religion as both a narcotic and an illusion, because it offers fantasy satisfaction of needs that cannot find real satisfaction. At the same time religion functions as a deterrent to an active change of reality, and thus keeps the lower classes from demanding their rights. "To sum up, religion has a threefold function: for all mankind, consolation for the privations exacted by life; for the great majority of men, encouragement to accept emotionally their class situation; and for the ruling classes, relief from guilt feelings caused by the suffering of those whom they oppress."[4]

---

[1]This is the reason why he called Marx an "atheistic-religious" philosopher. (Fromm: "Einige post-marxsche und post-freudsche Gedanken über Religion und Religiosität" *Concilium* 8 (1972), 472) In the same essay (op.cit., 473) Fromm stated that Freud - contrary to Marx - was "in keiner Weise ein religiöser Mensch", while he had earlier claimed that Freud's attitude of opposing religion in the name of ethics "can be termed 'religious'". (Fromm: *Psychoanalysis and Religion*, 20) And in a lecture held in 1953 he called Freud a "profoundly religious man in a deeper sense". (Fromm: "Mental Health in Contemporary Society" Lecture 6.1 1953 at HUC - JIR)

[2]Fromm: *Psychoanalysis and Religion*, 34. Cf. p. 17-20 for a critical discussion of Jung's definition of religion.

[3]Fromm: *To have or to be?*, 135. The same definition is given in slightly different words in Fromm: *Psychoanalysis and Religion*, 21.

[4]Fromm: *The Dogma of Christ* 14, see p. 11-14. Five years later - at the time when he was moving away from orthodox Freudianism - Fromm's view of religion was still very negative as can be seen from his letter to Max Horkheimer 17.7 1935. (Horkheimer: *Gesammelte Schriften* *15*, 371-374.

Twenty years later Fromm returned to the question of the function of religion. Now his attitude to religion is totally different.[5] There is no more talk about either narcotic or illusion. He now sees religion as an expression of man's real existential needs. According to him, there are five basic needs common to all men. These are the need for relatedness, transcendence, rootedness, sense of identity, and the need for a frame of orientation and devotion.[6] The task of a religion is to satisfy these needs, especially the need for a frame of orientation and an object of devotion giving meaning to man's existence and to his position in the world. Religion is thus an expression of a basic human need, and therefore all human cultures have, always had, and will always have a religion.[7] "Religion is the formalized and elaborate answer to man's existence..."[8] All people need a religion, in one form or another. Therefore it is not a question of religion or not, but of what kind of religion - good or bad, one that furthers man's development, the unfolding of his human powers, or one that paralyzes them.[9]

Man's need for a frame of orientation and an object of devotion is, in Fromm's opinion, desperate. "We cannot live in this world without trying to make some sense of it. The sense may be nonsense but subjectively the nonsense is sense. It can be better or worse but it must be something, and again you have all the whole range from the most irrational to the most rational frames of orientation, and from the most admirable to the most terrible objects of devotion."[10]

Sometimes there is a discrepancy between the real and the "official" religion of a person. "If, for instance, a man worships power while professing a religion of love, the religion of power is his secret religion, while his so-called official religion, for example Christianity, is only an ideology."[11] This can be true not only for individuals, but also for a whole society. Thus the Western world is not, in Fromm's opinion, in reality Christian. Its conversion to Christianity was only

---

[5]It is unbelievable that in a book written in 1977 Pöhlmann, when dealing with Fromm's critique of religion, only analyzes Fromm's work from 1930 and does not even mention what he later wrote about religion. (Pöhlmann: *Der Atheismus oder der Streit um Gott*, 133-135)
[6]Fromm: *The Sane Society*, 27-66. Cf. Fromm: "Values, Psychology, and Human Existence". In: Maslow (Ed.): *New Knowledge in Human Values*, 151-162. For a stimulating, although sometimes one-sided attempt to present Christian faith as a mature answer to these basic needs, see Forsyth - Beniskos: "Biblical Faith and Erich Fromm's Theory of Personality" *RUO* 40 (1970), 69-91.
[7]Fromm: *To have or to be?*, 135; Fromm: *Psychoanalysis and Religion*, 21.
[8]Fromm: "Psychoanalysis and Zen Buddhism". In: Suzuki - Fromm - de Martino: *Zen Buddhism and Psychoanalysis*, 91.
[9]Fromm: *Psychoanalysis and Religion*, 25-28; Fromm: *Die Pathologie der Normalität*, 34.
[10]Fromm: "Beyond Egotistical Religion". Lecture in 1957.
[11]Fromm: *To have or to be?*, 136.

superficial. Christianity has been the official ideology, but deep in its heart the Western world has been pagan, worshipping power and success.[12]

2.1.1. Progressive and regressive religions

As a non-theistic humanist Fromm looks at religion from a this-worldly perspective. What is important is not whether the dogmatic claims of a religion are true or not, but whether a religion promotes freedom, personal growth, and a striving towards social justice. Those religions which do this are progressive, those which do not are regressive. "If religious teachings contribute to the growth, strength, freedom, and happiness of their believers, we see the fruits of love. If they contribute to the constriction of human potentialities, to unhappiness and lack of productivity, they cannot be born of love, regardless of what the dogma intends to convey."[13] On the question of what religious answers to man's quest for meaning and devotion are better or worse, Fromm emphasized that "better" and "worse" must always be considered "from the standpoint of man's nature and his development."[14]

One saying quoted by Fromm on different occasions[15] is this, made by Abbé Pire: "What matters is not the difference between believers and unbelievers, but between those who care and those who do not care." People who care for their own freedom, for social justice and for the future of mankind - that is what Fromm is interested in. Therefore he admired people of different kinds, from history the anticlerical Karl Marx and the monk Meister Eckhardt, from his own time the believer Albert Schweitzer and the aggressive atheist Bertrand Russell. Though their religious beliefs were different, they were all humanists.

Religions try to give an answer to the existential question of man, which according to Fromm is how to overcome the separateness of man. According to him, this is done in two fundamentally opposite ways. One is characterized by regression to a preconscious unity with nature. Examples of this are the old

---

[12]op.cit., 139-146. Cf. Fromm: *Psychoanalysis and Religion*, 28f.

[13]Fromm: *Psychoanalysis and Religion*, 64.

[14]Fromm: "Values, Psychology, and Human Existence". In: Maslow (Ed.): *New Knowledge in Human Values*, 162.

[15]Quoted from Foreword II - written in 1967 - to Fromm: *Psychoanalysis and Religion*, viii. In *You shall be as gods*, 53f., *The Revolution of Hope*, 135, and *On Being Human*, 93, Fromm gives the same quotation in slightly different words.

German religion and animistic and totemistic religions. This answer to man's existential problem can be found not only in history. Although official totemism and animism are rare today, they exist, but under other names. Fromm mentions pathetic patriotism and clinging to an ideology (e.g. fascism or Stalinism) as examples of modern totemism.[16] The other solution to man's existential dilemma is to try to develop the human capacity of reason and love, and to find a new harmony between man and nature, and between man and man. The great world religions are examples of this.[17]

Fromm considers the period between 1500 BCE and 500 BCE as a remarkable one in human history that produced several great teachers: Ikhnaton in Egypt, Moses, Lao-tse in China, the Buddha in India, Zarathustra in Persia, the philosophers in Greece, and the prophets in Israel. Christianity and Islam later built on the foundations laid by Moses and the prophets during this period.[18]

What are the common denominators which Fromm commends in listing these religions? According to him, they give the right answer to man's basic problem of transcending separateness and achieving unity. The solution lies in the "full developement of all *human* forces, of the humanity within oneself".[19] On another occasion Fromm writes about the capacity of the religions to double liberation - from the dominance of greed and from the shackles of illusion.[20] To overcome greed, to love one's neighbor and to know the truth are said to be the common goals of all Western and Eastern philosophies and religions.[21] The great teachers all preached the unity of man, reason, love and justice as the goals man must strive for.[22] As an "approximate description" of the common core of the

---

[16]Fromm: *Psychoanalysis and Religion*, 31f.

[17]Fromm: "Psychoanalysis and Zen Buddhism". In: Suzuki - Fromm - de Martino: *Zen Buddism and Psychoanalysis*, 92-94. Cf. Fromm: *Beyond the Chains of Illusion*, 157f., 174f.; Fromm: *The Sane Society*, 49f.

[18]See, e.g. Fromm: *The Heart of Man*, 118f. The list of religions given by Fomm differs slightly from one work to another, but the basic thing is that practically all the so-called world religions are included. Hinduism - or "Indian Vedic religion" - is mentioned in e.g. Fromm: *The Art of Being*, 6, and Confucius and Quetzalcoatl in Fromm: *The Sane Society*, 51, 354. Concerning Quetzalcoatl Fromm said in a lecture in 1957 ("Beyond Egotistical Religion") that the wide-spread opinion that the religion of the Aztecs was a very cruel one might be simplified, and that the original teaching of Quetzalcoatl - of which we unfortunately know very little - perhaps resembled that of Christ. Fromm added that this is just a theory, but one "which has impressed me quite a bit".

[19]Fromm: *The Heart of Man*, 118. Cf. Fromm: *The Art of Human Destructiveness*, 257f.

[20]Fromm: *The Art of Being*, 6.

[21]Fromm: *The Revolution of Hope*, 89.

[22]Fromm: *The Sane Society*, 354.

humanistic religions and philosophies Fromm presents the following: "... man must strive to recognize the truth and can be fully human only to the extent to which he succeeds in this task. He must be independent and free, an end in himself and not the means for any other person's purposes. He must relate himself to his fellow man lovingly. If he has no love, he is an empty shell even if his were all power, wealth, and intelligence. Man must know the difference between good and evil, he must learn to listen to the voice of his conscience and to be able to follow it."[23]

Some may find it strange that Fromm stresses the similarities between the different religions so strongly. He has explicitly stated that the differences between the religions "are by far not as great as the adherents of these religions believe and want others to believe".[24] But we must remember that he totally ignores dogmatics, and only takes into account the ethics and the practical results of the teaching of a religion.[25] The essence is the same; what differs is the language. The conceptualizations differ, but they all point to the same reality. Some - like Moses - speak of a supreme being, others - like Lao-tse and the Buddha - do not speak of a god at all, while the Greek philosophers speak of a principle or a primordial substance.[26]

2.1.2. Authoritarian and humanistic religions

Another distinction that Fromm makes is that between authoritarian and humanistic religions. This is a distinction that makes a division within the group of great world religions and even within one religion, i.e. within the scope of e.g. Christianity, both authoritarian and humanistic parts can be found. Authoritarian religions are characterized by the concept of a higher power outside man to which man should show obedience, reverence and worship; humanistic religions are centered on man and his possibility. Virtues in humanistic religions are strength and self-realization, in authoritarian religions powerlessness and subservience. The prevailing mood in humanistic religions is that of joy, in authoritarian

---

[23]Fromm: *Psychoanalysis and Religion*, 76.
[24]Fromm: "Beyond Egotistical Religion" (lecture in 1957).
[25]"In trying to give a picture of the human attitude underlying the thinking of Lao-tse, the Buddha, the Prophets, Socrates, Jesus, Spinoza, and the philosophers of the Enlightenment, one is struck by the fact that in spite of significant differences there is a core of ideas and norms common to all of these teachings." (Fromm: *Psychoanalysis and Religion*, 76) In *The Sane Society*, 69, Fromm writes that the great founders of religions "have postulated the same norms for human life, with only small and insignificant differences."
[26]Fromm: *Beyond the Chains of Illusion*, 171.

religions that of sorrow and guilt. While humanistic religion is characterized by humility, authoritarian religion is characterized by self-humiliation. In authoritarian religion man humiliates himself by projecting everything good on God and feels evil himself, a total sinner. "He is caught in a painful dilemma. The more he praises God, the emptier he becomes. The emptier he becomes, the more sinful he feels. The more sinful he feels, the more he praises his God..."[27] There is a big difference between humility and self-humilation. "To understand realistically and soberly how limited our power is is an essential part of wisdom and of maturity; to worship it is masochistic and self-destructive."[28]

Fromm thought - according to the Marxist view - that there was a correlation between the social structure and the kind of religion that was dominant in a certain society. Humanistic religion developed among poor, marginalized groups, while authoritarian religion was the result of religion allying itself with secular power. Christianity was an excellent example of this. In the beginning it was a religion of the poor masses and very humanistic, but once it had become the religion of the rulers, the authoritarian trend became dominant.[29]

Fromm's distinction between humanistic and authoritarian religion is problematic. According to him, God in humanistic religon "*is not a symbol of power over man but of man's own power... God is the image of man's higher self, a symbol of what man potentially is or ought to become...*"[30] Yet still Fromm counts early Christianity, for example, as a humanistic religion. But did Jesus and the first Christians really see God as only a symbol of man's own powers? And when, in the 1960's, Fromm sees a humanistic renaissance within both Catholicism and Protestantism (see 2.5.4.), it does not mean that Pope John XXIII or Karl Rahner have abandoned traditional theism and have seen God as a pure symbol. In sum, Fromm describes a humanistic religion as his ideal religion but in fact he counts as humanistic more forms of religion than just those that suit his description.[31]

Calvinism is, according to Fromm, an excellent example of an authoritarian religion,[32] while early Buddism, Taoism, the teachings of Isaiah, Jesus, Socrates

[27]Fromm: *Psychoanalysis and Religion*, 51.
[28]op.cit., 53.
[29]op.cit. 52f., cf. 48.
[30]op.cit., 49, cf. 37.
[31] Fromm's idea of God as a symbol of man's own powers is also problematic. Friedman has commented: "If man is a being made in the likeness of God and God is a symbol of the powers of man, we have a perfect circle!" (Friedman: *To Deny our Nothingness*, 234)
[32]Jeremias has claimed that the most prominent Calvinist theologian in the 20th century, Karl Barth, is an excellent example of Protestant authoritarianism. Jeremias quotes the beginning of

and Spinoza, certain trends in the Jewish and Christian religions (particularly mysticism) and the religion of Reason of the French Revolution are examples of humanistic religions.[33] In the history of mankind Fromm sees a humanistic line starting with the founders of the great religions, stretching over the Renaissance and Enlightenment, culminating in the humanist socialism founded by Marx and flourishing in the late 19th and early 20th century, "the most important genuine religious movement of the last hundred years".[34] This movement was betrayed when the socialist leaders were carried away by nationalist fever in 1914. Nationalism almost totally destroyed this non-theistic "religious" movement. "Only in small circles and among a few individuals did the humanist spiritual tradition continue; its greatest representatives in our times are men like Gandhi, Einstein, and Schweitzer."[35] Fromm could make the most fantastic comparisons. Once he compared the Buddha and Moses with the great artists and scientists as well as with Freud and Marx, praising them all as the destroyers of illusions and seekers of reality.[36]

Fromm's concept of humanistic and authoritarian religion has been heavily criticized by Walter Kaufmann, who demonstrates that there are also authoritarian traits in the religions Fromm counts as humanistic. His conclusion is: "There never has been any 'humanistic religion' in Fromm's sense: there have only been humanistic tendencies in most religions..."[37] Although Kaufmann is right in many of his observations, he makes one substantial mistake. Fromm never saw humanistic religion as a religion without any authority, but he did make a

---

Barth's *Der Römerbrief*, where Barth speaks of Paul as a slave of Christ, tied to his hands and feet (in the first edition of the book, in later editions Barth softened the language). Jeremias further calls Barth's distinction between Christianity and religion Christian racism. (Jeremias: *Die Theorie der Projektion im religionskritischen Denken Sigmund Freuds und Erich Fromms*, 196 n.141)

[33]Fromm: *Psychoanalysis and Religion*, 34-38. For a theologian's comment on Fromm's distinction between authoritarian and humanistic religion, see Sölle: *Die Hinreise*, 87-90. That Fromm sometimes included movements that he did not know enough about in the rank of humanistic religions is shown by the fact that - in the German version of *To have or to be?* (*GA II*, 383) - he mentions the Hutterites as an example of radical humanism. Jeremias (*Die Theorie der Projektion im religionskritiscken Denken Sigmund Freuds und Erich Fromms*, 377-381) and Hardeck (*Vernunft und Liebe*, 73) have shown that the Hutterites, despite many radical traits, in many respects represent an authoritarian religion.

[34]Fromm: *Beyond the Chains of Illusion*, 172.

[35]ibid. Cf. also pp.182-185.

[36]op.cit., 173.

[37]Kaufmann: *Critique of Religion and Philosophy*, 345, see p. 331-339. Similarly Banks: "A Neo-Freudian Critique of Religion: Erich Fromm on the Judaeo-Christian Tradition" *Religion* 5 (1975), 120f.

distinction between rational and irrational authority.[38] Rational authority is present in humanistic religion, irrational authority is not.[39] And when Kaufmann ironically writes that the prophets "did not tell man to 'develop his power of reason' but rather demanded obedience to God",[40] this must be contrasted with Fromm's claim that obedience to God is reverence for reason, conscience, law, moral and spiritual principles, and also the negation of submission to man.[41] Thus understood, obedience to God is not in conflict with developing one's own power of reason.

2.1.3. The reality beyond the religions

Religions are, in Fromm's opinion, different conceptualizations of a human experience, attempts to put into words something that is beyond our capacity to verbalize. "A concept can never adequately express the experience it refers to. It *points* to it, but it *is* not it. It is, as the Zen Buddhists say, 'the finger that points to the moon' - it is not the moon."[42] The advantage with concepts and symbols is that they permit people to communicate their experiences; the danger with them is that they easily lend themselves to an alienated use. People start to think that the finger is importnat, and after a while they lose sight of the moon.[43]

The moon the fingers try to point to, the reality beyond the conceptualizations of religions, Fromm sometimes calls x, sometimes the ONE. In the history of religion it has been expressed with several names: God, Brahman, Tao, Nirvana. Common to them all is the belief that there is the ONE as opposed to the manifoldness of things and phenomena, the ONE who "represents the supreme value and the supreme goal for man: the goal of finding union with the world through full development of his specifically human capacities of love and reason".[44]

---

[38]See, e.g., Fromm: *Man for Himself*, 9f.; Fromm: *The Sane Society*, 95-98; Fromm: "Psychoanalysis and Zen Buddhism". In: Suzuki - Fromm - de Martino: *Zen Buddhism and Psychoanalysis*, 120f., 124f.; Fromm: *To have or to be?*, 36-39.

[39]"Fromm ist kein 'Antiautoritärer' in dem Sinn, dass er jede Autorität ablehnen würde! Er betont die Notwendigkeit von Erziehung, von Vorbildern, von Lebe-Meistern und Lehrern..." (Hardeck: *Vernunft und Liebe*, 57)

[40]Kaufmann: *Critique of Religion and Philosophy*, 333.

[41]Fromm: *You shall be as gods*, 73.

[42]Fromm: *You shall be as gods*, 19.

[43]op.cit., 20; Fromm: "Beyond Egotistical Religion" (lecture in 1957).

[44]Fromm: *You shall be as gods*, 22. Cf. Fromm: Antwort auf das Referat von Prof. Dr. Auer zum Thema: "Gibt es eine Ethik ohne Religiosität?" (transcript).

On the level of thought, the principle of one-ness means developing one's reason so that one can see that behind the manifoldness of phenomena there is a unity. On the level of feeling it means the experience of solidarity between all human beings, that we are all one, that in every one of us is everyone else, as the Talmud so beautifully says, "Whoever saves one individual is as if he had saved all of humanity." (Sanh. IV, 5) On the level of devotion, the concept of one-ness means that there is one goal which is of supreme value - one "ultimate concern", as Tillich put it - and that is the full birth and full humanization of man, the full development of his capacity to love and to use his reason.[45]

The ONE has always been expressed and conceptualized in the categories of contemporary society. Therefore God in the Old Testament was seen as a tribal king, an absolute ruler, the king of Kings. But the Old Testament also expresses one very important thing, that this ONE is - unlike the idols - not a thing. It is a principle without a name that cannot be reproduced (see 4.4.). The history of Western religion is an effort to cleanse the concept of the ONE of its accidental-historical remnants. This has been especially successful in the mystical tradition.[46]

The intricate question, "Is God dead?" Fromm divides into two aspects: "Is the *concept* of God dead or is the *experience* to which the concept points, and the supreme *value* which it expresses, dead?"[47] The concepts are always conditioned by time, and in the present world the God-concept has lost its philosophical and social basis. The atheism of the 19th century made the same mistake as many religions, i.e. made the concept the main issue rather than the values which it symbolizes. A more central issue than the death of God is today, Fromm continues, the question whether man is dead.[48] "He is in danger of becoming more and more alienated, of losing sight of the real problems of human existence and of no longer being interested in the answer to these problems. If man continues in this direction, he will himself be dead, and the problem of God, as a concept or as a symbol of the highest value, will not be a problem any more."[49]

---

[45]Fromm: "Beyond Egotistical Religion" (lecture in 1957).

[46]Fromm: Antwort auf das Referat von Prof. Dr. Auer zum Thema: "Gibt es eine Ethik ohne Religiosität?" (transcript).

[47]Fromm: *You shall be as gods*, 228.

[48]When in an earlier work (*The Sane Society*, 360) Fromm wrote that the problem of the 19th century was that God is dead and the problem of the 20th century is that man is dead, Tillich asked: "Is there not a connection between the two problems?" (Tillich: "Erich Fromm's *Sane Society*" *Past Psych* 6 (1955), 16.

[49]Fromm: *You shall be as gods*, 229. Cf. Fromm: *Psychoanalysis and Religion*, 9; Fromm: "Die psychologischen und geistigen Probleme des Überflusses" *GA V*, 327f.; Fromm: *On*

This danger is the central issue today, Fromm proclaims. We need fundamental socio-economic changes and a humanistic renaissance focusing on the reality of experienced values rather than on the reality of concepts and words. And then Fromm concludes his most thorough book on religion by asking a question that he does not answer, or cannot answer: "What could take the place of religion in a world in which the concept of God may be dead but in which the experiential reality behind it must live?"[50]

2.1.4. Religion in contemporary society

A teaching that is liberating can be falsified and turned into an ideology that oppresses, and this is what happened with the teachings of the persons mentioned. As soon as a religion becomes a mass organization governed by a religious bureaucracy, freedom is perverted. While the founders led man from the bondage of Egypt, the followers have led him back toward a new Egypt though calling it the Promised Land. According to Fromm this has happened in all religions.[51] What happens in such a deteroriation process is that the ideal is transformed into an ideology, administered by bureaucracies, and that instead of having authentic experiences, people slowly begin to have purely cerebral, alienated thoughts.[52]

As a social critic Fromm often describes how religion is used in an alienating way in modern society. Writing in the Western world, this criticism is mainly directed at Christianity, but also at religon as a whole, or - to be precise -at modern society, which damages even the best things. "Religion has become an empty shell; it has been transformed into a self-help device for increasing one's own powers for success. God becomes a partner in business."[53] Modern man thinks he is a Christian or a Jew or whatever he may be, but in fact he is practicing idolatry by worshipping things, production, success. "Some people even try to combine religion and materialism until religion becomes a do-it-yourself method to greater success."[54]

Disobedience, 53.
[50]Fromm: *You shall be as gods*, 229.
[51]Fromm: *Psychoanalysis and Religion*, 85f.; Fromm: "Interview with Richard Heffner" *McCalls* 92 (Oct. 1965), 218.
[52]Fromm: *May Man Prevail?*, 122-124.
[53]Fromm: *The Dogma of Christ*, 73. This statement is directed against Rev. Norman Vincent Peale, whose book *The Power of Positive Thinking* was very famous at the time when Fromm wrote this.
[54]op.cit., 127.

One feature that characterizes religion in modern society is, according to Fromm, commercialism. He quotes Bishop Sheen and Billy Graham, who speak about the Christian gospel as a product to sell.[55] The idea of monotheism is not compatible with the calculating mentality of capitalism. But religion has abandoned its radical roots and fallen to idolatry by worshipping an idol named "God", who "has been transformed into a remote General Director of Universe, Inc."[56] "Is there any greater sacrilege than to speak of 'the Man upstairs', to teach to pray in order to make God your partner in business, to 'sell' religion with the methods and appeals used to sell soap?"[57] The churches should be the most ardent critics of modern capitalism, but instead they normally belong to the most conservative parts of our society. The churches should call the present idolatry by its right name, instead of using God's name in vain.[58]

Commercialism has, according to Fromm, influenced religion in many ways. "I think many people, if they were honest with their concept of heaven, would imagine heaven to be a tremendous department store in which they could buy something new every day and perhaps a little more than their neighbors."[59]

According to Fromm, religions have fulfilled a double function, providing us with an explanation of the natural world and giving us moral principles, an ethic. Since the breakthrough of the natural sciences, especially since Darwin, the first function has no longer been valid. Creation is no longer a mystery. The other function has become problematic because the spirit of the modern world is incompatible with Christian and Jewish morality. This leads to ambiguity and double standards. We praise altruism and love for mankind, but in society egoism is the primal virtue. Still we claim to be a Christian society, but in fact we worship idols, especially the idol of technology.[60]

---

[55]Fromm: *The Sane Society*, 118.
[56]op.cit., 176.
[57]op.cit., 176f.
[58]op.cit., 177
[59]Fromm: *On Disobedience*, 119f. The same idea was already expressed in Fromm: *The Sane Society*, 135. Cf. Fromm: *For the Love of Life*, 20.
[60]Fromm: *For the Love of Life*, 27-29. Fromm sees an example of how technology has become a religion in the spectacle of the first journey to the moon, which even Christian newspapers described as the most important event since creation. A Christian view would be to see the Incarnation as the most important event in human history. (op.cit., 29f.)

2.2. The religious experience

As a psychoanalyst Fromm was interested not only in the history and the ideas of different religions, but also in the religious experience. According to him one of man's basic needs is to devote himself to something. But what happens when man devotes himself to God or to some other power?

Fromm states that a religious experience is a human experience open to all people - not only religious or theistic persons. The experiential substratum is the same, what differs is the conceptualization of the experience. Because the word "religious" is often considered to be synonymous with "theistic", Fromm, in his book *You shall be as gods* of 1966, chose to use another neutral word for this kind of experience, the *x experience*.[61] In his earlier works, however, he talked about the "religious" experience. Later he expressly wrote that he uses quotation marks to denote "religious" in the experiental, subjective orientation, just because there is no word for the experiential content of religion aside from the conceptions of institutional religion. He further refers to Ernst Bloch's *Atheismus in Christenthum* as the most profound and boldest treatment of atheistic religious experience.[62]

According to Fromm, it is "exceedingly difficult if not impossible" to formulate the decisive factor of religious experience. "Only those who experience it will understand the formulation, and they do not need any formulation."[63] In an interview in 1958 he was asked, "What is a religious experience?", and answered: "I would say: to have a sense of 'ultimate concern' - to quote Dr. Tillich - for the spiritual values in man, for our love for man, for our reason, for truth, and to experience this development of ourselves as the most - and only - important aim of life."[64]

It is evident that Fromm thought that the religious experience correlates with the refusal to try to comprehend God. "X" can be experienced if one is free of all images of God, all recognition of God, all knowledge about God. As Funk put it:

---

[61]Fromm: *You shall be as gods*, 57. The only other work where Fromm uses the x terminology is "Die psychologischen und geistigen Probleme des Überflusses" *GA V*, 317-328.

[62]Fromm: *To have or to be?*, 139. In a speech at a symposium in 1975 Fromm talked about the linguistic problem for a radical humanist. "Religious", "spiritual", and the other adjectives all have their problems. He would prefer to use the expression "x experience". (Fromm: Antwort auf das Referat von Prof. Dr. Auer zum Thema: "Gibt es eine Ethik ohne Religiosität?" (transcript).)

[63]Fromm: *Psychoanalysis and Religion*, 94.

[64]Fromm: "Interview with Mike Wallace" *Survival and Freedom* No. 5 (1958), 10.

"The moment of experience is understood by Fromm to be the negation of every attempt to grab hold of God."[65]

In *You shall be as gods* Fromm then, as stated above, writes about the x experience. He does not make a thorough psychological analysis of it, but writes briefly about it in five points:[66]

(1) The x person experiences life as a problem and is seeking an answer. As Fromm wrote many years earlier: "Existence, one's own existence and that of one's fellow men, is not taken for granted but is felt as a problem, is not an answer but a question. Socrates' statement that wonder is the beginning of all wisdom is true not only for wisdom but for the religious experience."[67]

(2) For the x experience there exists a definite hierarchy of values, with the optimal development of one's own powers of reason, love, compassion, and courage as the highest value.

(3) For the x person, man alone is an end and never a means, and he is constantly striving towards self-transformation in the direction of becoming more human.

(4) The x attitude is a kind of letting go of one's "ego", of being open to the outside world.

(5) The x experience has to do with transcending the ego, leaving the prison of one's selfishness and separateness.[68]

In sum, "the analysis of the x experience moves from the level of theology to that of psychology and, especially, psychoanalysis."[69] It is evident that with his concept of the x experience Fromm means experiencing the full potentiality of one's humanity, the thing to which he devoted most of his time. This means overcoming incestuous ties, narcissism, and necrophilia in order to experience

---

[65]Funk: "Biophilia and Fromm's Criticism of Religion". In: Eletti (Ed.): *Incontro con Erich Fromm*, 215.

[66]Fromm: *You shall be as gods*, 58-60.

[67]Fromm: *Psychoanalysis and Religion*, 94. Cf. Fromm: "Die psychologischen und geistigen Probleme des Überflusses" *GA V*, 326.

[68]In an earlier study Fromm mentions three characteristics of the religious experience: an attitude of wonder, of concern, and of oneness. (Fromm: *Psychoanalysis and Religion*, 94f.)

[69]Fromm: *You shall be as gods*, 60.

freedom, love, and biophilia. Because this is not a study of Fromm's psychological ideas, we will not deal further with these issues.[70]

2.3. Buddhism

Fromm showed a great interest in Buddhism. What interested him was not Buddhism as it was practiced in Buddhist countries, but the philosophy of the Buddha and later interpretations of it. How much he actually knew about the real life of the masses in Buddhist countries is difficult to say; probably not very much. His knowledge was based on reading and discussions with Buddhist teachers in the West.[71]

Fromm's first encounter with Buddhism was in the middle of the 1920's through the books of Georg Grimm, the reading of which contributed to his renunciation of Jewish orthodoxy.[72] What attracted Fromm in Buddhism was, of course, the fact that it was an atheistic religion, where the salvation of man is totally dependent on his own effort, not on any power outside himself. "The Buddha is a great teacher, he is the 'awakened one' who recognizes the truth about human existence. He does not speak in the name of a supernatural power but in the name of reason. He calls upon every man to make use of his own reason and to see the truth which he was only the first to find."[73]

---

[70]For a discussion of Fromm's concept of the x experience from a Christian perspective, see Kügler SJ: "Religiöse Erfahrung - humanistisch und christlich" *SZ* 203 (1985), 125-136.

[71]Torres has criticized Fromm heavily for his enthusiasm for Buddhism, mainly for two reasons: meditation is a privilege for the well-to-do, and Buddhism has contributed to the oppression of the lower classes by encouraging resignation and escapism. (Torres: *El irracionalismo en Erich Fromm*, 51-61, 103-114). Torres neglects the fact that a religion can have many valuable features although it has been used in history for negative purposes. As a matter of fact, Fromm expressively stated that Buddhism has - like Christianity - been used for evil purposes, has been "ideologized". But the "task of critique is not to denounce the ideals, but to show their transformation into ideologies, and to challenge the ideology in the name of the betrayed ideals." (Fromm: *Beyond the Chains of Illusion*, 145) And that when it came to Buddhism Fromm was distinguishing between the original teaching of the founder and the religion based on it, is also shown by the fact that he mentions as an example of humanistic religions not Buddhism but *early* Buddhism. (Fromm: *Psychoanalysis and Religion*, 37f.) And in all great religions - including Buddhism - one can see an ambiguity between narcissistic and antinarcissistic tendencies. (Fromm: *The Heart of Man*, 81)

[72]Funk: *Erich Fromm*, 51; Fromm: *For the Love of Life*, 105.

[73]Fromm: *Psychoanalysis and Religion*, 38. Cf. Fromm: *The Revolution of Hope*, 87; Fromm: *On Disobedience*, 52.

For Fromm the Buddha was not only one of mankind's great teachers, he was an extraordinary advocate of truth. Many great teachers have emphasized the fact that the truth makes us free, but nobody perhaps with such radicalism as the Buddha.[74] The radical demand in Buddhism for giving up the having orientation is based on the personal decision of the Buddha to leave his life of luxury and all his possessions.[75] And the principle - common to all great humanistic religions - that the goal of man is to overcome his narcissism is perhaps nowhere expressed more radically than in Buddhism. The Buddha taught that man must wake up from his illusions and become fully awake.[76]

The branch of Buddhism that most attracted Fromm was Zen Buddhism, which, according to him, "was expressive of an even more radical anti-authoritarian attitude" than Buddhism.[77] In the 1940's he met Dr. D.T. Suzuki, the man who introduced Zen Buddhism to a larger audience in the West, at Columbia University in New York. Suzuki made a lasting impact on Fromm as a person who did not teach Zen Buddhism but lived it.[78] Fromm's encounter with Zen Buddhism was of great importance to him. In 1957 he stated that "having read and heard about Zen Buddhism for the last few years, my own thinking has been greatly stimulated and influenced. I've learned a great deal from the radical emphasis on experience which you have in Zen Buddhism which really is much more than I ever had imagined possible before I got acquainted with it."[79]

In the late 1950's Fromm tried to persuade Suzuki to settle more permanently in Cuernavaca, close to him. He really admired Suzuki as can be seen from the statement that "the joy and benefit for my wife and myself in being near you, and in seeing you enjoy a congenial environment, would be so great".[80] After the death of Suzuki in 1967 Fromm wrote a commemorative essay in which he praised Suzuki for his never-failing kindness, love of life, absence of vanity, inner joy, ever-present interest in everything around him, and his child-like quality.[81]

---

[74]Fromm: *Greatness and Limitations of Freud's Thought*, ix. Cf. Fromm: *Man for Himself*, 35f.

[75]Fromm: *To have or to be?*, 103, 109, 163. Fromm also believed that this criticism of the having orientation was stronger in "classic Buddhism" than in the Old and New Testaments (op.cit., 59).

[76]Fromm: *The Heart of Man*, 88f.

[77]op.cit., 40.

[78]Funk: *Erich Fromm*, 114-116. Cf. Fromm: *The Art of Being*, 12.

[79]Fromm: "Beyond Egotistical Religion" (lecture in 1957).

[80]Letter Fromm - Suzuki 18.10 1956.

[81]Fromm: "Memories of Dr. D.T. Suzuki" *The Eastern Buddhist* New Series II (August 1967), 86-89.

In August 1957 Fromm arranged a congress on "Zen Buddhism and Psychoanalysis" at his home in Cuernavaca, Mexico. Three of the papers presented there were later published in a book with the same title. The first essay in the book was written by Suzuki, the second by Fromm.

In his essay Fromm compares Zen Buddhism with psychoanalysis. Both have a theory about human nature and a praxis that leads to well-being. But the differences are great: psychoanalysis is a scientific method, Zen Buddhism a religion. Despite this, there is a growing interest in Zen Buddhism among psychoanalysts. Fromm himself says that Zen Buddhism has been of "vital significance" to him, and could be so for every student of psychoanalysis.[82] Why?

According to Fromm, the goal of both the great Western religions and the great Eastern religions is the same: "overcoming the limitations of an egotistical self, achieving love, objectivity and humility and respecting life so that the aim of life is living itself, and man becomes what he potentially is."[83] The advantage of the Eastern religions over the Western is that they do not carry the ideas of a transcendent father-savior. Zen Buddhism basically gives the same answer to man's searching as do the Western religions, but in a way that is not contradictory to Western rationality. "This is precisely the reason why Eastern religious thought, Taoism and Buddhism - and their blending in Zen Buddhism - assume such importance for the West today."[84]

Later in his essay Fromm returns to the issue of the difference between Eastern and Western religions, between Zen Buddhism and Christianity. Both preach that one should give up one's will and be totally open and receptive. But in Christianity this emptiness has come to mean that one has to surrender to an omniscient, omnipotent God. This is not being open and responsive, it is being obedient and submissive. "To follow God's will in the sense of true surrender of egoism is best done if there is no concept of God. Paradoxically, I truly follow God's will if I forget about God. Zen's concept of emptiness implies the true meaning of giving up one's will, yet without the danger of regressing to the idolatrous concept of a helping father."[85]

---

[82]Fromm: "Psychoanalysis and Zen Buddhism". In: Suzuki - Fromm - de Martino: *Zen Buddism and Psychoanalysis*, 77f. In a letter to Suzuki 14.12 1963 Fromm wrote that "in our continued endeavor to reach deeper insight what you have said in your writings, and personally, about Zen Buddhism are some of the essential bases."
[83]Fromm: "Psychoanalysis and Zen Buddhism". In: Suzuki - Fromm - de Martino: *Zen Buddhism and Psychoanalysis*, 80.
[84]ibid.
[85]op.cit., 95.

When Fromm turns to the principles of Zen Buddhism he first states that he himself has not experienced enlightenment (*satori*). Therefore he cannot speak from experience, but only on the basis of what he has read and heard. Furthermore, the experience of *satori* cannot be taught or transmitted in words. Nevertheless, he tries to present the basic principles of Zen Buddhism.[86]

The ultimate goal in Zen Buddhism is enlightenment, *satori*.[87] This, according to Fromm, means achieving full productivity, being creative and active, enjoying total security and freedom from fear. He summarizes Dr. Suzuki's description of the aims of Zen Buddhism as follows: "Zen is the art of *seeing into the nature of one's being*; it is a way *from bondage to freedom*; it *liberates our natural energies*; it *prevents us from going crazy or being crippled*; and it impels us to express our faculty for *happiness and love*."[88] The goal of psychoanalysis is to make the unconscious conscious. If we cling to this goal to its utmost consequences, Fromm writes, we come very close to the goal of Zen Buddhism.[89] Other similarities between psychoanalysis and Zen Buddhism are that both consider the overcoming of greed as very important, both insist on freedom from every authority, both offer an experienced person as a guide (the Zen master and the analyst, respectively) and both strive to get people to take the plunge from thinking to experiencing.[90] Where psychoanalysis and Zen Buddhism differ from each other is in their methods.[91]

At the end of his essay Fromm states that psychoanalysis has a lot to learn from the Zen Buddhist conception of *satori* and expresses his gratefulness for "this precious gift from the East" and to Dr. Suzuki, who has succeeded in explaining what Zen Buddhism is to the Western world.[92] In another work Fromm has mentioned the importance of Zen Buddhism in helping him to overcome the attitude of judging which his biblical background had created in him.[93]

----

[86]op.cit., 113-121.

[87]In mainstream Buddhism the goal is called *nirvana*. This term was also used by Freud, but in Fromm's opinion in an unsuccessful way. *Nirvana* is not a state of lifelessness but a state of supreme joy when greed and egoism have been overcome. Fromm: *Greatness and Limitations of Freud's Thought*, 114n. Cf. Fromm: *To have or to be?*, 118.

[88]Fromm: "Psychoanalysis and Zen Buddhism". In: Suzuki - Fromm - de Martino: *Zen Buddhism and Psychoanalysis*, 115.

[89]op.cit., 135.

[90]op.cit., 123-126.

[91]op.cit., 139f.

[92]op.cit., 141.

[93]Fromm: *Gesellschaft und Seele*, 144.

In a later work Fromm called Zen Buddhism "the most highly sophisticated, anti-ideological, rational, psychospiritual system I know and which developed all the forms of a 'nonreligious' religion".[94] He further states that it is no surprise that Zen Buddhism has become popular among intellectuals and young people. It could have a deep influence on the Western world but "it would have to undergo new and unpredictable forms of transformation to become the equivalent of a religion in the West".[95] In this statement we can see a criticism of Zen Buddhism for not, in its actual form, being able to become a religion for the masses, but rather being a solution for an elite.[96]

Fromm's understanding of Zen Buddhism is totally dependent on Suzuki. But Suzuki is not an authority beyond all criticism. On the contrary, he has been criticized for overemphasizing the psychological at the expense of the religious and metaphysical in order to "westernize" Zen Buddhism.[97]

In old age Fromm's Buddhist interest was again directed at classical Buddhism. This was due to his friendship with Nyanaponika Mahathera, a German Jew of about the same age who converted to Buddhism and became a Buddhist monk in Sri Lanka. Fromm met him in Switzerland in the late 1960's and remained in close contact with him for the rest of his life. Nyanaponika used to spend his summers in Switzerland, where he met Fromm. They also corresponded regularly. Fromm was very impressed by Nyanaponika and regarded him as an extremely stimulating and very alive person without any mark of death.[98] For one hour every morning Fromm began to do breathing and concentration exercises he had learned from Nyanaponika.[99] During his long illnesses and periods of

---

[94]Fromm: *The Revolution of Hope*, 138 n.21.
[95]ibid.
[96]In *The Crisis of Psychoanalysis*, 2, Fromm writes about how "a few" seem to have found new frames of orientation in surrealism, radical politics, or Zen Buddhism. Hausdorff (*Erich Fromm*, 109f.) claims that Fromm never raised the question of the real applicability of Zen in the West and adds that it can hardly be any more than "an exotic fetish for a tiny minority". The statements by Fromm referred to here show that he was not far from Hausdorff on this matter.
[97]See, e.g., Benz: *ZEN in westlicher Sicht*, 21-26; Dumoulin: *Zen. Geschichte und Gestalt*, 267-270, 274-279. That Fromm was aware of this critique is sure; the book by Benz is in Fromm's library with many ticks in the margin of precisely the passages where Suzuki is criticized. But this book appeared in 1962, and after that Fromm did not write very much about Zen Buddhism.
[98]Fromm: *The Art of Listening*, 180.
[99]In letters to Nyanaponika on 8.9 and 4.12 1972 Fromm says how helpful Buddhist meditation has been both for himself and his wife. In *The Art of Listening* he writes enthusiastically about this method (p.179f.).

convalescence in the 1970's the writings of Nyanaponika became especially important to him. In a letter he writes about some essays by Nyanaponika: "We have read them by now many times during the three months of my illness and it has opened our minds to essential things in Buddhist thought which we had never fully grasped until we read your papers."[100]

In 1976 Fromm wrote an essay for the *Festschrift* in honor of the 75th birthday of Nyanaponika Mahathera.[101] In it he praises Nyanaponika in the way typical of a *Festschrift*. The Buddhist monk is praised both as a teacher and as a curer for being objective, unfanatical, reliable to the smallest detail, and modest. Fromm even calls the writings of Nyanaponika a "Guide for the Perplexed" for its time, thus alluding to the classic work by Maimonides.

I would like to stress two interesting details in this essay. Firstly, Fromm states that there are points where he differs from Buddhist doctrine. Unfortunately he confines himself to saying that a detailed description of the difference between radical humanism and Buddhist teaching can only be solved in the frame of reference of a special book, a book that was never written.

The other interesting detail is that Fromm says what it is about Buddhism that is attractive for modern Western man: rationality, independence, the giving up of illusions and submission to authorities, and the full grasp of inner reality. Christianity and Judaism do not, according to Fromm, appeal to the young generation. Buddhism, being an anti-authoritarian, rational religion, is more attractive. The works of Nyanaponika Mahathera may become one of the most important contributions to the spiritual renewal of the West.[102]

Fromm's posthumously published book *The Art of Being* - originally written in the 1970's - is intended to be a kind of guide to productive self-awareness. In this book is a chapter about Buddhist meditation, the aim of which, according to Fromm, is "*maximum awareness* of our bodily and mental processes".[103] This chapter consists to a large extent of a description of Buddhist meditation according to Nyanaponika Mahathera's *The Heart of Buddhist Meditation*. But beside the descriptive parts Fromm briefly writes about his own evaluation of Buddhism and of Buddhist meditation.

---

[100]Letter Fromm - Nyanaponika 1.12 1975.
[101]Fromm: "Die Bedeutung des Ehrwürdigen Nyanaponika Mahathera für die westliche Welt" *GA VI*, 359-361.
[102]In another of his books Fromm refers to the works of Nyanaponika Mahathera for a "penetrating understanding of Buddhism". Fromm: *To have or to be?*, 59n.
[103]Fromm: *The Art of Being*, 50.

Fromm states that he is not a Buddhist but is deeply impressed by the core of Buddhist teaching. What attracts him in Buddhism is its emphasis on overcoming greed, hate, and ignorance, and its demand for optimal awareness of the processes inside and outside oneself.[104] This is all familiar from his earlier writings. But what is more interesting is that he now also - although in passing - reveals what he does not accept in Buddhism. He does not agree with the doctrine of reincarnation, with a certain life-neglecting tendency in Hinayana Buddhism,[105] and with "techniques suggested to convince oneself of the futility of craving by imagining the foulness of the dead body..."[106]

The most systematic and detailed treatment of Buddhism by Fromm was written in the 1970's. Unfortunately it was never published. In this manuscript Fromm explicitly discusses some of the intricate issues raised by his earlier writings on Buddhism.

He starts by listing the common prejudices against Buddhism: that its ideal is an ascetic life and a nihilistic attitude to life, that the Buddha is a kind of God whose commands must be obeyed, that the dogma of rebirth is central and that Buddhism is opposed to rational thought. All this is, Fromm claims, wrong, although Buddhism has in the course of its history been distorted to contain all these traits. Westerners have difficulty in understanding real Buddhism because it is an atheistic religion. Also, Westerners do not usually pay any attention to the fact that Buddhism was a revolutionary movement directed against the polytheistic Hinduism and its powerful priesthood.[107]

According to Fromm Buddhism was strictly antiauthoritarian. Studying and deciding for oneself are important, not blind obedience. This lack of a supreme authority is also the reason why Buddhism does not recognise the concept of sin, only the concept of error, which is the cause of "illbeing" (dukkha). Buddhism is

---

[104]op.cit., 52f.
[105]It is interesting that Fromm uses the term Hinayana, which is not accepted by the followers themselves. In his essay in honor of Nyanaponika Mahathera he uses the more "politically correct" term Theravada. Fromm has been criticized (Hausdorff: *Erich Fromm*, 109f., Knapp: *The Art of Living*, 106) for failing to observe the egocentric leanings and the escapist tendencies in Buddhism and Easterns mysticism as a whole. These critics had not read this passage by Fromm, because it was first published in 1989.
[106]Fromm: *The Art of Being*, 52.
[107]Fromm: *Buddhism* (unpublished manuscript), 1f. Torres (*El irracionalismo en Erich Fromm*, 52f.) sees the relation of Buddhism to the Hindu priesthood in a totally different way. According to him Buddhism had from its very beginning the full support of the clergy and the nobility because it promoted escapism and resignation.

not based on tradition, revelation of God's commands, but on an anthropological-psychological examination of human existence aiming at human wellbeing.[108]

The only dogmatic element in Buddhism is, in Fromm's opinion, the belief in rebirth. But the reason for this is that the Buddha was so greatly influenced by the belief in the transmigration of souls that he could not think the unthinkable ("after death there is nothing"). Instead he expressed the negation of the Hindu doctrine by revising it, stating that the wheel of transmigration can stop. The Buddhist belief in rebirth is thus "a historically conditioned piece of baggage which has nothing to do with the central teaching of Buddhism".[109]

What is central in Buddhism is, Fromm continues, the idea of suffering and liberation. Suffering means illbeing and is caused by being dominated by greed, hatred and craving. Overcoming these leads to wellbeing. It is a grave misunderstanding to claim that Buddhism is ascetic or nihilistic; its aim is wellbeing, peace and joy, but not pleasure in a hedonistic sense. Another central idea in Buddhism is liberation from illusions. Through Buddhist meditation, which is essentially self-analysis, one can be liberated from self-deception and gain real self knowledge and knowledge of others. The Buddha and Buddhist teachers were wise enough to formulate two goals: the radical goal of reaching Nirvana, and the limited goal of achieving wellbeing by optimal though not total liberation from greed, hatred and illusion.[110]

Fromm's conclusion is clear: "If one discards dogmatic and historically accidental elements such as rebirth, it seems to me that Buddhism is by far the most rational system which can liberate man from unnecessary illbeing from the having mode of existence to wellbeing, the being mode of existence. Of course also Judaism and Christianity if one discards the historically conditioned concept of God, could have the same function; but with greater difficulty because the whole system is more pervaded by the spirit of authority and by many particular rituals and myths, while Buddhism speaks in the universal language of human beings, and of life."[111]

---

[108]Fromm: *Buddhism* (unpublished manuscript), 2f.
[109]op.cit., 4. It is interesting to note that after the death of Fromm Nyanaponika Mahathera claimed that had he had the opportunity he thinks he would have been able to convince Fromm of the psychological credibility of reincarnation. (Appel: "Erich Fromms Dialog mit dem Buddhismus". In: von Werder (Hrsg.): *Der unbekannte Fromm*, 82)
[110]Fromm: *Buddhism* (unpublished manuscript), 5-8.
[111]op.cit., 8.

The claim that Buddhism encourages resignation and escapism and thus contributes to social injustice - expressed so strongly by Torres[112] - is neither discussed nor answered by Fromm. The liberation from greed, hatred and illusion that he claims to be the central idea in Buddhism could indirectly promote social justice. But it is a fact - which Fromm recognizes - that the Buddhist teachers "had no visions of a radically different society, as the prophets had."[113] Maybe this is why the Buddhist element in Fromm's thinking was supplemented by prophetic messianism, just as his Freudianism was supplemented by Marxism.

To say that Fromm was a devoted Buddhist[114] is not totally incorrect, but neither is it correct. Fromm himself once stated that he did not belong to any religion, but that if he was forced to answer he would say that he was a Buddhist, because it wass the institutionalized religion to which he felt closest.[115] In his attitude to Buddhism Fromm was - as always - eclectic. He adopted what he esteemed as valuable in it, and ignored the rest.[116] By deliberately interpreting Buddhism in a way that suited himself, and by ignoring or denying the significance of the important disagreements, on, for example, reincarnation and karma, Fromm in fact seems to be more Buddhist than he really was.[117]

2.4. Transcendental Meditation

Other Eastern religions from China and India - especially Taoism - are now and then mentioned in Fromm's works, but he does not present any further analysis of them. He sometimes quotes Tao-te-king, especially as an expression of paradoxical logic,[118] and in the Hindu tradition he especially appreciated the Upanishads, representing "one of the deepest wells of wisdom for mankind in any

---

[112]See note 71 above. Similarly Y. Suzuki: *An Examination of the Doctrine of Man of Erich Fromm and Reinhold Niebuhr*, 305.
[113]Fromm: *Buddhism* (unpublished manuscript), 7.
[114]Knapp: *The Art of Living*, 206.
[115]Interview with Guido Ferrari 8.3 1980.
[116]Browning has a very accurate and very funny statement about Fromm's eclecticism: "Fromm moves through the world's religions somewhat like a butcher, cutting out the good pieces and throwing the rest in the dump heap of history." (Browning: *Generative Man: Psychoanalytic Perspectives*, 131)
[117]See Hardeck: *Vernunft und Liebe*, 167-171.
[118]Fromm: *The Art of Loving*, 73-75; Fromm: "Psychoanalysis and Zen Buddhism". In: Suzuki - Fromm - de Martino: *Zen Buddhism and Psychoanalysis*, 102; Fromm: *Beyond the Chains of Illusion*, 120.

time and place."[119] The new Eastern cults that became popular among young people in the West in the 1960's and 1970's did, however, arouse his interest.

The interest in the oriental religious tradition was perceived by Fromm as a reaction to the materialist culture of the West. Unfortunately, this interest was not only directed at the genuine religious traditions. Instead a bunch of "Indian fakirs" and nonserious and sometimes even dishonest cults misused this interest for their own purposes.[120] Many good ideas have been exploited by swindler gurus and false prophets of happiness and sex.[121]

The only modern Indian cult or guru teaching dealt with by Fromm at any lemgth is Transcendental Meditation (TM), founded in the 1950's by Guru Maharishi and very popular in the West from the 1960's onwards.[122] Fromm's judgement of this movement is devastating. The meditation method, which is much older than Maharishi, is good and effective, but the business mentality seeking to sell the method is a grave danger. TM is superficial, it promises profound change when it can, in fact, offer only a method for relaxation. Real change demands time, but for PR reasons TM is offered as a quick no-effort solution.[123] Despite the favorable effect of the meditation, the total effect of TM is negative. It is an idolatrous cult that represents the commercialization of values. The success of this movement is evidence of the fact that the spirit of big business has made inroads into the field of spiritual development.[124]

Fromm - who in his own words had a very old-fashioned musical taste[125] - disliked the Beatles. Beside the emptiness of their music, another bluff pulled by

---

[119]Fromm - Xirau (Eds.): *The Nature of Man*, 25.

[120]Fromm: "Einführung in H.J. Schultz: *Psychologie für Nichtpsychologen*" *GA VIII*, 90; Fromm: "Die Bedeutung des Ehrwürdigen Nyanaponika Mahathera für die westliche Welt" *GA VI*, 357.

[121]Fromm: *On Being Human*, 139. In 1977 Fromm stated that this guru religiosity is "zum grossen Teil reiner Schwindel". (Fromm: Interview with Michaela Lämmle and Jürgen Lodemann in 1977; cf. Fromm: "Ich habe die Hoffnung, dass die Menschen ihre Leiden erkennen: den Mangel and Liebe" *Der Stern* 27.3 1980, 307)

[122]Fromm: *The Art of Being*, 15-19.

[123]Fromm always opposed every notion that real change can occur very rapidly and without great effort. In a lecture for young people in 1970 he ironically spoke about those that are asking for "instant Zen". (Fromm: "The Myth of the Paradise" (lecture in 1970).)

[124]Fromm's view of the religious element in the hippie movement was much more positive. See Fromm: *The Revision of Psychoanalysis*, 84-87.

[125]Fromm: *For the Love of Life*, 108.

the four megastars was, in his opinion, their enthusiasm for the "swindler guru" Maharishi.[126]

Fromm's criticism of the "swindler gurus" is a frequent theme of his many interviews in the 1970's. Spiritual salvation has become a market, using all the sales arguments of the market, he says. Man is not interested in what is true, but in what works, be it meditation, God, or the devil.[127]

2.5. Scientology

In 1950 Fromm wrote a review of L. Ron Hubbard's book *Dianetics*, the "bible" of the Church of Scientology. Fromm's verdict on Hubbard's mixture of psychoanalysis, religion and philosophy is devastating. He was clear-sighted. The history of Scientology has since been full of ruined lives, court cases and scandals.

According to Fromm, Hubbard's book cannot be taken seriously as a contribution to human knowledge, but it must be taken seriously as a symptom of a dangerous trend that views man as a machine that can be treated by engineering, "on a push-button basis", as Hubbard himself put it. Everything is simplified in Hubbard's world; all you need to know is written in *Dianetics*. Fromm's conclusion is that this book is dangerous. "The mixture of some oversimplified truths, half truths and plain absurdities, the propagandistic technique of impressing the reader with the greatness, infallibility and newness of the author's system, the promise of unheard of results attained by the simple means of following *Dianetics* is a technique which had had most unfortunate results in the fields of patent medicines and politics; applied to psychology and psychiatry it will not be less harmfull [sic]."[128]

Three years later Fromm briefly touched upon Scientology in a lecture. He stated that it is incredible how even intelligent people admire Hubbard, the author of the totally insane book *Dianetics*. But this is just one more expression of man's desperate need for something to believe in and devote himself to.[129]

---

[126]Fromm: *Ethik und Politik*, 38.
[127]Fromm: Intrerview with Alfred A. Häsler: "Der Unbekannte denken und das Mögliche tun" *Ex libris* 22 (No.5 1977), 19. Similar criticism also in Fromm: Interview with Heiner Gautschy in 1979, Fromm: Interview with Micaela Lämmle and Jürgen Lodemann in 1977.
[128]Fromm: "For Seekers of Prefabricated Happiness. Review of L. Ron Hubbard: *Dianetics*" *New York Herald Tribune* 3.9 1950, 7.
[129]Fromm: *Die Pathologie der Normalität*, 38f.

2.6. Christianity

Living in a society so deeply influenced by Christianity led Fromm to make frequent comments on this religion. His criticism of religion in modern society (see 2.1) was based on his experience of Christianity, especially in its American form. But he also made more thorough studies of Christianity, its history and its theology.

2.6.1. Early Christianity

In 1930 - while studying at the Psychoanalytic Institute in Berlin - Fromm wrote an essay entitled *Die Entwicklung des Christusdogmas*, that was published in English translation thirty years later. It is an interesting study of early Christianity from two perspectives, a sociological and a psychoanalytical. From a sociological point of view Fromm tries, as a good Marxist[130], to show how the changing social basis of the early Christians influenced the Christian dogma. From a psychoanalytical point of view he wants to reveal the unconscious motives behind the different theological concepts. "Every attempt to understand the origin of Christianity must begin with an investigation of the economic, social, cultural, and psychic situation of its earliest believers."[131]

The early Christians were, according to Fromm, from "the masses of the uneducated poor, the proletariat of Jerusalem, and the peasants in the country", who "longed for a happy time for themselves, and also harboured hate and revenge against both their own rulers and the Romans".[132] The core of the first Christian teaching was that the kingdom of God is at hand, which would mean that "the poor would be rich, the hungry would be satisfied, and the oppressed would attain authority. This hope was understood in a completely literal and material sense."[133] Fromm states that the first Christians were filled with the same hatred of the ruling class as were the revolutionary movements. The only difference was that the Christians did not fight, but waited for the overthrow of the present order through a divine intervention.[134]

---

[130]I believe that in writing about the lowest stratum of the proletariat, the so-called *Am-Haarez*, that "they had nothing to lose and perhaps something to gain" (Fromm: *The Dogma of Christ*, 17f.) Fromm is deliberately alluding to the famous final words of the *Communist Manifesto*: The Proletarians have nothing to lose but their chains. (*MEW 4*, 493)
[131]Fromm: *The Dogma of Christ*, 15.
[132]Op.cit., 25.
[133]op.cit., 28.
[134]op.cit., 29-31.

According to Fromm, the first Christian community's concept of Christ was adoptionist, "He was a man chosen by God and elevated by Him as a 'Messiah', and later as 'Son of God'."[135] "In the early community of enthusiasts, Jesus was thus a man exalted after His death into a God who would soon return in order to execute judgment, to make happy those who suffer, and to punish the rulers."[136]

Fromm then turns to the question of the psychological motives for this Christian "fantasy". According to him, behind the conscious hatred for the rulers, the authority with "fatherly" power, was an unconscious hatred and desire to see God the Father dead. The concept of the suffering son who becomes God conceals a form of Oedipus wish. "The belief in the elevation of a man to God was thus the expression of [an] unconscious wish for the removal of the Divine Father."[137]

But the adoptionist view of Christ was soon replaced by the Pauline idea of the Son of God who was born as a divine being, who was always God and existed before all creation. Why did this change take place? With Paul, people who belonged to the well-to-do middle class and were educated started to enter the Christian community. During the next few centuries there was a dramatic change in the adherents of the new faith as regards nationality and more important social composition. "Indeed, slaves, artisans, and the shabby *proletariat*, that is, the masses of the lower classes, still constituted the bulk of the Christian community, but Christianity had simultaneously become the religion also of the prominent and ruling classes of the Roman Empire."[138]

This sociological change transformed Christianity during its first centuries in many ways. The eschatological expectations disappeared, the establishment of the kingdom was postponed to the distant future. A shift from the outward to the inward happened, salvation became a spiritual, unhistorical, individual matter. The ethical rigorism faded away. The state was no longer seen as an enemy; the Church became a state-supporting power. In sum, Christianity transformed from the religion of the oppressed to the religion of the rulers.[139] "As the first Christians were imbued with hatred and contempt for the educated rich and the rulers, in short, for all authority, so the Christians from the third century on were imbued with reverence, love, and fidelity to the new clerical authorities."[140]

---

[135]op.cit., 32. The main evidence for this assumption is the statement of Acts 2:36: "God has made him both Lord and Christ."
[136]op.cit., 33.
[137]op.cit., 35.
[138]op.cit., 41f.
[139]op.cit., 43-46.
[140]op.cit., 46.

Simultaneously, the view of Christ changed. The adoptionist view disappeared and was replaced by the homoousian doctrine. Instead of believing in a man becoming God, the Church taught that God became man. According to Fromm, this happened because of the changing social situation. The adoptionist view suited the lower classes, which hated the ruling class, while the new doctrine fitted the ruling class because in this dogma there is no Oedipus crime, the father remains untouched in his position. The aggressiveness towards the father and the authorities is now directed toward the individual self. The suffering of Christ made it easier to bear one's own sufferings. At the same time a certain feminization of Christianity occurred. The Church was seen as a mother, and Mary, who was in early Christianity in no way elevated beyond the sphere of ordinary mortals, now became the object of worship.[141]

Further in his essay Fromm briefly deals with some specific phenomena in the first centuries of the Christian church: Montanism, Gnosticism, the Logos Christianity, Monarchianism and Arianism. All these phenomena he describes according to his basic distinction between the revolutionary tendencies hostile to the father-god and the conformist movement supporting father and state.[142] Before the conclusion of the essay he compares his study with a similar one made by his teacher, Theodor Reik.[143]

What can be said of young Fromm's essay? First of all, it reveals a good knowledge of its subject. Fromm seems to have read a lot about early Christianity, although his main sources of information were the standard works by Johannes Weiss and Adolf Harnack. His sociological remarks are interesting, but not unique, he stands in a Marxist tradition with Engels and Kautsky as the most important names.[144] The really creative thing in his essay is the psychoanalytical interpretations. But to state that certain unconscious motives lay behind the dogmatic change in early Christianity is highly speculative;[145] it cannot be proved

---

[141]op.cit., 47-52. Fromm connects the feminization of Christianity with the homoousian doctrine, because in real life there is only one instance of two individuals sharing the same substance, being two beings and at the same time one, and that is a child in its mother's womb.
[142]op.cit., 54-62.
[143]op.cit., 62-68.
[144]Beit-Hallahmi describes Fromm's essay as "in itself a brilliant Marxist exercise". (Beit-Hallahmi: "Religiously based differences in approach to the psychology of religion: Freud, Fromm, Allport and Zilboorg". In: Brown (Ed.): *Advance in the Psychology of Religion*, 24. For a discussion of the similarities and differences between Fromm and Kautsky on this issue, see Bentley: "Three German Marxists Look at Christianity: 1900-30" *JCS* 22 (1980), 511-517.
[145]Bentley (op.cit., 513) writes that at this point in Fromm's analysis "the fantasies of contemporary psychoanalysis started to take over." On the other hand, Theissen has claimed that Fromm's analysis of the oedipal conflict is much less speculative than Freud's because

and it cannot be disproved. It is a claim beyond verification or falsification. A person can be psychoanalyzed and his or her unconscious can be revealed. But a big group that lived centuries ago can only be psychoanalyzed from a distance, and what one says of its unconscious remains pure speculation.

But what if we compare Fromm's analysis with present-day knowledge about early Christianity?

First of all, Fromm has in this essay tackled a very intricate issue. Christology has not only given rise to intense scholarly debate; it has also been the reason for denominational splits.

In order to support his theory Fromm makes exegsis and Church history too easy. Thomassen has pointed out three historical problems in Fromm's theory:[146] 1) The origin of the different Christologies. That the oldest Christological view was the adoptionist view which was later replaced by the homoousian doctrine is a clear simplification. Thomassen is totally correct in this. According to most scholars, many Christological views existed side by side from very early times.[147] The Logos doctrine is based on the first chapter of the Gospel of John, and although John is younger than most of the other New Testament books, it does not date from a time when the middle and upper classes had come to dominate the church.[148] That Acts 2:36 expresses the oldest doctrine of Christ[149] is a highly speculative statement. The book of Acts is younger than Paul's letters, but it is, of course, possible that this statement in Acts reflects a very old doctrine. Fromm does not argue this, however; he takes it for granted.[150] 2) That Fromm makes

---

Fromm studies them in a historical context, Freud only in a family context. (Theissen: *Psychologische Aspekte paulinischer Theologie*, 31 n.32)

[146]Thomassen: *Erich Fromm's 'Entwicklung der Christusdogma' ist darzustellen und historisch und dogmatisch zu beurteilen* (unpublished dissertation), 32f.

[147]Knox claims that there are three different types of Christology within the New Testament: 'adoptionism', 'kenotism', and 'docetism'. Knox: *The Humanity and Divinity of Christ*, 1-18. Cf. Pollard: *Johannine Christology and the Early Church*, 3-6. Fromm was told that adoptionism is not the oldest form of Christology in a letter from Thomas Merton on 12.11 1955. After that he never discussed the issue, so we do not know whether he was convinced by Merton or not.

[148]That Fromm is too definite in dating the New Testament books is shown by the fact that he dates the Epistle of James to the middle of the second century (Fromm: *The Dogma of Christ*, 29). There is no consensus among scholars about the dating of James. Some regard it as a very early book, while others place it very late, but no later than 130. (Paulsen: "Jakobusbrief" *TRE* 16, 492)

[149]Fromm: *The Dogma of Christ*, 31.

[150]Dunn writes that the statement in Acts 2:36 most likely is "one of several primitive christological emphases which Luke has faithfully preserved and reproduced." Dunn:

hatred the central element in early Christianity, but does not even mention the commandment to love one's neighbor, even one's enenmy. Here I cannot follow Thomassen's argument. Fromm's whole point is that the hatred is unconscious, repressed and rationalized. It was precisely because the first Christians were commanded to love that their hatred had to be repressed.[151] 3) That the return of Christ did not take place did not assume the importance to the change of Christianity which Fromm believes it did. Thomassen might be right here but the delay of the return of Christ is not a central point in Fromm's theory.

Although Fromm's theory is based on a simplified description of the historic development, he is correct in claiming that the homoousian doctrine is younger than the adoptionist, although it is not as late as he seems to believe. Fromm is also correct when he describes how the homoousian doctrine became the official dogma of the church. The merit of his essay is that he connects the success of the homoousian doctrine to the changed social basis of the Christian community. That the doctrinal development was determined - or at least influenced - by sociological changes can not be proved, but there is much that speaks in its favor. Anyway, most of the later theologians who have dealt with this issue seem to have totally ignored this theory,[152] while Fromm's theory has been considered among psychoanalysts as a pioneering study in psychology, religion, and historical sociology.[153]

Christology in the Making, 36. Cf. Robinson: *Twelve New Testament Studies*, 139-153; and Knox: *The Humanity and Divinity of Christ*, 8.

[151]Thomassen refers to Theissen's *Soziologie der Jesusbewegung*, but I find Theissen's discussion of aggression among the early Christians (p. 93-103) to be in accordance with Fromm.

[152]I have checked about twenty major theological works on the beginning of Christology - all written after 1963 when Fromm's essay was published in English - and Fromm's essay is not mentioned in even one of them. Some theologians who have not dealt with Christology but with critique of religion have commented Fromm's theory. Glen (*Erich Fromm. A Protestant Critique*, 46) states that Fromm's picture of how Christology developed in the early Church cannot be sustained. Greinacher ("Erich Fromm". In: Schmidt (Hrsg.): *Die Religion der Religionskritik*, 31) calls Fromm's ideas interesting, but very problematic from a historical and exegetical point of view. Schneider-Flume ("Fromm". In: Weger (Hrsg.): *Die Religionskritik von der Aufklärung bis zur Gegenwart*, 118) calls it original but not tenable. Pröpper (*Der Jesus der Philosophen und der Jesus des Glaubens*, 67) thinks that the historical basis for Fromm's theory is too narrow. Banks ("A Neo-Freudian Critique of Religion: Erich Fromm on the Judaeo-Christian Tradition" *Religion* 5 (1975), 128) calls Fromm's description of Christology in the early church questionable. It is interesting that in an extensive anthology on political interpretations of the Bible, Fromm is referred to in one essay - an essay about Marxist reading of the Bible - but his work on early Christianity is not taken into consideration. (Gottwald (Ed.): *The Bible and Liberation*).

[153]For references, see Burston: *The Legacy of Erich Fromm*, 32.

When in his other works Fromm sometimes mentions the church fathers, he most often emphasizes their social criticism. They managed to preserve some of the radical features of the Old Testament teaching and of the message of Jesus. Fromm praised them for their radical criticism of the existing state,[154] and for their conviction that man should never be a means but always an end.[155] He also points out that some of the church fathers - he mentions Origines, Maximus Confessor, and surprisingly also Augustine - had a humanist concept of sin as being a destruction of unity.[156]

But what attracted Fromm most in the church fathers was their radical condemnation of the materialist lifestyle, or the having mode, as he put it. He recognizes that there are differences in the degree of radicalism between the church fathers, and that the radicalism grew weaker as the church became more powerful. But nevertheless, the church fathers were prophetical in their condemnation of private property and egoistic use of any possession. Fromm quotes Justin, the Letter of Diognetus, Tertullian, Basilian, and John Chrysostomus.[157]

The greatest of the church fathers, Augustine, was the exception to the rule, a church father whom Fromm disliked. Although he does make some positive statements about him,[158] Augustine is mostly seen as the father of the doctrine of original sin that Luther and Calvin later deepened, and thus as an advocate of authoritarian religion.[159]

---

[154]Fromm: *Marx's Concept of Man*, 65.
[155]Fromm - Xirau: "Introduction". In: Fromm - Xirau (Eds.): *The Nature of Man*, 12.
[156]Fromm: *To have or to be?*, 124.
[157]op.cit., 57-59. One detail must be mentioned about Fromm's treatment of Tertullian. He mentions that the sentence "Credo quia absurdum est" (I believe because it is absurd) is a popular though somewhat distorted version of a sentence by Tertullian. What is interesting is that Fromm evaluates the irrational faith expressed in this sentence in two totally opposite ways. On the one hand (Fromm: "Faith as a Character Trait" *Psychiatry* 5 (1942), 311; Fromm: *Man for Himself*, 203f.) irrational faith is a fanatic conviction rooted in submission to an irrational authority. On the other hand, however, (Fromm: "The Philosophy Basic to Freud's Psychoanalysis" *Past Psych* 13 (1962), 28) irrational faith is seen as the unbiased openness to new "irrational" ideas, an attitude displayed by Freud and other great scientists.
[158]See, e.g., Fromm - Xirau: "Introduction". In: Fromm - Xirau (Eds.): *The Nature of Man*, 14.
[159]Fromm: *Man for Himself*, 150, 211; Fromm: *Psychoanalysis and Religion*, 48f.; Fromm: *The Forgotten Language*, 54f.; Fromm: "Humanism and Psychoanalysis" *Cont Psycha* 1 (1964), 73f.; Fromm: *The Crisis of Psychoanalysis*, 42.

2.6.2. Thomas Aquinas

One might imagine that a person who opposed dogmatics and ecclesial hierarchy as much as Fromm did would not be positive in his opinion of Thomas Aquinas, the chief dogmatist of the Catholic church. But in Fromm's case this is not true. He was surprisingly positive in his view of the great scholastic.

Fromm praised Thomas Aquinas as an excellent psychologist,[160] and in his book about dreams he devoted three pages to the dream theory of Thomas Aquinas.[161] Other ideas of Thomas Aquinas mentioned by him in passing are the concepts of self-knowledge,[162] rationality,[163] activity,[164] and *habitus*.[165]

Fromm contrasted the medieval Catholic theology with Protestantism, and sympathized with the Catholics. Despite the fact that Augustine's view of man's corruptness had triumphed over Pelagius' opinion, the late Middle Ages witnessed an increasing belief in man's dignity, power, and natural goodness. The scholastics did not rebel against outer authorities, instead advocating inner freedom, man's share in the determination of his fate, his strength and his dignity.[166] Thomas Aquinas, although never as radical as Pelagius, had a more optimistic view of man's nature than Luther and Calvin, who revived the Augustinian position.[167] Thomas Aquinas was forced to use complicated constructions to reconcile two contrasting doctrines: that of predestination, and that of man's freedom of will. Although Fromm does not find these constructions intellectually tenable, the total impact of the theology of Thomas Aquinas for man's dignity is much better than that of Luther and Calvin.[168]

Thomas Aquinas' concept of authority and sin also receives praise from Fromm. In the history of Christian theology Fromm discovers two different interpretations of sin: the authoritarian where sin is disobedience, and the nonauthoritarian where sin is unresolved estrangement. Thomas Aquinas is perceived as a representative of the nonauthoritarian or humanistic interpretation, where sin is a violation of

---

[160]Fromm: "Einführung in H.J. Schultz: *Psychologie für Nichtpsychologen*" *GA VIII*, 74.
[161]Fromm: *The Forgotten Language*, 134-136.
[162]Fromm: "Einige post-marxsche und post-freudsche Gedanken über Religion und Religiosität" *Concilium* 8 (1972), 473.
[163]Fromm: *The Anatomy of Human Destructiveness*, 263 n.30.
[164]Fromm: *To have or to be?*, 93.
[165]Fromm - Xirau: "Introduction". In: Fromm - Xirau (Eds.): *The Nature of Man*, 7.
[166]Fromm: *Escape from Freedom*, 100.
[167]Fromm: *Man for Himself*, 211f.
[168]Fromm: *Escape from Freedom*, 70.

human growth and wellbeing. But Fromm adds that, being an obedient son of the church and a supporter of the existing social order, Thomas Aquinas had to stop half-way and could not become a pure representative of nonauthoritarian ethics.[169]

The ethics of medieval theology is for Fromm in many ways more attractive than the ethics of modern society. In the Middle Ages economic behavior was still determined by ethical principles, hence, for example, Thomas Aquinas' qualification to the concept of "just price".[170] And in his view of private property Thomas Aquinas - although battling against the communists sects - followed the tradition of the church fathers (see 2.6.1.) and saw private property as justified only inasmuch as it best served the purpose of satisfying the welfare of all.[171]

Both Thomas Aquinas' ethics and the concept of man were progressive for their time and more humanistic than, say, those of Luther and Calvin, although not as radically humanistic as those of Fromm's favorite, Meister Eckhart. Fromm can thus give Thomas Aquinas a place in the history of the development of the humanist idea,[172] and mention Thomism as one of the forerunners of the Marxist and other forms of socialism.[173]

But when it comes to the heart of theology, the concept of God, the nontheist Fromm disagrees totally with the chief theologian of the Catholic church. By trying to reconcile faith and reason, Thomas Aquinas started a development that has in Fromm's opinion proven to be terrible or even disastrous for religion. Making religion an issue of the head instead of an issue of the heart paved the way for the future decline of religion. When science from Galilei to Darwin tore the rational basis for religion to pieces, nothing remained. One can only speculate, Fromm concludes, what would have happened to Christianity if the No-Theology of Meister Eckhart had become its basis instead of the theology of Thomas Aquinas.[174]

---

[169]Fromm: *To have or to be?*, 121-125.
[170]op.cit., 7.
[171]op.cit., 58f.
[172]Fromm: *On Being Human*, 65.
[173]Fromm: *Marx's Concept of Man*, 68.
[174]Fromm: *On Being Human*, 134-136.

48

2.6.3. The Reformation

In his famous study on freedom - *Escape from Freedom* (1941) - Fromm devotes one chapter to "Freedom in the Age of the Reformation".[175] In it he describes the economic changes during the transition from the Middle Ages to the Modern Era, how these changes affected different classes in society, and how the teaching of Luther and Calvin suited the 16th century middle class.

At the time of Luther's appearance man was at the same time gaining and losing freedom. The individual was becaming economically and politically freer, but was losing his fixed place in a closed world and the security that followed from this. "Paradise is lost for good, the individual stands alone and faces the world - a stranger thrown into a limitless and threatening world. The new freedom is bound to create a deep feeling of insecurity, powerlessness, doubt, aloneness, and anxiety."[176]

Luther's theology was directed at this powerless, humiliated man. But first Fromm turns to Luther as a person. He does not psychoanalyze Luther's personality thoroughly - this was done later by Erik H. Erikson[177] - but in his brief statement he does not hesitate to use strong words. Luther is said to have been a typical representative of the "authoritarian character"; he had an ambivalent attitude towards authority, was filled with doubts and with an extreme feeling of powerlessness, wickedness, and hatred of both himself, others, and life.[178]

Luther's own character determined his theology, the inner core of which is - according to Fromm - the belief in man's innate evilness. Man's nature is totally vicious, he is completely incompetent to do anything good on his own merits. His only chance is total submission to God. While freeing individuals from the authority of the Pope and the Church, Luther at the same time makes them submit to another, higher authority, God. This corresponds to the situation of the middle class at the time; freed from the authority of feudalism, but subordinated to the higher powers of emerging capitalism. For many people feeling very alone and powerless, Luther's theology was a way to handle this feeling, something that

---

[175]Fromm: *Escape from Freedom*, 40-102.
[176]op.cit., 63.
[177]Erikson: *Young Man Luther*.
[178]Fromm: *Escape from Freedom*, 66. In later works Luther is characterized with the following attributes: "obsessional, hoarding (anal), father centered, unloving, and isolated", (Fromm & Maccoby: *Social Character in a Mexican Village*, 234) and as "a man of fear, superstition, and hate". (Fromm: "Humanism and Psychoanalysis" *Contemporary Psychoanalysis* 1 (1964), 73.

could give them hope to find a new security through complete submission and self-humiliation.[179]

Calvin's theology resembles that of Luther in many ways. The submissive feature is even more prevalent in Calvin, "self-humiliation and the destruction of human pride are the *Leitmotiv* of his whole thinking."[180] Of the differences between Luther and Calvin Fromm brings out only two: Calvin's deepening of the doctrine of predestination and the greater emphasis on moral effort and a virtuous life. The idea of predestination is for Fromm the utmost expression of the insignificance of the individual, and a motive for the basic inequality of men[181] which found its most vigorous revival in Nazi ideology.[182] By emphasizing a virtuous life and unceasing effort Calvinism became crucial for the development of capitalism, as proved by Max Weber in his famous work on Protestant ethics and capitalism.[183]

The picture Fromm gives of the doctrines of Luther and Calvin is not a beautiful one, and many Protestants would certainly protest against it.[184] But it should also be mentioned that Fromm gives the Reformators credit for freeing man from the

---

[179]Fromm: *Escape from Freedom*, 74-84.
[180]op.cit., 84. In a later work Fromm summarizes the ideas of Luther and Calvin as follows: "To be aware of one's powerlessness, to despise oneself, to be burdened by the feeling of one's own sinfulness and wickedness are the signs of goodness." (Fromm: *Man for Himself*, 150)
[181]The Calvinist idea of predestination is in Fromm's opinion in blatant contradiction to the idea of God's love (Fromm: *Psychoanalysis and Religion*, 62f.), and the anxiety it creates can be seen as a severe defect. (Fromm: "Individual and Social Origins of Neurosis" *American Sociological Review* 9 (1944), 383; Fromm: *Man for Himself*, 222) Fromm compares the anxiety that this doctrine creates to the experience of being condemned without knowing the reason that the main character K. experiences in Kafka's *The Trial*. (op.cit., 168)
[182]Jeremias totally agrees with Fromm on this point: "Die Seligen und die Verdammten, vorherbestimmt vom imaginären Gott, säkularisierten sich im Hitler-Deutsch zu 'Ariern' und 'Nicht-Ariern', die man vom 'Blut', von der 'Rasse', von der 'Erbmasse' her prädestiniert sind, 'selig' oder 'vedammt' zu sein." (Jeremias: *Die Theorie der Projektion im religionskritischen Denken Sigmund Freuds und Erich Fromms*, 200; cf. p. 195)
[183]Fromm: *Escape from Freedom*, 84-94. Fromm was very familiar with the ideas of Max Weber from his time as a young student in Heidelberg, where he had Max Weber's brother Alfred as his teacher. (Funk: *Erich Fromm*, 46) He gave a more detailed description and criticism of Weber's theory in an essay written in 1937 and published posthumously. (See Fromm: *Gesellschaft und Seele*, 87-91. Cf. Fromm: *Escape from Freedom*, 296f.)
[184]See, e.g., the review of *Escape from Freedom* by Boisen in *Psychiatry* 5 (1942), 113-117, which is a defence of religion in general and Protestantism in particular against Fromm's interpretation. Banks ("A Neo-Freudian Critique of Religion: Erich Fromm on the Judaeo-Christian Tradition" *Religion* 5 (1975), 129) interestingly states that it is easier to defend Calvin than Luther. He then defends Calvin but acknowledges that Fromm put his finger on areas where there are inconsistencies and dubious elements in Calvin's theology.

authority of the Church and for giving all responsibility to the individual.[185] But to Fromm the humanist, for whom the idea of the dignity of man is central, the Protestant doctrine of man's innate evilness is something repulsive. The difference between Luther and humanism is that according to humanism, man's perfectibility is dependent on his own efforts,[186] and freedom is not only freedom from political servitude but also freedom to realize one's humanity.[187]

In other works, too, Fromm comments on Luther and Calvin. As we have already seen (chapter 2.1.) he regards Calvinism as a typical example of an authoritarian religion. Another feature he ascribes to Protestantism is that of patricentrism and patriarchalism. One important source for Fromm's thinking was the studies about matriarchal societies by the 19th century scholar Johann Jakob Bachofen. Fromm was already writing about Bachofen's theories in the early 1930's and later frequently returned to them. From Bachofen he got the concept of the difference between motherly and fatherly love. Motherly love is unconditional, while fatherly love is dependent on the child's behavior. The mother loves all her children unconditionally, while the father loves the child most that resembles him most.[188]

The Protestant idea of salvation totally dependent on God's grace without any personal effort corresponds to motherly love, while the Catholic idea that man can contribute to his salvation corresponds to fatherly love. In the later development, however, Protestantism became more and more patriarchal, while Catholicism holds many matriarchal characteristics: the idea of the mother Church, the reverence for the Virgin,[189] and the unmarried priest who can function as both father and mother.[190]

---

[185]Fromm: *Escape from Freedom*, 74; cf. p.38. In a later work Fromm commends Luther for his fight against the clerical authority who denied man direct access to God. "This Lutheran tradition is one of the bases of our modern concept of freedom and individuality." (Fromm: "Freedom in the Work Situation". In: Harrington -Jacobs (Eds.): *Labor in a Free Society*, 6).

[186]Fromm: "Introduction". In: Fromm (Ed.): *Socialist Humanism*, vii.

[187]Fromm: "Humanism and Psychoanalysis" *Cont Psycha* 1 (1964), 73.

[188]This idea is elaborated in Fromm: *The Art of Loving*, 41-46, and expressed in several other works.

[189]Luther's elimination of the mother figure inspired Fromm to make an interesting comment. Fromm accused Freud of totally neglecting or misunderstanding women, and thus doing for psychology what Luther did for religion. "Properly speaking, Freud is the psychologist of Protestantism." (Fromm: *The Sane Society*, 44 n.12) On another occasion Fromm compares Luther to Jung. (Fromm: "C.G. Jung: Prophet of the Unconscious" *SA* 209/3, 283)

[190]Fromm & Maccoby: *Social Character in a Mexican Village*, 113 n.8, 115 n.9. Cf. Fromm: "Die sozialpsychologische Bedeutung der Mutterrechtstheorie" *GA* I, 105-107; Fromm: *The Art of Loving*, 66f.; Fromm: *To have or to be?*, 145f.

Patriarchalism is, according to Fromm, characterized by a strict superego, guilt feelings, compliant love for fatherly authority, a desire to rule over weaker persons, the acceptance of suffering as punishment for one's guilt, and a disturbed capacity for happiness. Matriarchalism, on the other hand, is characterized by optimistic confidence in unconditional motherly love, fewer guilt feelings, a less strict super ego, and a better capacity for happiness and pleasure.[191] Despite this characterization, patriarchalism is not only something negative. The renaissance of the patriarchal spirit initiated by the Reformation is seen by Fromm as having both negative and positive aspects. The negative aspect is the submission to authority and hierarchy, the positive rational thought and individualism.[192]

In dogmatics, it is the doctrine of original sin that repels Fromm in Protestantism. This doctrine is older than the Reformation, but it was given a new depth and importance by Luther, while humanists, including Marx, have had a more optimistic view of the human soul.[193] The doctrine of original sin led Luther and Calvin to claim that man should do everything to humiliate himself. This doctrine is rooted in self-contempt and self-hatred and stands in total contradiction to the biblical commandment to love not only one's neighbor but also oneself.[194] The Protestant idea that man must suppresss his self-interest and be an instrument for a higher purpose became, in a secularized version, the norm for modern society, where man is a tool for industrial progress.[195] In this way Luther and Calvin "psychologically prepared man for the role which he had to assume in modern society: of feeling his own self to be insignificant and of being ready to subordinate his life exclusively for purposes which were not his own. Once man was ready to become nothing but the means for the glory of God who represented neither justice nor love, he was sufficiently prepared to accept the role of a servant to the economic machine - and eventually a 'Führer'."[196]

All those familiar with Protestant theology know very well how Luther and Calvin can be defended against the claims of Fromm. Let us look closer at one

---

[191]Fromm: "Die sozialpsychologische Bedeutung der Mutterrechtstheorie" *GA* I, 104.

[192]Fromm: *The Sane Society*, 56. For a discussion of how patriarchalism and Protestantism were seen not only by Fromm but also by the other "Frankfurt Theorists" (including Tillich), see Hammond: "Patriarchy and the Protestant Conscience: A Critique" *Journal of Religion and Ethics* 9 (1981), 84-102.

[193]Fromm: *The Heart of Man*, 20f. Cf. Fromm: *You shall be as gods*, 122.

[194]Fromm: *Man for Himself*, 119f. Cf. Fromm: "Selfishness and Self-Love" *Psychiatry* 2 (1939), 507f.

[195]Fromm: *Man for Himself*, 134f.

[196]Fromm: *Escape from Freedom*, 111. Earlier in this book (p.38f.) Fromm also connects the Protestant idea of the unworthiness of the individual, his fundamental inability to rely on himself, and his need to submit with Nazism.

Protestant defence. Professor J. Stanley Glen - a Protestant theologian and minister of the Presbyterian (Calvinist) Church - has written a whole book defending Luther and Calvin and criticizing Fromm's humanistic religion.[197]

The basic mistake in Fromm's interpretation of Protestantism is, in Glen's opinion, that he postulates a reciprocal opposition between God and man. The more God is, the less man is. The Protestant position is thus seen by Fromm as a "God everything - man nothing" relation, equal to a tyrannical master-slave relation. But the relation between God and man cannot be compared to a relation between two men, because God is infinite and man is finite. The elevation of God, then, does not mean the degradation of man. God is not everything in order to make man nothing, God is not high so that man can be made low, God is not omnipotent so that man is a robot. On the contrary, the idea of salvation by grace alone (*sola gratia*) is to make man free, free from servitude to the church hierarchy as a possessor of divine grace (indulgence) and free from condemnation and guilt.[198]

On this basis Glen examines the two Protestant doctrines which Fromm abhorred, i.e. predestination and man's total depravity. Fromm has misunderstood both, he claims.

The doctrine of predestination is not the same as the philosophical doctrine of determinism. It does not mean that everything has been fixed in advance by God and that man is deprived of all responsibility, as Fromm interprets it. What does it mean then? It is interesting to note that Glen is more explicit about what predestination is not than about what it is. He constantly stresses how it should not be understood, i.e. as Fromm did, but is singularly brief about how it should be understood correctly. But in this he seems to tread in the footsteps of Calvin himself, because God's predestination "remained a mystery to Calvin",[199] and he did not find "final answers"; nor did he always succeed "in avoiding the extremes he recognized as dangerous".[200] And how can the statement by Calvin that when man falls he does so "according to the appointment of Divine Providence, but he falls by his own fault"[201] be interpreted in a non-deterministic way?

The only hint at how the doctrine of predestination could be interpreted in a non-deterministic way is an analogy that even in Glen's own opinion is

---

[197]Glen: *Erich Fromm: A Protestant Critique*.
[198]op.cit., 50-74.
[199]op.cit., 61.
[200]op.cit., 64.
[201]Quoted in op.cit., 63.

"oversimplified". It goes like this: " Assuming that the law of the state makes murder a crime, there are two possibilities. The state can rescind its law and make every murderer innocent, or it can retain its law and make every murderer guilty. But in doing this, it foreordains every murderer to execution or life imprisonment but without being responsible for the crime. Similarly with God - he can rescind his law and procure salvation for all. But he rejects this possibility because his grace would then be lawless and therefore completely permissive of evil."[202]

That the Calvinist doctrine of predestination is difficult to defend is clearly shown by this awkward attempt by Glen.[203]

In speaking of the Protestant doctrine of man's total depravity Glen has a stronger point. Luther and Calvin never taught that man is intrinsically or ontologically evil, only that man is totally incapable of earning salvation. Man's depravity is in the religious sphere alone. In the secular sphere, as a citizen and as a being created in the image of God, man is able to obey laws, do good, create and produce.[204]

What can be said of Glen's critique of how Fromm interpreted Reformatoric theology? Obviously a Protestant theologian will have a deeper knowledge of Luther and Calvin than a Jewish psychoanalyst. The claim that Fromm's interpretation is biased and one-sided and sometimes totally wrong is probably correct. But in my opinion Fromm also has a point in his criticism. It is possible to differentiate between Glen and Fromm by saying that what Glen is looking at is what Luther and Calvin really meant, while Fromm is more interested in the consequences of their doctrines for the common man.[205] And it is a truth beyond any doubt that the doctrine of predestination has been interpreted and understood by generations of Calvinist laypeople and also clergy as meaning that God has fixed everything in advance. The doctrine of man's total depravity has, furthermore, frequently resulted in people feeling totally condemned and

---

[202]op.cit., 63.
[203]For Fromm's more extensive discussion of the philosophical problem of determinism, see Fromm: *The Heart of Man*, 115-150.
[204]Glen: *Erich Fromm. A Protestant Critique*, 66-70.
[205]Dellbrügge has pointed out that Fromm probably did not know Luther and Calvin well enough, but that he understood their "Wirkungsgeschichte". (Dellbrügge: "Impressionen eines Theologen beim Lesen Erich Fromms". In: Evangelischer Studienzentrum Heilig Geist (Hrsg.): *Erich Fromm und der christliche Glaube*, 74.)

worthless.[206] Even Glen recognizes that Luther and Calvin are not entirely free from responsibility for creating these popular impressions.[207]

Glen criticizes Fromm in many other respects, too, such as for his acceptance of Weber's theory of the relation between capitalism and Protestantism,[208] his concept of authoritarian or sado-masochistic religion,[209] and his dependence on Feuerbach in the idea of religion as a projection.[210] Two of Glen's points for criticism I wish to discuss further: the claim that Luther and Calvin were great haters, and Fromm's ignorance of Italian and Spanish fascism.

Fromm claimed that Luther and Calvin "belonged to the ranks of the greatest haters among the leading figures of history, certainly among religious leaders."[211] Glen, naturally, opposes this and stresses the positive features of Protestant theology and the fact that the aim of the Reformators was the liberation of man. Behind Fromm's harsh statements is a sophisticated psychoanalytical theory about repressed hostility to the father which is then expressed as hatred of oneself and/or somebody or something outside oneself. Without going into this theory, suffice it to say that the statement that Luther and Calvin were great haters can, of course, be disputed. But it is a fact that Luther expressed himself in very aggressive words when attacking his enemies, be it the Pope or the rebelling peasants. One fact that Fromm does not, surprisingly enough, mention - and Glen does not therefore touch upon either - is Luther's antisemitism. The hatred of Jews shown in Luther's *Von den Juden und ihren Lügen* is an additional argument for the claim that Luther was indeed a great hater.[212]

---

[206]In 1934 Fromm already reviewed Sandford Fleming's book *Children and Puritanism*, which shows how young children in a Puritan Protestant context are taught how to feel like great sinners, and how this creates anxiety, doubt, submission and guilt. (Fromm: "Review of Sandford Fleming: *Children and Puritanism*" ZSF III (1934), 277)

[207]Glen: *Erich Fromm. A Protestant Critique*, 71-74.

[208]op.cit., 78-91.

[209]op.cit., 92-112.

[210]op.cit., 113-136. Glen claims that Fromm nowhere acknowledges his indebtedness to Feuerbach (p. 115). This is true only insofar as he does not make an explicit acknowledgement. Indirectly he does it, however, by stating that 1) he himself was heavily influenced by Marx (this he has done many times), and 2) Marx was influenced by Feuerbach (see, e.g., Fromm: "Marx's Contribution to the Knowledge of Man" SSI 7 (1968), 8; Fromm: *Beyond the Chains of Illusion*, 44).

[211]Fromm: *Escape from Freedom*, 95.

[212]In this book "the reformer rails against the Jews in his powerful, lusty style, with a torrential outpouring of passion that makes the diatribes of his predecessors seem languid, and that no one else, perhaps, has matched to this day." (Poliakov: *The History of Anti-Semitism I*, 216)

Fromm's reason for including Calvin among the ranks of great haters is predominantly his doctrine of predestination. The belief that some people are destined before birth to eternal damnation "represented psychologically a deep contempt and hatred for other human beings."[213] Against this it may be said that the reason for the doctrine of predestination was not hatred of anybody; it was the rational conseqence of a radical *sola gratia* belief. If man can do *nothing* for his salvation, he cannot believe, choose or receive, because believing, choosing, and receiving are also works of man. Such rational considerations lay behind the doctrine of predestination. But it is, of course, possible for a psychoanalyst to claim that the unconscious motive was hatred.

Glen asks the very well-justified question why Fromm does not discuss the issue of Spanish and Italian Fascism. If Protestantism is the root of Capitalism and indirectly resulted in Nazism, then what is the root of the Fascism "in the two nations of Western Europe in which Protestantism has had the least influence"?[214] Although Glen's claim that Franco and Mussolini are never mentioned in *Escape from Freedom* is wrong (Mussolini is mentioned on p.232), it is legitimate to ask why Fromm never analyzed the psychological conditions of Fascism in general, but concentrated solely on Nazism. Two things must be remembered. First, this choice can easily be understood as resulting from personal reasons. Fromm came from Germany and had personally suffered under the Nazis (exile). Secondly, although Fascism and Nazism share a contempt for democracy and authoritarianism, there is a difference between Italian and Spanish Fascism on the one hand and German Nazism on the other. The latter was racist, while obscure theories about superior and inferior races played almost no role in Italian and Spanish Fascism. In his analysis of Protestantism there are two features which Fromm connects with Nazism: the readiness to submit to an authority,[215] and the principle of the basic inequality of men that is an implication of the doctrine of predestination.[216] While the former is common to all forms of Fascism, the latter applies to German Fascism, i.e. Nazism, only.

I do not have any reason to defend Fromm on this point, however. Glen is right in his claim that an analysis of how the Renaissance, the Catholic Church, and medieval society contributed to the origin of capitalism would have nuanced the picture.[217]

---

[213]Fromm: *Escape from Freedom*, 89.
[214]Glen: *Erich Fromm: A Protestant Critique*, 84.
[215]Fromm: *Escape from Freedom*, 38f., 111.
[216]op.cit., 89.
[217]Glen: *Erich Fromm: A Protestant Critique*, 81-84.

Before ending the discussion of Fromm's view of the Reformation, I would like to mention an interesting study made by Lester C. Lee.[218] He wanted to know whether there is any truth in Fromm's claim that Protestantism, and especially Calvinism, is an authoritarian religion. He therefore created a questionnaire to measure the degree of agreement with typical authoritarian Calvinist teaching (the questions were approved by Fromm) and compared its results with another scale measuring the degree of dogmatism or authoritarianism. 177 active Presbyterians participated in the study. Such a study cannot *prove* or *refute* Fromm's claim, but the result was nevertheless interesting. "Thus it appears that the conclusions of Erich Fromm are supported. That is, those individuals who are believers in the teachings of the two major Reformation leaders, Martin Luther and John Calvin, are themselves authoritarian."[219]

2.6.4. Contemporary Christianity

As we have seen earlier (chapter 2.1.), Fromm was critical about the use of religion as an ideology in modern society. In this chapter we will look more closely at his comments on specific Christian phenomena in his own time.

When Fromm looks at contemporary Christianity, what he appreciates is the Christian humanism. Although the mainstream of humanism has in the past few centuries been outside religion, there are and always have been humanists within Christianity. Fromm mentions the Quakers as one example of this in his own day.[220] He had come into contact with the Quakers through his engagement in the peace movement[221] and during his study of a Mexican village.[222] The silent meetings of the Quakers held a great appeal for him. He recognized the need for some kind of ritual, and saw the "rational humanistic rituals" of the Quakers as an attractive alternative.[223]

---

[218]Lee: *An Investigation of Erich Fromm's Theory of Authoritarianism.*
[219]op.cit., 91.
[220]Fromm: *Marx's Concept of Man*, 65f.
[221]See his commendation of Quaker involvement in the struggle for peace, in Fromm: *On Disobedience*, 102, 112. Fromm's little book *War Within Man* of 1963 was published by a Quaker organization, the American Friends Service Committee.
[222]Fromm & Maccoby: *Social Character in a Mexican Village*, XIII.
[223]Fromm: *Psychoanalysis and Religion*, 111 (for a psychological interpretation of religious rituals, see op.cit., 106-111). In *The Revolution of Hope* he draws on the meetings of the Quakers when he writes about the meetings of the radical humanistic clubs that he suggests as a tool for radical change in society (p. 158-162). He also encourages his readers by saying that important movements in history have always started with small groups, and mentions as examples the first Christians, the first Quakers, and - more surprisingly - the first Free Masons

In the late 1960's Fromm greeted with enthusiasm the "humanist renaissance that is taking place within the Roman Catholic and the Protestant churches".[224] This humanist renaissance had been greatly stimulated by the late Pope John XXIII.[225] Fromm continues that this humanist renaissance has led to a new dialogue, not only between Catholics and Protestants, but also between theistic and non-theistic humanists. By this he means the dialogue between Christians and Marxists.[226] As further representatives of Catholic humanism he mentions Teilhard de Chardin,[227] Hans Küng, and Karl Rahner.[228] He notes with satisfaction that since the second Vatican council - summoned by Pope John XXIII - there have been theologians who believe that non-believers can also gain salvation. Their ideas to some extent resemble Karl Rahner´s concept of "anonymous Christians".[229]

John XXIII was succeeded as Pope by Paul VI. Although he, too, published some radical statements, e.g. about the peace issue, he did not impress Fromm as much as his predecessor. In 1966 Fromm appealed to the Pope to arrange a world conference for peace. To Fromm's disappointment the Catholic leadership did not

---

(p.160). In a campaign speech that Fromm wrote for Eugene McCarthy in 1968 he makes the same point, and mentions as examples - beside these three - the Essenes, the monastery groups, the Jesuits, and the early socialists and anarchists. (Fromm: *On Being Human*, 58, cf. 59-61.)
[224]Fromm: "Foreword II". In: Fromm: *Psychoanalysis and Religion* 2. ed., vii; cf. Fromm: *On Disobedience*, 48. In *You shall be as gods*, 229, he also mentions - beside Catholic, Protestant and Marxist humanism - Jewish humanism.
[225]Later Fromm mentioned John XXIII - together with Schweitzer and Einstein - as an example of the small minority "in whom there is no trace of necrophilia, who are pure biophiles motivated by the most intense and pure love for all that is alive." (Fromm: *The Anatomy of Human Destructiveness*, 367) And Fromm quoted with approval a statement from John XXIII's encyclica *Pacem in terris*. (Fromm: *Ethik und Politik*, 199)
[226]Fromm: *On Disobedience*, 49.
[227]In *You shall be as gods*, 134 n. and in *The Revolution of Hope*, 18 n.12, Fromm compares Teilhard de Chardin's idea of the vertical and horizontal with the idea of Leo Baeck. And in *The Anatomy of Human Destructiveness*, 220, he mentions Teilhard de Chardin as one of the authors who have made contributions to the problem of the nature of man from an evolutionary standpoint. And in Fromm - Xirau "Introduction". In: Fromm- Xirau (Eds.): *The Nature of Man* Teilhard de Chardin is referred to concerning his ideas of man as the author of his own history (p.6), the development of human nature (p.8), and freedom (p.14).
[228]The Jesuit Rahner was mentioned not only in two lists of Catholic humanists, but also as a prominent humanist together with Einstein, Schweitzer, Bertrand Russell, Georg Lukacs, and Ernst Bloch. (Fromm: Preface; in Arasteh: *Rumi the Persian*, vii)
[229]Fromm: *On Being Human*, 138. Fromm himself asked Jesuits he met in Europe about the salvation of a non-believer who does God's will, and was very pleased when the answer was that the salvation of such a person is no problem (Letter Fromm- Merton 10.9 1963). Another version of this event is that Fromm asked this question in the first person: "I am a Marxist atheist, but I try to do God's will to the best of my knowledge... What do you think about my salvation?" (Fromm: "Doubts and Certainties" TV-Interview with Oliver Hunkin)

react.[230] The late 1960's saw the birth of liberation theology within the Catholic church. Fromm saw this - he mentions Archbishop Dom Helder Camara and "hundreds of Catholic priests", mostly in Latin America - as an example of humanistic non-idolatrous Christianity where the struggle for love, justice, and responsibility for each other is more important than dogmatics.[231]

Fromm seems to have had a special sympathy for the Jesuits; this is no great surprise because the Jesuits are - despite the solid negative image of them in Protestant countries - among the most radical groups in contemporary Catholicism. Fromm's positive attitude toward the Jesuits was probably influenced by the Jesuit Ivan Illich, one of his closest friends.[232] Anyway, as was stated above, Fromm met and discussed with many Jesuits. And in 1965 he stated in an interview: "Now, I don't belong to any religion, and I am a nonbeliever in any theological sense. However, I find myself very often in a profound understanding with liberal Jesuit priests, because we share a common concern that what matters is man's soul and that if he loses his soul, no riches he gains will save him."[233]

As representatives of Protestant humanism Fromm mentions Dietrich Bonhoeffer,[234] Karl Bultmann,[235] and "in a less radical sense", Paul Tillich. Tillich was a theologian whom Fromm not only read, but also met and cooperated with. They both shared the destiny of forced emigration from Germany to the USA, both had a background linked to the Frankfurt Institute of Social Research, and they had a common interest in a humanist interpretation of Marx. In *Marx's Concept of Man* Fromm several times quotes or refers to the writings of Tillich. In his many references to Tillich in all his works he only once declares his disagreement, and that is about the term "self-love".[236] He seems to have adopted one of his central religious ideas, the combination of the biblical concept of idolatry with the Marxian theory of alienation (see 4.4.1.), from Tillich.[237] Tillich

---

[230]op.cit., 93-98.

[231]Fromm: *Om Being Human*, 137f.

[232]See Fromm's praise of Illich in Fromm: "Introduction". In: Illich: *Celebration of Awareness*, 7-10.

[233]Fromm: "Interview with Richard Heffner" *McCalls* 92 (1965), 214.

[234]In *You shall be as gods*, 57 n., Fromm very briefly writes about some recent trends within Protestant theology - he mentions Tillich, Bonhoeffer, Bultmann, Th.J.J. Altizer, and John A.T. Robinson - and refers to Suzuki in order to show "the essential identity between Western theistic and Eastern nontheistic mystical attitudes.

[235]This is an error; Bultmann's first name is Rudolf.

[236]Fromm: *The Art of Loving*, 57 n.13. Tillich's critical comment on Fromm's idea of self-love was given in Tillich: "Erich Fromm's *The Sane Society*" *Past Psych* 6 (1955), 14.

[237]Fromm: *Marx's Concept of Man*, 44 n.1.

also reviewed two of Fromm's books. In his sympathetic, though critical, review of *Psychoanalysis and Religion* he claims that theistic Christianity can be understood in a way that avoids the dangers of authoritarian religion. What Fromm is fighting against, Tillich states, is not theism as such, but a heteronomous, supranaturalistic theism, a fight that is also a genuine theological concern, a fight against idolatry in which theology and psychotherapy are allies.[238]

The resemblances between the ideas of Tillich and Fromm are great, as has been shown in several studies.[239] When, after an interview about man's needs, Fromm had the opportunity to suggest further reading, he recommended two of his own books, one by Lewis Mumford, and Tillich's *The Courage to Be*.[240] He nevertheless wrote in a letter to James Luther Adams: "Tillich's and my attitudes I think were rather far apart although we had always a sufficient strong basis for an open and fruitful discussion of all problems that interested both of us."[241] According to Rainer Funk, who knew Fromm very well during the last years of his life, Fromm was positive about the ideas of Tillich, but was somehow distrustful about his character. When the memoirs of Tillich's wife openly revealing Tillich's erotic adventures were published, Fromm felt confirmed in his evaluation of Tillich's character.[242]

Another contemporary Protestant theologian who did not gain as much praise as Tillich from Fromm was Reinhold Niebuhr. Niebuhr's emphasis on original sin was repellant to Fromm,[243] because it was precisely this doctrine that Fromm

---

[238]Tillich: "Review of Erich Fromm: *Psychoanalysis and Religion*" *Past Psych* 2 (1951), 62-66.
[239]There are several studies comparing Fromm's and Tillich's thinking from different perspectives, e.g. Rössler: "Zwei Pole in Gott" *EvK* 15 (1982), 259-262; Hammond: "The Conscience-less Society and Beyond: Perspectives from Erich Fromm and Paul Tillich" *NZSThR* 25 (1983), 20-32; Hammond: *Man in Estrangement*
[240]Fromm: "Interview with Huston Smith: Man's Needs" *Science and Human Responsibility*, 13.
[241]Letter Fromm - Adams 2.5 1977. In the same letter Fromm also writes that Tillich "seemed to take a very sharp negative attitude to *The Dogma of Christ*."
[242]Personal communication from Rainer Funk 12.4 1997.
[243]Fromm: *Marx's Concept of Man*, vi; Fromm: *Die Pathologie der Normalität*, 87f.; Fromm: *On Being Human*, 74. It is interesting to note that a *Festschrift* for Niebuhr contains two very different Jewish contributions. Rabbi Alexander J. Burnstein claims that Niebuhr's views of man's evilness are not compatible with either the Old Testament or the Jewish tradition. (Burnstein: "Niebuhr, Scripture, and Normative Judaism". In: Kegley - Bretall (Eds.): *Reinhold Niebuhr. His Religious, Social and Political Thought*, 411-428) Abraham I Heschel, a philosopher rooted in the Hasidic movement, claims that Niebuhr and the Jewish tradition are basically compatible. (Heschel: "A Hebrew Evaluation of Reinhold Niebuhr". In: op.cit., 391-

disliked most in Protestant theology. But Fromm had to admit that this neo-orthodox Lutheran position assumed, paradoxically, by Niebuhr was combined with a progressive political philosophy.[244]

Looking at the names Fromm mentions as humanist theologians one may also wonder at those which might have been expected but are missing. I am surprised that neither Jürgen Moltmann nor Harvey Cox are mentioned. Fromm once referred to Cox as a "profound American theologian" who has expressed in religious language the idea - very important to Fromm - that man has become a slave to his machines.[245] Considering the enormous impact of Cox's *The Secular City* (1965), one might have expected more comment from Fromm. Cox for his part wrote a very positive review of *You shall be as gods*[246] and professed himself "a great admirer" of Fromm, "...this great man, whom I met and admired intensely..."[247] Moltmann's *Theologie der Hoffnung* one might have expected Fromm to quote or refer to in his *The Revolution of Hope*. Moltmann wrote of Fromm's book: "As I read Erich Fromm's new book, on almost every page I had the auspicious feeling that the theology of hope had to be continued in this 'revolution of hope'."[248]

The contemporary Christian theologian whom Fromm admired most was Albert Schweitzer. This extraordinary theologian, physician, musician, and missionary was praised by Fromm as "one of the great representatives of the love of life - both in his writings and in his person",[249] as (together with Einstein) manifesting "the highest development of the intellectual and moral traditions of Western culture",[250] as being a pure biophile "motivated by the most intense and pure love for all that is alive",[251] and as an enlightened non-idolater.[252]

Fromm must have seen in Schweitzer a kindred spirit. In many ways they shared the same convictions. Schweitzer's philosophy of "reverence for life" is almost

---

410)

[244]Fromm: *Man for Himself*, 212 n.67. In 1955 Niebuhr supported an initiative by Fromm appealing to the President of the USA not to engage in any military operations against China, a crucial issue at that time. (See Fromm: *Ethik und Politik*, 235-256)

[245]Fromm: *The Condition of the American Spirit. Are We Fully Alive?* (manuscript), 13.

[246]Cox: "A Test of Faith" *NYTBR* 27.11 1966, 10 and 12.

[247]Cox: "Fromm's Eclecticism" *NYT* 7.5 1980.

[248]Moltmann: "The Impossible Dream?" *Critic* (Febr./March 1969), 80.

[249]Fromm: *War Within Man*, 15 n.9; Fromm: *The Heart of Man*, 47 n.9; Fromm: *The Anatomy of Human Destructiveness*, 366 n.35.

[250]Fromm: *The Sane Society*, 229.

[251]Fromm: *The Anatomy of Human Destructiveness*, 367.

[252]Fromm: *The Revision of Psychoanalysis*, 52.

identical with Fromm's idea of biophilia as the optimal orientation in life. Or - as Fromm himself put it - "reverence for life" is the ethics of biophilia. *"Biophilic ethics* have their own principle of good and evil. Good is all that serves life; evil is all that serves death. Good is reverence for life, all that enhances life, growth, unfolding. Evil is all that stifles life, narrows it down, cuts it into pieces."[253]

As a social critic, too, Fromm felt spritually akin to Schweitzer. Both shared a deep antipathy toward the dehumanizing features of modern society. According to Fromm, Schweitzer "belongs to the few who saw in all clarity what modern progress in the bourgeois sense of maximal production and consumption would do for the substance of man, how it would make man passive, suggestible, fragmentised, and he did this as early as the first 15 years of this century..."[254] When in *The Sane Society* Fromm gives a pessimistic diagnosis of the "pathology of normality" in modern society, he includes a long quotation from Schweitzer.[255] And again, in *To have or to be* Fromm quotes Schweitzer's radical criticism of industrial society.[256] Both Fromm and Schweitzer opposed the atom bomb and struggled for nuclear disarmament.

Schweitzer's radical criticism of modern society was the focal point for the essay Fromm wrote on the centenary of Schweitzer's birth. In this essay on the ambiguity of progress Fromm seeks a third way between the conservatives, who want no progress, and the "progressives", who uncritically accept every development in technology and economics. The representatives of the third way - the radical humanists or the "antiprogressive progressives" - see the problems of industrial and economic progress, but they do not want to return to past eras but have their sights directed at the future. Schweitzer was the person who - according to Fromm - expressed this view most clearly and may serve as the prophet for those struggling for the humanization of modern technology and economics.[257]

In his religious beliefs as well Fromm tried to make Schweitzer his ally. According to him Schweitzer was a metaphysical sceptic who was attracted to Buddhism and saw the meaning of life as something man has to give himself, not something given by a supreme being. He even makes Schweitzer a representative

---

[253]Fromm: *The Anatomy of Human Destructiveness*, 365f. Cf. Fromm: *War Within Man*, 15; Fromm: "Essay". In: *Summerhill: For and Against*, 254; Fromm: *The Revolution of Hope*, 88f.
[254]Letter Fromm - Darmstadter 7.6 1975.
[255]Fromm: *The Sane Society*, 229-232.
[256]Fromm: *To have or to be?*, 161-163.
[257]Fromm: "Die Zwiespältigkeit des Fortschritts" *EvK* 8 (1975), 757-758.

of godless religiosity. Evidence for this is to be found in a statement in a private letter that "the religion of love can exist without a world-ruling personality".[258]

In the 1970's Fromm planned a work on non-theistic religiosity in Buddhism, Meister Eckhart, Marx and Schweitzer. Unfortunately he was not able to fulfil his plans and only produced some fragments dealing mainly with Meister Eckhart. Writing about Schweitzer as a representative of non-theistic religiosity, Fromm says "we have his own words to go on"[259], but he does not give any references. Hence the only evidence of Schweitzer's non-theism presented by Fromm is the quotation from the letter mentioned above.

To anyone used to viewing Schweitzer as a Christian theologian and missionary, Fromm's idea of him as a non-theist might seem exaggerated. But Fromm's claim is not as radical as one might think. In fact, many scholars have recognized Schweitzer's very unorthodox tendencies and have, with different moderations, called him an agnostic.[260]

Beit Hallahmi[261] makes the peculiar claim that Fromm "has become a representative of liberal Protestantism", that he is "much closer to liberal Protestantism" than to orthodox Judaism, and that "he has been associated with this movement", i.e. liberal Protestantism. Fromm can indeed be associated with liberal Protestantism and is in many regards close to Schweitzer and Tillich, who can both be regarded as representatives of this movement. But making Fromm a *representative* of liberal Protestantism as well is a definite exaggeration which Fromm himself would have soundly denounced. Fromm represented no religion, he had a humanistic world view with elements taken from Buddhism, Judaism and other religions and philosophies. The fact that this humanistic belief to a certain extent resembles liberal Protestantism should not allow us to jump to conclusions.

---

[258]Fromm: *To have or to be?*, 163.

[259]Fromm: Fragments on Meister Eckhart. In: Frederking: *Durchbruch vom Haben zum Sein*, 454.

[260]See, e.g., Picht: *Albert Schweitzer. Wesen und Bedeutung*, 74-78; Kantzenbach: *Albert Schweitzer. Wirklichkeit und Legende*, 12f.

[261]Beit-Hallahmi: "Religiously based differences in approach to psychology of religion: Freud, Fromm, Allport and Zilboorg". In: Brown (Ed.): *Advances in the Psychology of Religion*, 24.

2.7. Mysticism

Zen Buddhism and mysticism were the religious phenomena that attracted Fromm most deeply. He defined his own religious position as "nontheistic mysticism",[262] and stated that the mystic movements - both Eastern and Western - have been carriers of the antiauthoritarian humanistic spirit.[263]

2.7.1. What is mysticism?

According to popular opinion mysticism is more or less the same as "mystification", connected with trance, ecstatic experiences, and a flight from everyday reality. For Fromm, however, mysticism is something totally different, although he recognizes that there are mystics for whom the popular belief is more or less correct. But for Meister Eckhart and certain other mystics it is completely false; their mysticism is the highest development of rationality in religious thinking. To support this view, Fromm quotes Schweitzer's statement: "Rational thinking which is free from assumption ends in mysticism."[264]

For Fromm mysticism is something existential and nondogmatic. Compared with mainstream religion there is in mysticism a shift from dogmatics to ethics, from believing to experiencing, from having to being. Fromm connects mysticism with the being mode of faith, where a person is said to *be in* faith rether than to *have* faith.[265] Fromm thinks that it is impossible to make any statement about God in the way conventional Western theology does. But mysticism, "the consequent outcome of monotheism" and "the logical consequence of theology", has given up every attempt to know God by thought, and is instead striving to experience union with God without any room or need for knowledge *about* God.[266]

---

[262]Fromm: *You shall be as gods*, 19. He probably got this designation from Thomas Merton. In a letter to Merton on 9.10 1961 Fromm wrote: "You once called me an atheistic mystic, and I think quite rightly so..."
[263]See, e.g., Fromm: *To have or to be?*, 140; Fromm: *The Anatomy of Human Destructiveness, 234*.
[264]Fromm: *Psychoanalysis and Religion*, 93f. n.9. Cf. Fromm: *The Art of Loving*, 32; Fromm: *On Being Human*, 159. In "The Nature of Dreams" *SA* 180/5 (1949), 45, Fromm seems - at least to a certain extent - to compare the mystic *Versenkung* with abnormal states of mind (like states of hypnotic trance) although he adds that the mystic himself considers this state as the highest awareness.
[265]Fromm: *To have or to be?*, 43.
[266]Fromm: *The Art of Loving*, 32.

The nondogmatic character of mysticism is the reason why the mysticisms of different religions resemble each other so much. The conceptualizations differ, but the basic experience in Zen Buddhism, in Christian, Jewish, and Islamic mysticism is the same,[267] one of feeling oneness with oneself, with one´s fellow men, with all life, and with the universe. This experience of oneness with all does not mean self-denial or self-effacement. On the contrary, it is at the same time the fullest experience of individuality and of belonging.[268]

Fromm further distinguishes between narcissistic and sound mystical experience. Both resemble each other, but there is a decisive difference: while the narcissistic mystical experience is characterized by a loss of ego, an "oceanic feeling", the sound mystical experience of Buddhist, Christian, Jewish, and Islamic mysticism is characterized by a realistic relation to reality.[269]

Fromm carries the nondogmatic trend in mysticism so far as to claim that the mystics were nontheists (see 2.7.3.). This is the reason why he can state that there is no contradiction between so-called theistic, i.e. Christian, Jewish, and Islamic, mysticism and nontheistic mysticism, i.e. Zen Buddhism and his own eclectic religion.[270] This is also the reason why he so often compares Marx with the mystics.[271]

2.7.2. Islamic mysticism

Fromm makes a distinction between Western and Eastern mysticism, Zen Buddhism and Taoism being representatives of the latter. The Western tradition takes in Christian, Jewish, and Islamic mysticism. Fromm seems to have been most familiar with Christian mysticism (and especially his favorite, Meister Eckhart). Leaving Jewish mysticism to chapter 3, we will now turn to Fromm's treatment of Islamic mysticism.

---

[267]Fromm: *You shall be as gods*, 57; Fromm: *On Disobedience*, 52f.
[268]Fromm: *Psychoanalysis and Religion*, 95.
[269]Fromm: *The Revision of Psychoanalysis*, 79.
[270]Fromm: "Die psychologischen und geistigen Probleme des Überflusses" *GA V*, 327.
[271]"Marx's atheism is the most advanced form of rational mysticism..." (Fromm: *Marx's Concept of Man*, 64) Cf. Fromm: "Marx's Contribution to the Knowledge of Man" *SSI* VII (1968),11; Fromm: "Einige post-marxsche und post-freudsche Gedanken über Religion und Religiosität" *Concilium* 8 (1972), 472; Fromm: *The Dogma of Christ*, 110.

Fromm had very little to say about Islam. It appears in the lists of humanistic religions (see 2.1.), indicating that he was basically sympathetic towards a religion that has so often been demonized in the West.

The only phenomenon within Islam in which Fromm showed slightly more interest was Islamic mysticism. It appears a few times just as a label beside Jewish and Christian mysticism,[272]and twice Fromm discusses it briefly. In a footnote about the relation between Maimonides and the mystics he notes the influence of al-Farabi and his school on Maimonides, adding that Maimonides' son Abraham was the author of a number of antirational works which drew on Islamic mysticism.[273]

Of greater interest to the scholar is Fromm's second comment on Islamic mysticism. Fromm wrote a brief foreword to A. Reza Arasteh's book on the Persian mystic Rumi, a book that appeared in 1965. In it he notes that very little is known about Islamic humanism and Islamic mysticism in the Western world, that Arasteh has done contemporary man a real service by publishing this book by one of the greatest Islamic humanists and mystics. He further notes the similarities with Meister Eckhart, and states that Rumi was expressing the idea of religious tolerance 200 years before the Renaissance humanists. Rumi had a profound insight into the nature of man and was one of the great lovers of life. All his works are said to be imbued with this love of life.[274]

Having read this effusive praise, one can only be surprised that Fromm used the ideas of Rumi so little in his writings.[275] Was the enthusiasm expressed in this foreword really true?

---

[272]Fromm: *You shall be as gods*, 57; Fromm: *On Disobedience*, 53.
[273]Fromm: *You shall be as gods*, 37 n. Fromm's argument is somewhat vague here because al Farabi - a 10th century Islamic philosopher - was not a mystic.
[274]Fromm: "Foreword"; in Arasteh: *Rumi the Persian*, viiif.
[275]In *The Sane Society* a saying by Rumi is used as a motto for the book together with sayings from the Bible, Seneca, Emerson, and Léon Blum. In *Greatness and Limitations of Freud's Thought*, 9, the enthusiasm of Rumi - as well as of Meister Eckhart, Shakespeare, and Schweitzer - is mentioned as an example of love that is often banalized in psychoanalytical literature. And in *The Art of Loving*, 34f., Fromm quotes a poem by Rumi that expresses the polarity of the male and female principle. This is all Fromm has to say about Rumi in his extensive writing.

2.7.3. Meister Eckhart

Although the five most important influences on Fromm's thinking were - according to Fromm himself[276] - prophetic Judaism, Marx, Bachofen's theory of matriarchy, Buddhism, and Freud[277], his favorite authors were Marx and Meister Eckhart.[278] To anyone not familiar with Fromm's works these two may seem an odd pair, but Fromm stressed the close points of similarity between the socialist philosopher and the medieval Catholic monk several times.[279] He called Meister Eckhart "one of the boldest and most radical of thinkers",[280] and "one of the greatest masters of living".[281] He was quoted by Fromm very frequently and he appears together with the Buddha, Jesus, and other great personalities in Fromm's lists of great humanists,[282] of revolutionary characters,[283] and of non-idolaters.[284] In a letter dated 1974 Fromm wrote that Meister Eckhart was "a writer whom I have read practically uninterruptedly for the last twenty years. By that I do not mean that I read him every day but half an hour to an hour every week, together with my wife."[285]

I cannot clearly demonstrate when Fromm got to know Meister Eckhart. Chronologically the first reference to him is in 1947 and after appearing regularly in his writings, Meister Eckhart becomes the object of intense analysis in the mid-1970's.

Frederking - who has made a detailed and thorough study of Fromm's Meister Eckhartreception - has divided Fromm's treatment of the medieval mystic into two periods, the first being the 1950's and 1960's, the second the 1970's.[286] During the 1950's and 1960's Meister Eckhart appears in Fromm's writings as a

---

[276]Fromm: *For the Love of Life*, 105.

[277]Schultz has commented: "Das ist kein Synkretismus, das ist Universalismus." (Schultz: "Humanist ohne Illusionen" *EvK* 9 (1976), 37)

[278]op.cit., 108.

[279]E.g. Fromm: *Marx's Concept of Man*, 64; Fromm: *The Dogma of Christ*, 110; Fromm: "Einige post-marxsche und post-freudsche Gedanken über Religion und Religiosität" *Concilium* 7 (1972), 472; Fromm: *For the Love of Life*, 103.

[280]Fromm: *For the Love of Life*, 103.

[281]Fromm: *The Art of Being*, 9.

[282]Fromm: *Psychoanalysis and Zen Buddhism*, 136.

[283]Fromm: *The Dogma of Christ*, 115.

[284]Fromm: *The Revision of Psychoanalysis*, 52.

[285]Letter Fromm - Mieth 27.6 1974. In Fromm's library there are 34 books by or about Meister Eckhart.

[286]Frederking: *Durchbruch vom Haben zum Sein*, 223f.

representative of negative theology[287] and of paradoxical logic[288], and in his discussion of the love of God[289], the x experience[290], and the concept of self-love.[291]

In the 1970's Fromm devoted himself to the intensive study of Meister Eckhart. The result of this can be seen in *To have or to be?*, where he devotes one chapter to "Having and Being in the Old and New Testament and in the Writings of Master Eckhart", and in posthumously published manuscripts.

In *To have or to be?* Fromm analyzes Meister Eckhart's view of having and being. According to him, Meister Eckhart described and analyzed this issue "with a penetration and clarity not surpassed by any teacher".[292] Following a sophisticated exegesis of some statements in the sermons of Meister Eckhart, he states that the great mystic taught that being poor in spirit (Matthew 5:13) means overcoming greed and certainty and letting nothing, neither things and property nor good deed and knowledge, not even God become an object of craving. Instead man should strive towards productive activity, which is not the same as being busy, but an authentic activity that goes out of oneself. "Breaking through the mode of having is the condition for all genuine activity. In Eckhart's ethical system the supreme virtue is the state of productive inner activity, for which the premise is the overcoming of all forms of egoboundness and craving."[293]

Besides the chapter in *To have or to be?* Fromm wrote much more about Meister Eckhart in the 1970's. A longer study has been published posthumously[294] and Frederking has published several shorter fragments in an appendix to his book.[295]

The point Fromm makes in his analysis of Meister Eckhart is that the medieval mystic was a non-theist, like the Buddha, Marx, and Schweitzer.[296] To be able to

---

[287]Fromm: *Psychoanalysis and Religion*,116; Fromm: *The Dogma of Christ*, 137; Fromm: *You shall be as gods*, 31 n.
[288]Fromm: *The Art of Loving*, 77.
[289]op.cit., 80f.
[290]Fromm: *You shall be as gods*, 57. Fromm does not mention Meister Eckhart here, only Christian mysticism, but Meister Eckhart is for Fromm the Christian mystic *par excellence*.
[291]Fromm: *The Art of Loving*, 57-63.
[292]Fromm: *To have or to be?*, 59.
[293]op.cit., 65, see 59-65.
[294]Fromm: *On Being Human*, 114-170.
[295]Frederking: *Durchbruch vom Haben zum Sein*, 423-457.
[296]According to Fromm there are two forms of atheism: the materialistic-bourgeoisie and the revolutionary-mystical atheism. Meister Eckhart and Marx, naturally, represent the latter form. (Fromm: Interview with Alfred A. Häsler: "Der Undenkbare denken und das Mögliche tun" *Ex*

argue this, he introduces a method of literary analysis drawn from psychoanalysis. Because Meister Eckhart lived at a time when the idea that there is no God was not only unspeakable but also unthinkable, he clearly never explicitly denied the existence of God. His unmistakably non-theistic statements have traditionally been interpreted in a harmonizing way, as "allegories" or "images", in the light of his stated orthodoxy. But according to Fromm the real message is the one that is hidden. Just as in psychoanalysis one has to listen to the hidden content that is not intended to be expressed, the truth which the person is afraid to reveal, so a person's writings can be psychoanalyzed to find the "unconscious knowledge". A study with this method - Fromm describes in detail what to look for in the written text - shows that the non-theistic statements of Meister Eckhart are the revolutionary new insight, although they are veiled in the garments of orthodox formulations.[297]

According to Fromm, Meister Eckhart wrote on three levels. On the first his views conform with traditional scholastic thinking. On the second we find Meister Eckhart's negative theology, mainly influenced by Maimonides, the author he quoted more than any other. "On a third level, Eckhart, by implication, denies the being of the Christian God. He does that only in rare statements and in the form of minimizing the significance of the Trinitarian God of Creation in favor of what he calls the 'Godhead'."[298]

Meister Eckhart distinguished between the Christian God of the Bible (Gott) and the Godhead (Gottheit), which are as far apart as heaven and earth. The God of Creation, the God of the Bible is, Fromm states, treated by Meister Eckhart with "polite negligence". One of the bold statements made by the mystic is this: "How then shall I love him? Love him as he is, a not-god, a not-ghost, apersonal, formless. Love him as he is the One, pure, sheer and limpid, in whom there is no duality; for we are to sink eternally from negation to negation in the One."[299]

---

libris 22 (No.5, 1977), 18; Fromm: Interview with Micaela Lämmle and Jürgen Lodemann in 1977; Fromm: "Konsumreligion" *Neues Forum* 301/302 (Februar 1979), 13)

[297]Fromm: Fragments on Meister Eckhart. In: Frederking: *Durchbruch vom Haben zum Sein*, 450-452. A method like this is, of course, extremely problematic, although Fromm claims that it is not as difficult as it seems at first glance. An experienced psychoanalyst knows the method. Frederking comments that this method approaches "die Grenzen wissenschaftlichen Kommunizierbarkeit". (op.cit., 300)

[298]Fromm: *On Being Human*, 119, see 118f.

[299]Quoted in Fromm: Fragments on Meister Eckhart. In: Frederking: *Durchbruch vom Haben zum Sein*, 445.

The Godhead is the absolute Nothing which cannot be understood, described, or named, and is identical with the ground of man's soul (Seelengrund). Meister Eckhart asks the Godhead: "Please get me rid of God." Fromm's conclusion: "This view is not any longer Christian or theistic, but it is Eckhart's 'secret view', which came to his consciousness only a few times in sermons, when he seemed to have been inspired and in a semi-trancelike state. Only if one deals with Eckhart's writings as a closed system without immanent contradictions can one come to the conclusion that Eckhart's non-theistic statements can be ignored. If one understands Eckhart's writings as the utterances of a creative man, full of contradictions, and on rare occasions expressing his usually 'repressed' thoughts one can understand his role as one of the earliest representatives of non-theistic 'religiosity'."[300]

The monotheistic development culminated in Meister Eckhart, whose radical formualtion of negative theology led to a non-theology. "The God of Creation - the active god - lost his supreme role, and the 'Godhead', far above the God of Creation, was no god to think about, to talk about, or even to talk to. He was stillness and silence, he was no-thing. What alone mattered was man, the process of inner liberation, his efforts to become a just being."[301]

Having compared Meister Eckhart's mysticism with Marx's humanistic writings, Fromm comes to the conclusion: "There is little difference, except in terminology, between Eckhart's atheistic mysticism and Marx's concept of man as the highest being for himself. Both are atheistic, both speak against the idolization of man, for both the fulfillment of man lies in the unfolding of his essential power as a purpose in itself. If Eckhart was an atheistic mystic speaking in the language of theology, Marx was an atheistic mystic speaking in the language of post-Hegelian philosophy."[302] As an example of a scholar who has clearly seen the implicitly religious character of Marx's writings and the kinship between unalienated Christianity and unalienated Marxism, Fromm mentions Ernst Bloch.[303] Bloch was also interested in Meister Eckhart[304] and his Eckhart-interpretation shows many similarities, though also differences, with Fromm's.[305]

---

[300]op.cit., 122f.; cf. Fromm: Fragments on Meister Eckhart. In: Frederking: *Durchbruch vom Haben zum Sein*, 441.
[301]Fromm: *On Being Human*, 136.
[302]op.cit., 169f. For a more systematic comparison of Meister Eckhart and Marx, see Fromm: Fragments on Meister Eckhart, in Frederking: *Durchbruch vom Haben zum Sein*, 436f.
[303]Fromm: *On Being Human*, 115, 170.
[304]See, e.g., Bloch: *Das Prinzip Hoffnung*, 1534-1540; Bloch: *Zwischenwelte in der Philosophie-geschichte*, 156-163; Bloch: *Atheismus in Christenthum*, 92-95, 285-287.
[305]Frederking: *Durchbruch vom Haben zum Sein*, 99-101, 286f., 312, 388. Bloch and Fromm

Fromm was not the first to claim that Meister Eckhart was a non-theist. He himself refers to Schopenhauer[306] and to some other scholars, among them the Japanese scholars, including Suzuki, who have analyzed Meister Eckhart's affinity with Buddhism.[307] All have claimed that Meister Eckhart's view of God is that "God is nothing", in contrast to the other "God is being"-opinion. Frederking has claimed that Fromm is too bold in his conclusions here. The Japanese scholars have correctly noted that when Meister Eckhart states that "God is nothing", it is an epistemological and not an ontological statement. In contrasting God and the Godhead, Meister Eckhart does not eliminate the concept of God, he just relativizes and transcends it. Fromm's main point - that Meister Eckhart was, with his statements about the Godhead and "God is nothing", a non-theist - is not correct when it comes to the explicit utterances of the medieval mystic. But using the literary method of Fromm it is, of course, possible to claim that unconsciously Meister Eckhart was making an ontological statement and thus denying the existence of God altogether.[308]

2.7.4. Thomas Merton

Thomas Merton was a Catholic writer who lived as a monk in a Trappist monastery in Kentucky, but managed to become a well-known and influential thinker in the 1950's and 1960's. He wrote a letter to Fromm in 1954, and from then onwards they engaged in lively correspondence. Merton can be seen as a modern Christian mystic who shared with Fromm a deep mistrust of modern

---

were two Marxist writers with many similar ideas about Marxism and religion. They held a mutual appreciation of each other, but they met only once, when Fromm was very young. (Fromm: Letter to Karola Bloch. In: K. Bloch - Reif (Hrsg.): *"Denken heisst Über-schreiten"*. *In memoriam Ernst Bloch 1885-1977*, 317. In this letter to Bloch's widow Fromm writes that Bloch and he both stood in the revolutionary-mystical tradition.)

[306]Fromm: *On Being Human*, 119; Fromm: Fragments on Meister Eckhart, in: Frederking: *Durchbruch vom Haben zum Sein*, 447, 452, 454. The passage referred to is Schopenhauer: *Sämmtliche Werke 3*, 705. Other plausible utterances about Meister Eckhart that Fromm does not refer to are op.cit., 703f.; Schopenhauer: *Aus Arthur Schopenhauer's handschriftlichem Nachlass*, 432f,

[307]In a letter to Nyanaponika Mahathera dated 4.12 1972 Fromm refers to a sermon of Meister Eckhart and writes that it "seems to be clearly written in the Buddhist rather than in the Christian spirit." In his answer Nyanaponika Mahathera refers to a German Buddhist who called Meister Eckhart "the Buddha of the West". (Letter Nyanaponika Mahathera - Fromm 31.12 1972)

[308]Frederking: *Durchbruch vom Haben zum Sein*, 296-301. A similar criticism of Fromm's notion of the atheistic mystics is given by Isaac. (Isaac: "Review of Fromm: *You shall be as gods*" *Commentary* 43 (May 1967), 99)

society, a strong commitment to nuclear disarmament, and a great interest in Zen Buddhism. There were plans for a book by Fromm, Merton and Suzuki[309], but they were never realized.

In their correspondence Fromm and Merton show a great cordiality that is more than normal courtesy. As Fromm once wrote: "There are so few of us who keep their faith, and I feel from all you say that even though we speak often in different words, the faith is the same."[310] But they were never afraid of expressing their disagreements. The most interesting concerns the religiosity of the mystics. Merton writes that even though Fromm is correct in saying that true mysticism does not know God as "an object outside ourselves, as 'another being' capable of being enclosed in some human concept", it is not correct to claim that the mystics were non-theists. "...the majority of true mystics stand and fall with the existence or non-existence of God."[311] Unfortunately Fromm does not comment on this in his answer.

In 1963 Fromm wrote a short book named *War Within Man*. His text is then commented on by six persons, one of them Merton. In his comment[312] Merton declares his full agreement with Fromm and then adds some further thoughts. Fromm concludes his own response to the comments by thanking and praising Merton in a beautiful text that I want to quote at some length.

"To read Thomas Merton's comments was deeply satisfactory. First of all because he expresses with clarity and courage many truths which need to be said. Beyond this I am always happy to find that Thomas Merton reacts with a spirit of true charity to what he reads. Not only that he does not distort things and ignore others which have been said. He tries to transcend the *words* of the author and to understand what he means or even what he *might* mean if he were fully aware of the consequences of his own ideas.[313] Much as we differ in our religious concepts, I feel that more important than conceptualization (even though I do not mean to say that it does not matter) is the experience of that which can not be verbalized. Thomas Merton is a true religious humanist who seeks understanding and not arguments because he can see man behind his thoughts. I want to stress briefly how much I agree with Thomas Merton's emphasis on 'the overwhelming and almost totally neglected importance of exploring this spiritual unconscious of

---

[309]Letter Fromm - Merton 3.11 1960.
[310]Letter Fromm - Merton 30.1 1962.
[311]Letter Merton - Fromm 2.10 1954.
[312]Fromm: *War Within Man*, 44-50.
[313]The way of reading that Fromm here praises is very close to the literary method he described a decade later when dealing with the Meister Eckhartinterpretation (see 2.6.3.).

72

man.' I believe that any real change in man depends on this discovery of one's self and of exploring the depths of what he calls one's 'spiritual unconscious.' ...

Let me conclude with a reference to Thomas Merton's statement toward the end of his commentary. I too find hope in the fact that man is not alone.[314] The humanism expressed in Thomas Merton's comment is a greeting from man to man, a greeting beyond the barriers of separating thoughts, it is an affirmation of the humanity in which we all share."[315]

2.8. Conclusions

Fromm's view of religion is consistent, but also sometimes vague. While he commends all the great world religions for having humanistic ideals as their core, he can on other occasions be very critical of some of the central concepts of the same religions. One gets the impression that to be, say, a good Christian in Fromm's opinion one has to reject or ignore a good part of what has been considered as traditional Christianity. But still Christianity is a progressive religion and Jesus one of the greatest spiritual leaders of all times.

With some religious phenomena Fromm is very polemic. The best example of this is his treatment of the Reformation. On other occasions he interprets religion in a very symphathetic way, emphasizing the good traits and to a great extent ignoring the concepts he does not share. This is especially evident in his extensive writing on Buddhism, where he hardly mentions the central Buddhist ideas he cannot believe in. But when dealing with the Reformation, he acts in exactly the opposite way. Time after time he brings forth the negative, the concepts that he abhors.

Another notable trait in Fromm's religious writing is his interest in dogmatists. He is opposed to dogmatism, emphasizes the importance of ethics over dogmatics, and stresses that the important thing is not what you believe but what you do. But despite all this, he shows a great and positive interest in the chief dogmatist of the Catholic church, Thomas Aquinas. His great hero is Meister Eckhart, a member of the dogmatics-oriented Dominican Order, and not the non-dogmatic, saintly Francis of Assisi, who appears only once in passing in Fromm's writings.[316]

---

[314]This statement can be contrasted with what Fromm wrote more than a decade later about the non-theistic world view: "There is no God, no father, no king, no idea, no institution which takes care of us, consoles us, loves us, saves us. We are alone!" (Fromm: Fragments on Meister Eckhart. In: Frederking: *Durchbruch vom Haben zum Sein*, 454)
[315]Fromm: *War Within Man*, 55.
[316]op.cit., 53.

Analyzing Fromm's interpretation of religion raises the question whether he dreamt of creating a new humanistic religion stripped of all dogmatic superstructure. In fact, he was thinking about this alternative.

In *The Sane Society* Fromm describes the transformation he considers necessary to create a sane society. Transformation must take place not only in the economic and political sphere, but also in the cultural. And one cannot speak of a cultural or spiritual transformation without mentioning religion.[317] In the short run Fromm's suggestion is that believers and non-believers should join together in the struggle against idolatry. In the long run he expects the theistic concepts to disappear and give place to a new universalistic religion that will embrace the humanistic teachings common to all great religions. It would doctrinally be in line with present-day science, and it would be more oriented towards the practice of life than doctrinal beliefs. This religion will be born - just like all other great religions - with the appearance of a great new teacher when the time is ripe. "In the meantime, those who believe in God should express their faith by *living* it; those who do not believe, by living the precepts of love and justice and -waiting."[318]

Thirteen years later Fromm is more hesitant about the potential for a new religion without revelation or mythology. A religion is always born within a historic context, one cannot just put some principles together to form a religion. Fromm sees no new Moses or Buddha and this may even be good, because a new leader is quickly transformed into an idol and his religion into idolatry. Despite this Fromm is hopeful. The necessary transformations will lead to a spiritual renewal and perhaps one day to a "total and socially accepted system".[319]

In his third book with a vision for a new society - *To have or to be?* of 1976 - Fromm touches only very briefly upon the demand for a new, nontheistic, noninstitutionalized religiosity, a religiosity long prepared by the movement of

---

[317]Fromm believed that the reason for the failure of socialism was its neglect of the religious need for a frame of orientation and an object of devotion. Fascism and Stalinism in all their dreadfulness gave people this and therefore they were victorious in many countries. (Fromm: *Die Pathologie der Normalität*, 95f.)

[318]Fromm: *The Sane Society*, 352, see 351f. In a footnote to this passage Fromm refers to a similar suggestion for a new humanistic religion made by Julian Huxley. Huxley's view of religion resembled that of Fromm in many ways. See, e.g., his *Religion without Revelation*. Already in a lecture in 1953 Fromm referred to Huxley's idea of a new religion, and stated that the ideas of Huxley resemble his own very much. (Fromm: *Die Patholoige der Normalität*, 95f.)

[319]Fromm: *The Revolution of Hope*, 137f.

nontheistic religiosity, from the Buddha to Marx. He notes that such a religiosity is not a threat to the existing religions, and - very typical of his thinking - adds: "It does mean, however, that the Roman Catholic Church, beginning with the Roman bureaucracy, must convert *itself* to the spirit of the gospel."[320]

Betz has argued that Fromm was not only a secular prophet, but that he also functioned as a messiah, a founder of a new humanistic religion. He presents three arguments for this: "(1) the content and form of his writings have the character of a religious idom; (2) in his person Fromm goes beyond the prophetic role to that of the 'new leader' who perceives himself as destined to found a new religion; (3) in his activities, Fromm has searched for movements which would give him an effective platform from which to voice his new religion."[321]

Betz's first point is incontestably correct, but the fact that Fromm's writing is religious does not make him a founder of a new religion. There is also some truth in Betz's third point. Fromm entered and left many movements, including the psychoanalytical and the socialist movement, during his life. But so have many others. And what does it prove? Hardly that they have rejected the priestly role of maintaining the received doctrines for a prophetic role of developing new doctrines, as Betz suggests.[322] Disapproval of a social movement does not make one a messiah-to-be.

The crucial point in Betz's hypothesis is the claim that Fromm had a messianic self-image, that he might have been speaking about himself when he wrote about the new leader that will appear "when the time is ripe" (see page 60). Fromm is said to have many of the traits characteristic of a religious leader. He was a prophet, a moralist, a poet, a visionary, an eternal optimist, a good theologian and a good confessor (as against many religious leaders who are capable theologians but poor confessors). That Fromm was a religious leader can further be seen from the severity of the opposition of his critics. Fromm's Jewish origins also contributed to his aspirations for founding a new religion (cf. Spinoza, Marx and Freud), Betz claims.[323]

---

[320]Fromm: *To have or to be?*, 202.
[321]Betz: *An Analysis of the Prophetic Character of the Dialectical Rhetoric of Erich Fromm*, 313f.
[322]op.cit., 324.
[323]op.cit., 316-320. Schaar has alsopointed out Fromm's alleged ambitions to become a popular leader. "If Freud is the Moses who showed the people the way out of the Egypt of their own passions, Fromm is the aspiring Joshua who would lead them into the promised land of the sane society." (Schaar: *Escape from Authority*, 5). Schaar is a rabid Fromm-critic and his remark must be seen as a spiteful remark and nothing else.

In my opinion, Betz's claim is pure nonsense, although several of his comments are correct. There is nothing in Fromm's life or work that suggests that he dreamt of becoming a messiah or a religious leader. Quite the opposite: he was very anxious not to establish any kind of school.[324] Therefore there is no Frommian psychoanalytical movement or school today. It is, of course, possible to claim that deep in his heart he dreamt of a position as a religious leader or that his unconscious ambition was to be a messiah, but then we have left the field of scientific research and entered the world of speculation.

Saavedra - who studied psychoanalysis for Fromm and later wrote a very critical book about him - has also characterized Fromm as a religious leader of whom his disciples speak in religious terms and with veneration.[325] That some of Fromm's disciples use words like pilgrimage, preach, and salvation when they write about him might be considered unwise or silly. But one should not overinterpret this. It can also be seen as a pure expression of their great appreciation of Fromm. And at least it says nothing about Fromm's own aspirations.

Fromm's hesitation about a new humanistic religion springs from the fact that he was perfectly aware of the dangers with any institutionalized form of religion. His vision was a society without religion but instead a religious society. When the essence of religion - justice, freedom, and love - is being practiced in society as a whole, there is no need for religion as some institutional "extra". Religion is needed only when society is irreligious.[326] For Fromm the shell is nothing, the important thing is the content. Organizations and institutions are nothing, life is what matters. "*Die* Religion ist gar nichts. Religiös leben ist alles."[327]

---

[324]"... I have never wanted to found a school of my own." (Letter Fromm - Jay, in: Kessler - Funk (Hrsg.): *Erich Fromm und die Frankfurter Schule*, 251. Cf. Fromm: Interview with Heiner Gautschy)
[325]Saavedra: *La promesa incumplida de Erich Fromm*, 121-123.
[326]Fromm: "Konsumreligion" *Neues Forum* 302/302 (1979), 13; Fromm: Interview with Michaela Lämmle and Jürgen Lodemann in 1979. According to Fromm this was also the idea of Marx. His opposition to religion was only an oppositioin to institutionalized religion, not to authentic religious life, which he promoted. "I am sure that Marx was a nontheistic religious man. His idea was that as long as the world acts in a non-religious way religion necessarily must be apart from real life and therefore also distort its true kernel... As I see it, Marx's idea was the realisation of the religious values of [the] Eastern and Western tradition in modern society and this he called socialism." (Letter Fromm - Adams 1.10 1974)
[327]Fromm: Interview with Guido Ferrari 8.3 1980.

3. Fromm and Judaism

3.1. Biographical background

Erich Fromm was born into an orthodox Jewish family. Among his ancestors were many prominent rabbis and Talmudists. His grandmother was descended from the great medieval commentator on the Bible and the Talmud, Rashi, and her father was a famous German rabbi.[1] Fromm's father, Naphtali, was a wine-merchant and very active in Jewish life in his home town, Frankfurt.[2]

The young Fromm led a traditional Jewish life, followed all the rules, studied the Bible and Talmud. At the same time he went to a German school and took part in German culture just like all other Germans. But he always had a feeling of being a stranger. "... I feel glad to have this experience as the Old Testament once said: 'Love the stranger because you know the soul of the stranger for you have been [a] stranger in Egypt.' One can really understand the stranger only if one has been thoroughly a stranger and being a stranger means one is at home in the whole world."[3] Here we can see the roots of Fromm's later cosmopolitanism.

Fromm later wrote[4] that as a young man he had three important teachers, all great rabbinical scholars. The first was his mother's uncle, Ludwig Krause, "a traditionalist, little touched by modern thought"[5] whom he loved and admired very much.[6] He must have been really impressed by Krause, who spent his last years living with the Fromms in Frankfurt[7], because after graduating from school he wanted to go to Lithuania and study to become a Talmud teacher. He did not do so because of the fierce opposition from his father, not because his father had anything against the Talmud, but because he did not want his son to go all the way to Lithuania.[8]

---

[1]See the family tree in Funk: *Erich Fromm*, 18f.
[2]op.cit., 19-21.
[3]Fromm: Interview with Gerard Khoury 1979.
[4]Fromm: *You shall be as gods*, 12f.
[5]ibid.
[6]Fromm: Interview with Gerard Khoury 1979. Fromm mentions one episode that left a lasting mark on him. He once asked Onkel Krause what he thought would become of him. The answer was: an old Jew.
[7]Funk: "Die jüdischen Wurzeln des humanistischen Denken von Erich Fromm" (manuscript), 2.
[8]Fromm: Interview with Gerard Khoury 1979.

The second influential teacher was the Frankfurt rabbi Dr. Nehemia Anton Nobel, a learned teacher and an excellent preacher. Nobel was influenced by Jewish mysticism and was a humanist in the spirit of Goethe and Kant. The group of young men that gathered around him was heavily influenced by the Jewish Neo-Kantian Hermann Cohen, who regularly listened to Nobel in the synagogue up to his death in 1918.[9] After Nobel's sudden death in 1922 Fromm published a short note in the *Neue Jüdische Presse* in which he praised Nobel as a leader for the young generation. The feature that Fromm especially praised was not his deep knowledge, but the fact that he lived what he taught.[10]

In 1919 Fromm took part in the formation of a society for Jewish adult education in Frankfurt. The prominent Jewish philosopher Franz Rosenzweig was soon employed by the society and a "Freie Jüdische Lehrhaus" was established.[11] At this institute a lot of great Jewish scholars were teaching, such as Martin Buber, Gershom Scholem, Leo Baeck, Leo Löwenthal, and the later Nobel prize winner Samuel Josef Agnon.[12]

The death of Nobel in 1922 was a great loss for all his students, among them Fromm. But Fromm - who was at this time in the final stages of his studies at the University of Heidelberg - had in Heidelberg found another, his third important Talmud teacher and spiritual guide, Dr. Salman Baruch Rabinkow. For several years Fromm visited Rabinkow almost daily. Beside the Talmud he also studied Maimonides and Hasidism. Rabinkow was not only heavily influenced by Habad-Hasidism, he was also a socialist.[13]

---

[9]Funk: *Erich Fromm*, 29-33. In *You shall be as gods*, 13, Fromm describes Nobel as "deeply steeped in Jewish mysticism as well as in the thought of Western humanism."
[10]"...er *lebte*, was er sagte, und nur sagte, was er lebte." (Fromm: "Rabbiner Nobel als Führer der Jugend" *Neue Jüdische Presse* 2.2. 1922, 3. The note was anonymous, but the Leo Baeck Institute has ascribed it to Fromm, which is probably correct.)
[11]The society was founded by the liberal rabbi Dr. Georg Salzberger and Fromm, who also first suggested that Rosenzweig should be called to Frankfurt. (Salzberger: "Erinnerungen von Rabbinern Dr. Georg Salzberger an die 20er Jahre" (transcript of a radio programme).
[12]Funk: *Erich Fromm*, 33f. About the institute, see Sesterhenn (Hrsg.): *Das Freie Jüdische Lehrhaus - eine andere Frankfurter Schule*. Fromm's relation to Scholem cannot have been very close because in his memoirs - published in 1977 - Scholem later came up with the totally erroneous claim that Fromm later became an enthusiastic Trotskyite. (Scholem: *Von Berlin nach Jerusalem*, 197f.) Scholem also called Fromm a psychoanalytical Bolshevik. (In a letter to Walter Benjamin, published in Scholem: *Walter Benjamin - die Geschichte einer Freundschaft*, 285) Burston (*The Legacy of Erich Fromm*, 13, cf. 78) has claimed that there might be some truth in Fromm's alleged Trotskyism.
[13]Funk: *Erich Fromm*, 37-39. Cf. Fromm: *You shall be as gods*, 13.

Salman Baruch Rabinkow was a very special man. Born into a Hasidic family in Russia in 1882, he studied with several teachers before going to Heidelberg, where he lived as a Talmud teacher. Although he was formally trained as a rabbi, he never occupied any office because he wanted to stay away from all establishments.[14] During his time in Heidelberg he collected a group of young students around him - many of whom would become famous and influential - who admired him immensely.[15]

Due to his modesty Rabinkow never occupied any office and, despite his vast knowledge, wrote almost nothing. The only written work by him is an essay from 1929 on the individual and the community in Judaism.[16] It shows many similarities with Fromm's later works.[17] But to understand the influence of Rabinkow on Fromm one does not have to compare texts. One just has to look at Fromm's own statements.

In the 1970's Leo Jung asked some of Rabinkow's students - Fromm, Ernst Simon, Nahum Goldmann and others - to write their reminiscences of him. These were published as late as in 1987.[18] In his own essay[19] Fromm brings out Rabinkow's humility, kindness, realism, tolerance, honesty, humor, love of life, humanism and all-pervasive sense of freedom. "He was one of the most extraordinary, most gifted, and most interesting men I have ever met..."[20]

Fromm also acknowledged the deep influence of Rabinkow on him. His being is said to have "left the deepest impression on me" and he "has been one of the greatest influences in my life".[21] "Rabinkow influenced my life more than any other man, perhaps, and although in different forms and concepts, his ideas have remained alive in me."[22] That Fromm's relation to Rabinkow was one not only of

---

[14]Once he was offered the chair of Halakhah at the Hebrew University but turned the offer down. (Simon: "Reminiscences of Shlomo Barukh Rabinkow". In: Jung (Ed.): *Sages and Saints*, 119)

[15]Funk: *Erich Fromm*, 37; Honigmann: "Der Talmudistenkreis um Salman Baruch Rabinkow". In: Giovannini - Bauer - Mumm (Hrsg.): *Jüdisches Leben in Heidelberg*, 265-267.

[16]Rabinkow: "Individuum und Gemeinschaft im Judentum". In: Brugsch - Lewy (Hrsg.): *Die Biologie der Person IV*, 799-824.

[17]See Funk: *Erich Fromm*, 40-44.

[18]Schacter (Ed.): "Reminiscences of Schlomo Baruch Rabinkow". In: Jung (Ed.): *Sages and Saints*, 93-132.

[19]op.cit., 99-105.

[20]op.cit., 99. How extraordinary a man Rabinkow must have been is shown by the fact that the other writers give a similar description of him.

[21]op.cit., 100.

[22]op.cit., 103.

admiration but even of identification is shown by the fact that when Funk wanted to describe how he experienced Fromm, he quoted long passages from Fromm's description of Rabinkow, and stated that this was how Fromm was.[23]

In his reminiscences of Rabinkow Fromm did not write anything about his teacher's religious thinking. But in a letter to Leo Jung he wrote that "I had ever the feeling that his religious attitude was essentially a mystical one. He was strictly a man of the Halacha but I never heard him speak about God or in any 'theological' terms. His attitide [sic] was in this respect typically Chassidic which fits his Chabad background. In fact I think aside from my teacher Nobel, he was a great influence in my life in the direction of mysticism. I cannot really prove that, since he never talked about his belief even in this sense but it is a firm impression I have."[24]

Krause, Nobel and Rabinkow were the three teachers who influenced Fromm during his most formative years. Although he ceased to practice his childhood orthodoxy and to be a believing Jew, he could still write about these three teachers that "...my views have grown out of their teaching, and it is my conviction that at no point has the continuity between their teaching and my own views been interrupted."[25] And in a letter to Rabinkow's widow he wrote that although he was probably the only one of Rabinkow's disciples who had ceased practicing Jewish life, Judaism, as learnt from Rabinkow, was always part of him, and that an essential part of his development was due to the influence of Rabinkow.[26]

In the early 1920's Fromm encountered psychoanalysis. Through a friend he got to know the analyst Frieda Reichmann, a Jewess who had a psychoanalytical sanatorium where Jewish traditions were strictly upheld. Fromm started analysis with Reichmann and in 1926 they married. Not only because of the analysis, but also through other impulses - such as the encounter with Buddhism - Fromm dissociated himself from orthodox Judaism, as did his wife. In 1926 he ceased to obeserve Jewish traditions and no longer considered himself a theist.[27] The final

---

[23]Funk: "Der Humanismus in Leben und Werk von Erich Fromm. Laudatio zum 90. Geburtstag". In: Wissenschaft vom Menschen/Science of Man 3, 146-148.
[24]Letter Fromm - Jung 18.10 1972.
[25]Fromm: *You shall be as gods*, 13.
[26]Letter Fromm - Rabinkow-Rothbard 9.7 1964.
[27]Funk: *Erich Fromm*, 49ff. The fact that Fromm, Reichmann, and several of her clients gave up their orthodox praxis led Scholem to write that the result of the therapy was that the Orthodox Judaism of the clients was analyzed away. (Scholem: *Von Berlin nach Jerusalem*, 197f.)

step away from orthodoxy was a certain event in Munich in 1926. Like Eve before the tree with the forbidden fruit, Fromm stood before a street vendor's stall and could not resist the temptation to buy and eat a sizzling pork sausage. He thus ate non-kosher food for the first time in his life.[28]

Many features of Fromm's thinking have been seen as having their root in the orthodox Judaism of his childhood and youth. Among them are the following:

* His opposition to capitalism and commercialization. Fromm himself stressed the fact that his anti-capitalist views were indebted to the milieu he was born into. That milieu was prebourgeois, precapitalist, premodern. Very typical of this way of life was the story about one of his great-grandfathers, a shop-keeper who spent his days sitting in his shop studying the Talmud. "Whenever a customer came in, he would look up and snap at him: 'Isn't there some other shop you can go to?' That was the world that was real to me. I found the modern world strange."[29]

* His strong ethical orientation. Fromm had a very intense feeling for ethical values. Standing for truth and righteousness, serving life and opposing death, developing the art of loving were what he strove for in his own life and teaching. He recognized these values and goals as the basis of all humanitarian religions (see 2.1.). He himself first encountered them in the Judaism practiced in his home.[30]

---

[28]Funk: *Erich Fromm*, 44. This is the version Funk heard from Fromm. According to Frieda Fromm-Reichamnn, their first trespass was the eating of bread during the Passover in Heidelberg. (Fromm-Reichmann: Autobiographical tapes (transcript).)

[29]Fromm: *For the Love of Life*, 99. Cf. Knapp: *The Art of Living*, 3f.

[30]Beit-Hallahmi ("Religiously based differences in approach to the psychology of religin: Freund, Fromm, Allport and Zilboorg", in Brown (Ed.): *Advances in the Psychology of Religion*, 24) makes an interesting comparison with Freud: "Freud, who knew Jewish tradition more superficially, found in them and analyzed, ritual and mythology. Fromm, with his strict Talmudic training, found in Judaism (and in all other religions) an ethical concern worth preserving, and not much else." Knapp (*The Art of Living*, 10) writes about his Talmud studies that "the insights gained from these studies were to be integrated directly as the strong moralistic focus of his entire later works." For me the word "moralistic" has an unpleasant ring. Because I do not find any narrow moralism in Fromm's writings, I would replace it with "ethical". Knapp uses the words "moral" and "moralistic" alternately (see op.cit., 2f.). Chrzanowski ("Das psychoanalytische Werk von Karen Horeny, Harry Stack Sullivan und Erich Fromm". In: Eicke (Hrsg.): *Tiefenpsychologie 3*, 375f.) has also claimed that there is a dogmatic moralism in Fromm's thought. In a letter to Martin Jay Fromm wrote that he was often accused of moralism - especially by Adorno and Horkheimer - but that he found this accusation unjust. (Letter Fromm - Jay 14.5 1971. In: Kessler - Funk (Hrsg.): *Erich Fromm und die Frankfurter Schule*, 254.

* A messianic tendency. There is in Fromm's thinking an insistence on human renewal and societal change, a belief in the possibility of building a better world. This belief can be seen as a secular version of the belief in a messianic age (about this theme, see 4.6.2.). Messianism, ethical commitment and social justice are the themes that occupied not only Fromm but also Horkheimer and the other members of the Frankfurt school,[31] one of the most remarkable Jewish sects, as Scholem once called it.[32]

* His style of writing has also been seen as deriving from his early studies of the Talmud. Fromm is said to have had a peculiar way of reiterating his argument and starting with a summary of what is to come, thus trying to persuade the reader by rephrasing the important points. All this should be very similar to the literary style of the Talmud.[33]

3.2. The Jewish Law: dissertation of 1922

In 1922 Fromm wrote a doctoral dissertation at the University of Heidelberg entitled *Das jüdische Gesetz. Zur Soziologie des Diaspora-Judentums*. His "Doktor-Vater" was the well-known sociologist Alfred Weber. The dissertation was published as late as 1989.[34]

The aim of Fromm's work was to analyze how the Jewish Law was interpreted in three movements within Diaspora Judaism, i.e. Karaism, Reform Judaism, and Hasidism. It begins with a chapter on the meaning of the Law in Judaism.

What is it that has kept Judaism together through out the centuries without an organization, a state, or a common language? According to the young Fromm, it was the biblical belief in God, expressed in the words of Deut. 6:4: "Hear, o Israel, the LORD is our God, the LORD is one." This statement is undogmatic. The Jews believe in God and in the Messiah, not in statements (Aussagen) about God and the Messiah. The Jewish Law was very undogmatic and so is Judaism. The Karaites were the first to create dogmas within Judaism, and Maimonides was the first to make a dogmatic system. But the Jewish people was not influenced by the dogmatic efforts of some of its teachers.[35] Even at this early

---

[31]Tarr - Marcus: "Erich Fromm und das Judentum". In: Kessler - Funk (Hrsg.): *Erich Fromm und die Frankfurter Schule*, 218.
[32]Scholem: *Von Berlin nach Jerusalem*, 167.
[33]Knapp: *The Art of Living*, 44f.
[34]For the background facts, see Funk's foreword in Fromm: *Das jüdische Gesetz*, 9-13.
[35]Fromm: *Das jüdische Gesetz*, 18-28.

stage - while himself being a practicing Jew - Fromm already shows an antipathy towards dogmas, something that later became an important part of his humanistic religiosity.

The Jewish Law, which demands certain acts not beliefs, is meant for the whole community, not for a certain group or certain individuals. That the Law is equal for everyone is a sign of democracy. The Law wants to give people the chance to reach the goal, it is not a goal in itself. Therefore it is called *halacha*, a way.[36] The Law wants to change the surrounding world (Umwelt) first. This is shown by the Sabbath commandment. It does not say in what mood a Jew should celebrate the Sabbath, but it gives detailed prescriptions about what to do and not do. "Das Gesetz will die Umwelt verändern, um den Menschen die Möglichkeit zu geben, sich selbst zu ändern."[37] The Law is given to the people, its commandments should be practiced by the individual, the community, and the family. The Law has a twofold purpose: to be a guide for the control of this world (e.g. the dietary laws) and to help the individual to rest, to be free from the sorrows of this world (e.g. the Sabbath commandment). Rest in the Bible and in Rabbinical Judaism is not the same as doing nothing. The idea of the Sabbath is to give the individual a chance to direct his activity to the religious sphere.[38]

Next come two excursuses. The subject of the first is work and calling (Beruf) in Rabbinical Judaism. Taking Max Weber's theory about the connection between religious belief and the conception of work and calling as his starting-point Fromm seeks to show the truth in Weber's statement that there is a basic difference between Puritanism and Judaism. Judaism has a positive outlook on this world and is not ascetic. Work is not an end in itself but a means to earn one's living. Rabbinic Judaism has a traditionalistic or non-capitalistic view of economies. But work is also seen as something good that no-one should withdraw from without good reason. The legal position of the worker is also rigorously protected in Judaism. Fromm supports all his arguments with frequent and long quotations from the Bible and the Talmud. At the end of the excursus he argues against Werner Sombart, who claimed that Judaism was imbued by the spirit of capitalism and in fact a form of Puritanism. Sombart's basic mistake was, according to Fromm, that to support his claim he quoted 19th century German

---

[36]In a later work Fromm notes that *halacha* has the same meaning as Tao. (Fromm: *The Art of Loving*, 78)

[37]Fromm: *Das jüdische Gesetz*, 32.

[38]op.cit., 29-40.

rabbis, who in Fromm's opinion did not represent the Jewish religion but identified themselves with the capitalist culture.[39]

The second excursus deals with the Christian concept of revelation and the concept of the divinity (Göttlichkeit) of the Torah in Judaism. The Christian concept of revelation implies two beliefs: 1. The divinity of the book is based on its author and giver. 2. Every single commandment is sacrosanct and unalterable. Both these beliefs are in Fromm's opinion in strong opposition to historical Judaism. According to Rabbinical Judaism, all generations stood on the mountain of Sinai when the Law was given. Thus the historical event of the giving of the Torah is of no importance; each generation must itself experience it as a living reality. Historical Judaism has also changed several commandments in the Torah, e.g. concerning the death penalty and the levirate. Despite this the Christian concept of revelation has been adopted and adjusted to the Torah by the Neo-Orthodox wing of Judaism.

The divinity of the Torah has, according to Fromm, nothing to do with the historical event of its giving or with the unalterability of its commandments. "'Göttlichkeit' der Tora meint, dass alle einzelnen Bestimmungen der Tora Sinn und Bedeutung nur durch ihre Beziehung zum Göttlichen haben und dass sie nur in ihrer Totalität und in ihrer Bezogenheit zur Sphäre des Göttlichen gesehen werden können und dürfen."[40] The important thing is that there is a people that carries with it the Torah and makes it a living reality for each new generation. The branches of Judaism that have abandoned the idea of the people, i.e. the Karaites, the Neo-Orthodox and the Reform Jews, have also adopted the Christian concept of revelation. The Reform Jews have, furthermore, abandoned the practical consequences of the Law.[41]

3.2.1. The Karaites

The first branch of Diaspora Judaism which Fromm analyzes is Karaism, a Jewish sect founded in the 8th century in Babylonia by Anan ben David. After a short presentation of the sect[42] he examines the economic background to the birth of Karaism. According to him, the reason for the birth of this sect was political, not religious. Anan's brother was exilarch and Anan revolted against the institution of

---

[39]op.cit., 40-57.
[40]op.cit., 61.
[41]op.cit., 57-65.
[42]op.cit., 67-70.

a united exilarchy for the Jews in Babylonia. Because the Kalifate supported the exilarch, Anan was imprisoned as a a rebel. In that situation Anan was forced to claim that his religion was something different from Rabbinic Judaism. The Karaites were mainly wealthy people engaged in international trade. That such people accepted Karaism is easily understood because Rabbinic Judaism was critical of "big business". Through tradesmen Karaism spread very rapidly to many countries. It adjusted very easily to the surrounding culture and adopted ideas especially from Islamic theology but also from Christianity. The decline of Karaism in the 13th century was also due to economic reasons. In many countries the economic and legal situation of the Jews deteriorated and this development hit the Karaites in particular.[43]

The main difference between Rabbinic Judaism and Karaism was basically that the Karaites did not accept the Oral Law. Their only authority was the Bible. This "back to the Bible" idea led to an individualization of the Law. Instead of recognizing a community that interpreted the Law and shaped their differences to a uniform totality, the Karaites believed that every individual could read the Law and interpret it in his own way. This resulted in the creation of several Law Books written by different Karaite leaders. These books differed greatly from each other. Lacking a common interpretation of the Law, the Karaites attempted to create a common dogmatic system. Whereas Rabbinic Judaism advocated a collective understanding of the Law and individualism in faith and belief, Karaism advocated "Individualismus des Gesetzes" and "Kollektivismus des Glaubens".[44]

Although Fromm must have devoted considerable time to the study of Karaism, he never returned to it later. In all his later writings I have found only one mention of Karaism, in a footnote in which he compares the controversy between Karaism and Rabbinic Judaism with that between the Pharisees and the Sadducees.[45]

3.2.3. Reform Judaism

Fromm starts his chapter on Reform Judaism with a description of the emancipation of the European Jews.[46] Although the text is mostly soberly descriptive, his negative opinion of Reform Judaism is revealed when he states that there were two ways out of the difficult situation of isolation and

---

[43]op.cit., 70-83.
[44]op.cit., 83-96.
[45]Fromm: *You shall be as gods*, 39 n.
[46]Fromm: *Das jüdische Gesetz*, 97-106.

discrimination: liberation from within through spiritual renewal (which happened in Poland through Hasidism), and outward liberation (emancipation) through a movement (Reform Judaism) that - in the words of Simon Dubnow - in its moderate form resulted in the renewal of Jewish culture, and in its extreme form in the destruction of Jewish culture.[47]

When Fromm analyzes the birth of the Reform movement he once again stresses the sociological and economic background. The growing class of rich Jewish businessmen saw the Jewish traditions as ballast in their economic affairs. Therefore they wanted to get rid of the dietary laws and the duty to pray daily. The demand that Sunday and not Saturday be the day of rest was strictly economically motivated. Rich laymen were for a long time the leaders of the Reform movement, and only later were some rabbis ready to become the spiritual leaders of the new movement which the representatives of the richest capitalist layer had called for. Fromm's analysis cannot veil his own hostility towards Reform Judaism. There are several nasty sneers, and Fromm is not slow to remark about many leading representatives of the Reform movement that they later converted to Christianity.[48]

Having scrutinized the sociological background of Reform Judaism, Fromm turns to its theology. He starts with Moses Mendelsohn, the forerunner of the Reform movement. As regards theology, Mendelsohn was a representative of the national rabbinic Judaism, emphasizing the importance of the Law and the freedom of belief, but sociologically he became the pioneer of Reform Judaism by allying himself with the German intelligentsia.[49]

For the rich laymen who started the Reform movement the Jewish Law was an obstacle to their entrance into German capitalism. Therefore the Reform movement created the basic principle that the Law is unessential and Judaism is a community of believers. The central doctrine was the belief in ethical monotheism. By renouncing the Law, the Reform movement also denied the

---

[47]op.cit., 98.
[48]op.cit., 106-123. Cf. Fromm's statement more than fifty years later: "In fact, when the well-to-do Jews worked for 'emancipation' they threw away the pride and dignity that characterized them as long as they were poor. This, of course, is not an exclusively Jewish phenomenon. Pride and dignity, which are characteristics of most societies, necessarily disappear in the bourgeois class in which man is transformed into a commodity. Commodities have a price, but they do not have pride." (Fromm: *On Being Human*, 108f.)
[49]Fromm: *Das jüdische Gesetz*, 123-126.

national character of Judaism. The Jews do not form a nation, but a religious community (Glaubensgemeinschaft).[50]

By frequently quoting of leading Reform rabbis Fromm tries to show that the inner character of Reform Judaism is its effort to adjust to Christianity and to German society.[51] Everything in traditional Judaism that is not socially acceptable must be reformed. In its interpretation of Jewish Law the Reform movement is very imprecise and leaves great freedom for the individual to decide for himself. The result is the total individualization of the Law. In its attitude to the Law Reform Judaism shows, in Fromm's opinion, an enormous lack of principle. A commandment can be accepted because it is an old tradition among the Jews, while another equally solid tradition is rejected. Sometimes a statement is motivated by the Talmud, while the Talmud is otherwise considered to be irrelevant.[52]

Fromm ends his chapter on Reform Judaism with a brief discussion on its competitor, Neo-Orthodoxy.[53] According to him Neo-Orthodoxy is trying - exactly like Reform Judaism but in another way - to combine the spirit of Judaism with the spirit of capitalism. It does so by clinging to an interpretation of the Law that was made in a totally different society, instead of doing the only right thing, having its own Jewish administration of justice. Therefore Neo-Orthodoxy is not - contrary its own claims - the true representative of Judaism, either culturally or socially.

---

[50]op.cit., 127-133.

[51]Fromm also mentions a third form of adjustment: "Die Angleichung der Juden als Träger eines bestimmten Geistes an den Geist des Kapitalismus." (op.cit., 134) Unfortunately he does not expound this point any further, but his statement does come close to the famous claim by Marx in *Zur Judenfrage* that the spirit of Judaism is the spirit of capitalism, and that therefore the aim is the emancipation of society from Judaism, i.e. from capitalism. (*MEW 1*, 377) Fromm, however, does not mean that the true spirit of Judaism is capitalistic, only that the purpose of the Reform movement was to transform it into that. *Zur Judenfrage* aroused lively debate about Marx's attitude to Jews. Many consider him as very prejudiced against Jews or even anti-Semitic (see, e.g., Poliakov: *The History of Anti-Semitism III*, 421-426). Fromm found these accusations to be totally wrong. "Anyone who reads the book and who knows Marx's philosophy and literary style will recognize that this claim is absurd and false. It misuses some critical remarks on the Jews, which were made polemically in a brilliant essay dealing with the problem of bourgeois emancipation, in order to make this fantastic accusation against Marx." (Fromm: *Marx's Concept of Man*, x n.3) Similarly in a lecture in 1966, Fromm stated that "no objective person could dream of the fact that Marx was antisemitic, and of course, he wasn't a bit." (Fromm: "The Renaissance of Humanist Socialism" Lecture in 1966)

[52]Fromm: *Das jüdische Gesetz*, 134-150.

[53]op.cit., 154-156. Here Fromm also mentions the famous rabbi Seligmann Bär Bamberger, who was his own great grandfather.

3.2.3. Hasidism

As negative as Fromm was about Karaism and Reform Judaism as enthusiastically positive he was about Hasidism. We must remember that his Talmud teacher at this time, Dr. Rabinkow, had his roots in a branch of Hasidism, Habad-Hasidism.

Fromm starts by describing the social background of Hasidism. The economic, spiritual, and social despair of the poor Jewish masses in Poland gave birth to a movement that was totally democratic and whose leaders, the Zaddikim, were not above the people but one with it. As Fromm wrote later in life, the Hasidic movement "was a rebellion of the poor against those who had the monopoly of learning or of money".[54] The Polish Jews were not emancipated by some outer force, they emancipated themselves (Autoemanzipation).[55] Hasidism rose directly from the soul of historic Judaism. The reason for the decline of Hasidism was the alienation of the Zaddikim from the people. Many Zaddikim became rich and powerful, and instead of being based upon voluntarism, the office of Zaddikim became inheritable. With these worldly Zaddikim dynasties the revolutionary principle of Hasidism was lost.[56]

The spirit of Hasidism was anti-capitalistic. The capitalistic qualities of haste and restlessness are alien to Hasidism, as they are to Rabbinic Judaism. Instead Hasidism emphasized things like contemplation and music. Even the most rationalistic branch of Hasidism, Habad-Hasidism, was clearly anti-capitalistic. Hasidism was also hostile toward the political emancipation of the Jews, because it was considered to be a threat to their own nationally and religiously distinctive character.[57]

While the ideas of Karaism were based on hostility towards Rabbinic Judaism and the ideas of Reform Judaism on adjustment to the surrounding culture, Hasidism was able to produce its own creative ideas. But these ideas are all based on the Law, which is revered and followed in Hasidism. Why were there such bitter fights between Hasidism and the representatives of Rabbinic Judaism, the so called Mitnagdim, when Hasidism is in fact a true expression of historic

---

[54]Fromm: *Psychoanalysis and Religion*, 47.
[55]The Hasicid emancipation, in which there is no conflict between collective and individual liberation can be seen as prototypical of Fromm's later view of liberation, which was very holistic. (Sahler: "Die Dissertation Erich Fromms über das jüdische Gesetz aus dem Jahr 1922. Darstellung des Inhalts". In: *Erich Fromm. Zu Leben und Werk*, 12.)
[56]Fromm: *Das jüdische Gesetz*, 157-168.
[57]op.cit., 168-176.

Judaism? According to Fromm, the answer is the historical situation.[58] Shortly before Hasidism was born, the Eastern Jews witnessed the messianic movement around Sabbathai Zwi and Jakob Frank, and many rabbis were afraid that Hasidism would cause a similar catastrophe for the Jews as these movements did. This fear proved to be groundless. The last great Hasidic leader, Schneur Salman, was the expression of a synthesis between Hasidism and Rabbinism, although being a Hasid, Salman stressed the importance of Talmud study in a way similar to Rabbinic Judaism.[59]

Fromm preserved his appreciation for Hasidism his whole life through. Among friends he sometimes sang Hasidic songs.[60] In *You shall be as gods*, while writing about the Psalms, he describes the Hasidic songs as a late expression of the same tradition as the Biblical Psalms. Many of the Hasidic songs have the same inner movement - from sadness to joy - as the Biblical. As an example he mentions a famous song created by Schneur Salman, and in a footnote he adds that he learned many Hasidic songs from Rabinkow.[61]

Fromm not only sang Hasidic songs, he also told Hasidic stories. There is a Hasidic legend which he seems to have loved. At least he told it on different occasions.[62] It goes like this: A man was asked why he went to see his Hasidic master. Was it in order to listen to his words of wisdom? No, answered the man, not for that, I just want to see how he ties his shoelaces. The moral of this story is that your faith and attitude to life are best seen in your little, normal, every-day acts.

In a letter to Ernst Simon in 1973 Fromm writes that he has heard about a Habad kibbutz in Israel, and he asks Simon to tell him what he knows about it. He also writes that it would be one of the places he would be most interested to visit if he came to Israel (he never did). "I am interested almost in all aspects of their life, in one point especially, and that is whether they are as fanatical as the Chassidic or

---

[58]There is also a sociological reason for the schism. Hasidism represented the poor, unlearned masses, while the rabbis were learned. See Fromm: *You shall be as gods*, 41, where he also compares this conflict with the conflict between the poor unlearned followers of Jesus and the learned Pharisees.
[59]op.cit, 177-187.
[60]Rubins: *Karen Horney*, 219. According to Maccoby: "The Two Voices of Erich Fromm: The Prophetic and the Analytic" *Society* 32/5, 79, Fromm "often hummed chasidic music".
[61]Fromm: *You shall be as gods*, 220f.
[62]Fromm: "Memories of Dr. D.T. Suzuki" *Eastern Buddhist* New Series II (August 1967), 88; Fromm: *You shall be as gods*, 227; Fromm: *The Revolution of Hope*, 135; Fromm: "Die psychologischen und geistigen Probleme des Überflusses" *GA V*, 326.

whether there is a new, more tolerant spirit."[63] Having read Simon's answer that Habad Hasidism is a reactionary movement, and that even its founder, Schneur Salman, showed biological and racist tendencies,[64] Fromm remarked that he found this very interesting. "Having read with Rabinkow, and I assume we did it together, the Tanjah, and under the influence of Rabinkow's own chabad sympathies, I may have idealized the Raw or overlooked certain tendencies... Of course the Chassidim were reactionaries politically and opted for the Czar against Napoleon in reaction against progress. But in a sense they were right, because progress was to undermine their system and their world."[65]

What was it that attracted Fromm in Hasidism, "the most original development in postmedieval Jewish history"[66]? One thing was the central place it gave to joy and religious enthusiasm. "Their motto was the verse of the Psalms: 'Serve God in joy.' They emphasized feeling rather than intellectual accomplishment, joy rather than contrition; to them (as to Spinoza) joy was the equivalent of virtue and sadness the equivalent of sin."[67] The biblical reproach of the Hebrews that they did not serve their Lord with "joy and gladness of heart in the midst of abundance of all things" (Deut. 28:47) Fromm saw as the central sin of the Hebrews, and as a reproach that is also accurate for us in the well-to-do world today.[68]

Another thing that Fromm appreciated in Hasidism was its belief that man can challenge God.[69] Like Abraham in the story of Sodom many Hasidic masters dared to challenge God. Block - an orthodox Jew - has heavily criticized Fromm on this issue. The reason why Abraham and some Hasidic masters could

---

[63]Letter Fromm - Simon 21.7 1973.
[64]Letter Simon - Fromm 13.8 1973.
[65]Letter Fromm - Simon 9.10 1973. *Tanjah* was the most important of Schneur Salman's books. For a short but informative presentation of Habad Hasidism that clearly shows its conservative, even fundamentalistic tendencies, see Friedman: "Habad as Messianic Fundamentalism: From Local Particularism to Universal Jewish Mission". In: Marty - Appleby (Eds.): *Accounting for Fundamentalism*, 328-357.
[66]Fromm: *You shall be as gods*, 145.
[67]Fromm: *Psychoanalysis and Religion*, 47. Cf. Fromm: *You shall be as gods*, 148, 174f.
[68]Fromm: *War Within Man*, 15; Fromm: *The Heart of Man*, 47; Fromm: "Interview with Richard Heffner" *McCalls* 92 (Oct. 1965), 133; Fromm: "Essay". In: *Summerhill: For and Against*, 254 n.1; Fromm: *On Disobedience*, 120; Fromm: "Die psychologischen und geistigen Probleme des Überflusses" *GA V*, 323; Fromm: *To have or to be?*, 117; Fromm: *Die Pathologie der Normalität*, 104.
[69]Fromm: *You shall be as gods*, 79f.; cf. Fromm: *Psychoanalysis and Religion*, 47f. One of the Chasidic stories that Fromm tells in this context, about a man who challenged God by a formal juridical procedure that ended so that the ten judges rendered judgement in favor of the man, has served as a model for Elie Wiesel's play *Trial of God*.

challenge God was not a predilection for rebellion or ambition to free themselves from God, but the pure fact that they were men who were totally dedicated to serving God without the slightest tincture of hesitation or question.[70]

When it came to the Messianic expectations in Hasidism, Fromm stressed the importance of these against the notion of Gershom Scholem.[71]

Fromm's interest in Hasidism was most probably kindled by his encounter with Rabinkow. Another intermediary of knowledge about Hasidism was Martin Buber, whom Fromm had met in the "Freie Jüdische Lehrhaus". In his doctoral dissertation he frequently refers to and quotes Buber's works on Hasidism. Once he refers to the excellent (ausgezeichnete) description that Buber gives. But he ends his analysis of Hasidism by rejecting a claim by Buber. While Buber claimed that the rigid clinging to the Law weakened the renewing power of Hasidism, Fromm was of the opinion that the opposite was true. It was not the engagement for the Law that caused the decline of Hasidism, but the weakening of the movement which lead to a "Subjektivierung der Gesetze".[72]

Although the influence of Rabinkow on the thought of Fromm was, also according to Fromm himself, considerable, after his doctoral dissertation he does not in his writings deal very much with Hasidism and related issues. According to Funk[73], this must be due to personal reasons connected to his break with orthodox Judaism. But Funk has also shown[74] the similarities between Habad-Hasidism, as presented in the writings of Schneur Salman, and Fromm's humanistic religion.

Steinberg has written a thesis about the Hasidic elements in Fromm's thinking.[75] It is an extremely badly organized work (each chapter starts anew from page 1), but - which is more serious - the weakness of the work is not restricted to the outloook. Time after time Steinberg claims that on this or that issue Fromm is in

---

[70]Block: "Radical Humanism and the Bible" *Tradition* (Winter 1968), 134. Similarly Shapira: "Fromm and Judaism". In: Eletti (Ed.): *Incontro con Erich Fromm*, 234.

[71]Fromm: *You shall be as gods*, 148 n.

[72]Fromm: *Das jüdische Gesetz*, 186f. In a lecture in 1953 Fromm discussed the "very complex question" why a religious movement starting as spontaneous and progressive so easily degenerates into a reactionary movement, and he mentioned Hasidism as an example of this. Fromm does not know the answer to this question; he just says that the only thing we can do is to be aware of this risk and be on our guard. (Fromm: "Mental Health in Contemporary Society" Lecture 6.1 1953 at HUC - JIR, Cincinnati)

[73]Funk: *Mut zum Menschen*, 258 n.182.

[74]op.cit., 246-260.

[75]Steinberg: *Hasidic Elements in the Writings of Erich Fromm* (unpublished dissertation).

accordance with the Hasidic tradition, but without saying how or showing a Hasidic statement that corresponds to Fromm's utterance. There is almost nothing in Fromm's thinking that Steinberg does not explain as being drawn from Hasidic sources. A typical sentence is: "Fromm's emphasis on joy, his attitude towards authority, his spiritual conception of human nature, his optimism, his democratic orientation, his romantic conception of individuality, his mystical conception of love, his emphasis on the matriarchal aspects of religion, his protest against Freud's nineteenth-century patriarchal, rationalistic outlook - all prove to be deeply Hasidic in flavor and content."[76]

Despite the grave weaknesses of her work, Steinberg presents many good and interesting remarks. Many of the affinities she points out between Fromm's ideas and those of Hasidism are certainly correct. But one has to remember that Fromm's knowledge of Hasidism was based on reading and on what he heard from Rabinkow. Therefore it might to a certain extent have been biased, as is seen from what he wrote about Habad Hasidism in his letter to Simon (see above).

3.3. The Torah and the Talmud

The mature Fromm also dealt with the Jewish Law, although not as thoroughly as the young Fromm in his doctoral dissertation. The undogmatic character of the Torah and of Judaism is the feature that connects the young and the mature Fromm.

The core of Fromm's interpretation of the Bible and the Jewish tradition is that what it is all about is not knowledge *about* God but imitation of God, the right way of living, called *halakha*. "The task of man is to live and to act in the right manner, and thus to become like God. What matters from the standpoint of the Jewish tradition is whether a man fulfills the law, not what his views about God are."[77]

This can also be seen from the very word *torah*, meaning "direction", "instruction", and "law". *"The Torah is a Law which directs man to imitate God by instructing him in the right action."*[78]

---

[76]op.cit., chapter II, p.2f.
[77]Fromm: *You shall be as gods*, 187f.; cf. 40f.
[78]op.cit., 188.

The most fundamental biblical formulation of the law is the Ten Commandments, which are grouped by Fromm into four categories: 1) About God: God as the God of liberation, the prohibition of idolatry and of empty use of God's name. 2) The Sabbath commandment. 3) The commandment to honor one's parents. 4) The prohibitions against greed, envy, and hate of one's fellow man.[79]

What Fromm especially wants to emphasize is that there is no ritual commandment and no commandment "to love God or to have faith in him, but only the statement that God *is* and that he is the liberator of the people."[80] The post-biblical tradition enlarged and developed the biblical law and so the system of *halakha* came to cover every aspect of man's activities, as can be seen from Maimonides' classification of the *halakha* in *Mishneh Torah*.[81]

Many *mitzvot* (individual laws) have no rational and educational function, but most *mitzvot* direct man to act justly and lovingly, thus educating and transforming him. "The spirit of the law, as it was developed by the rabbis through the centuries, was one of justice, brotherly love, respect for the individual, and the devotion of life to one's human development."[82]

This is, in sum, Fromm's programmatic statement about the Jewish Law, both the written Law (Torah) and the oral Law, codified in the Talmud. As already noted, Fromm studied the Talmud very diligently for many years. Schwarzschild reported how, until they were old, Ernst Simon and Fromm, when they happened to be in New York at the same time, got together every morning to study the Talmud.[83] Although Fromm, being the modest man he was, stated late in life that "I have, unfortunately, never achieved anything close to real Talmudic knowledge",[84] his writings show a very good knowledge of the Talmud. In many

---

[79]op.cit., 189f.

[80]op.cit., 189. Maly has criticizesdthis statement and asks: "Does this mean, then, that we must ignore all of Deuteronomy's understanding of the Law and the prophetic insistence of faith (Is 7,9b is pretty difficult to explain away) in favor of the author's unusual understanding of the one passage?" (Maly: "Review of Fromm: *You shall be as gods*" *CBQ* 29 (1967), 620). Fromm's statement concerns the Ten Commandments only and is correct. Another thing is how Deuteronomy and many others understand the Law. Concerning the issue of faith, see Fromm: "Faith as a Character Trait" *Psychiatry* 5 (1942), 307-319.

[81]Fromm: *You shall be as gods*, 190f.

[82]op.cit., 193.

[83]Schwarzschild: "Remembering Erich Fromm" *The Jewish Spectator* (Fall 1980), 31.

[84]Fromm: "Reminiscences of Shlomo Baruch Rabinkow". In: Jung (Ed.): *Sages and Saints*, 102. Cf. Fromm: *The Anatomy of Human Destructiveness*, 417: "The Talmud is a large and difficult work and only someone who has devoted years to its study could have a 'remarkable knowledge' of it."

texts dealing with very different issues he can tell a Talmudic story or quote a saying from the Talmud. One theme in which Fromm showed a special interest was the interpretation of dreams in the Talmud.[85]

We are, however, interested not in individual stories or sayings but in Fromm's overall attitude to the Talmud. According to the traditional Jewish position, there is a total unity of the written and the oral Law; both were given by God on the Mount Sinai. Although Fromm does not share this belief, he agrees with the traditional view about the unity between the written and the oral tradition. Both contain a record of ideas expressed over a very long period, and the development that took place during this period is reflected in the text. In both the Old Testament and the oral tradition there are contradictions, and a split between nationalism and universalism, conservatism and radicalism, fanaticism and tolerance. An expression of this tension in the Talmud is the conflict between the schools of Hillel and Shammai.[86]

When in *To have or to be?* Fromm writes that the protest against the having structure is even more radical in the New Testament than in the Jewish tradition (see 4.8), he makes an interesting sociological comment. While the New Testament was the product of a group of the poor and socially despised, of the downtrodden and the outcast, the Pharisees, who were the learned men behind the Talmud, represented the middle class. Despite this they were imbued by the spirit of social justice, but they did not condemn wealth as evil or as incompatible with the principle of being.[87]

In sum, Fromm's attitude to the Talmud was positive, it was for him a source of wisdom, an expression of the genius of the same people that gave us the Bible. And his knowledge of the Talmud was - despite his claim to the contrary - good. As one of his relatives wrote about him: "Only an individual who had received traditional Orthodox training would have been able to analyze the statements found in Talmud and Midrash in such a precise and exact manner."[88]

---

[85]Fromm: *The Forgotten Language*, 127-130. The Talmudic statement that an uninterpreted dream is like an unopened letter (Berachot 55a) was frequently quoted by Fromm. (Fromm: *The Forgotten Language*, 10; Fromm: "Der Traum ist die Sprache des universalen Menschen" *GA IX*, 315; Fromm: "The Nature of Dreams" *SA* 180/5 (1949), 47)

[86]Fromm: *You shall be as gods*, 9-11. Hillel was seen by Fromm as the representative of the humanistic tradition and Fromm saw his famous statement about the essence of the Torah (Shabbat 31a) as an example of the value of affirmation of life so central in the Talmud. (op.cit., 180)

[87]Fromm: *To have or to be?*, 53f. Cf. Fromm: *The Dogma of Christ*, 17-19.

[88]I. N. Bamberger: "A Note on Erich Fromm's Rabbinic Roots" *Tradition* 29 (No.3 Spring

3.4. Fromm's Jewish mentors

Fromm's most importants mentors were Marx and Freud, both Jews. But let us here look closer at the persons who influenced Fromm and who were not only Jews but influenced him with their writings about Judaism.

3.4.1. Maimonides

Moses ben Maimon or Maimonides (1135-1204) was in Fromm's opinion - and in the opinion of many others - the greatest Jewish philosopher.[89] Fromm refers to him in his discussion of the Talmudic concept of the Noachites,[90] free will and hardening of one's heart,[91] and the classification of the *halakha*.[92] But Maimonides influenced Fromm most with his concept of the attributes of God - an idea Fromm called negative theology - but also, to a lesser extent, in the field of eschatology.

In his famous work *The Guide of the Perplexed*[93] Maimonides developed his negative theology, first formulated by the Hellenist Jewish philosopher Philo of Alexandria, but having its starting point in the biblical prohibition against giving God a name (see 4.4.). Negative theology states that it is not possible to make any positive statement about God's essence, only about God's actions. "Know that the master of those who know, *Moses our Master*, peace be on him, made two requests and received an answer to both of them. One request consisted in his asking Him, may He be exalted, to let him know his essence and true reality. The second request, which he puts first, was that He should let him know His attributes. The answer to the two requests that He, may He be exalted, gave him consisted in His promising him to let him know all His attributes, making it known to him that they are His actions, and teaching him that His essence cannot be grasped as it really is."[94] The thirteen characteristics traditionally attributed to God are not to be taken as God possessing moral qualitites, but as God acting in

---

1995), 54.
[89]Fromm: *Beyond the Chains of Illusion*, 158; Fromm: Interview with Michaela Lämmle and Jürgen Lodemann 1977. In *You shall be as gods*, 32f., Fromm calls him "the most important Jewish philosopher - or theologian - in the Middle Ages."
[90]Fromm: *You shall be as gods*, 51.
[91]op.cit., 116f., 164, 166f.
[92]op.cit., 190f.
[93]Originally written in Arabic, this book has in English been called both *The Guide of the Perplexed* and *The Guide for the Perplexed*.
[94]Maimonides: *The Guide of the Perplexed*, 123.

a way that resembles the actions that in men proceed from moral qualities. The utmost virtue of man is to imitate God's actions, as God commanded: "You shall be holy; for I the Lord your God am holy." (Lev. 19:2)[95]

Something may be stated about God's action, but when it comes to the essence of God, no positive attributes are possible, only negative ones. When one says that God is living, powerful, wise, and so on, it means that he is not dead, not powerless, not ignorant and so on. Because God is one, there can be no multiplicity in his essence, i.e. not a number of attributes that describe Him. "It has thus become clear to you that every attribute that we predicate of Him is an attribute of action or, if the attribute is intended for the apprehension of His essence and not of His action, it signifies the negation of the privation of the attribute in question."[96]

Maimonides further discusses some objections to his concept of the attributes of God. If one cannot know the true essence of God, how is it then possible that some people have a deeper knowledge of God than others? Maimonides' answer to this is that the true apprehension of God is directly related to the negating approach to the essence of God. The words of the Psalmist, "Silence is praise to Thee" (Ps. 65:2), Maimonides claims to mean silence with regard to Thee is praise.[97]

Another objection to the negative theology of Maimonides is that the Bible itself mentions positive attributes of God. But the Bible also speaks about God in an anthropomorphical way and still God is not corporeal. Neither should the attributes of God be taken literally. As the Talmud says, "The Torah speaks in the language of man" (Jebanoth 71a, Baba Metzia 31b), some statements in the Bible must be seen as concessions to man's traditions.[98]

This is, briefly, the negative theology of Maimonides. Fromm finds it slightly ambiguous. Maimonides was at the same time a bold philosopher influenced by Greek and Arab thought and a Talmudic traditionalist rabbi. "My own interpretation of Maimonides' theology is based on one aspect of this theology; it

---

[95]op.cit., 124-128. Funk emphasizes - contrary to Fromm - that adherence to this ethical concept of God is an expression of negative theology and the prerequisite for ethical statements about men. (Funk: *Mut zum Menschen*, 236f.)
[96]Maimonides: *The Guide of the Perplexed*, 136, see 134-137.
[97]op.cit., 137-140.
[98]op.cit., 119f. Maimonides later makes this point - that some elements of the Bible are concessions to man's traditions - very clear in speaking of cultic traditions like sacrifice, prayer, and fasting. (op.cit., 526f.)

seems to me that this is permissible if one does not ignore the fact that actually his position was slightly ambiguous."[99] Being less radical than the Buddha and Meister Eckhart, Maimonides still agrees with them on one point, "namely that to make any statement about God is idolatry."[100]

For Fromm, the negative theology of Maimonides is one important step in man's development towards freedom, including freedom from God, an attempt to find a purer concept of God stripped of every trace of positive description or definition of God. This is monotheism in its logical consequence, a guarantee for tolerance, "there can be no argument about the nature of God; no man can presume to have any knowledge of God which permits him to criticize or condemn his fellow men or to claim that his own idea of God is the only right one. The religious intolerance, which springs from such claims and, psychologically speaking, stems from lack of faith or lack of love, has had a devastating effect on religious development. It has led to a new form of idolatry."[101]

Another consequence of negative theology, in Fromm's opinion, is mysticism. "If I can have no full knowledge of God in thought, if theology is at best negative, the positive knowledge of God can be achieved only in the act of union with God."[102] It is not surprising that Meister Eckhart was enthusiastic about Maimonides (see 2.7.3.).

Maimonides did not, of course, deny the existence of God, only "our capacity to know *what* he is, but not our faith *that* he is."[103] But Fromm goes one step further. If the consequence of monotheism is not to mention God's name at all, not to speak *about* God, then "God becomes what he potentially is in monotheistic theology, the nameless One, an inexpressible stammer, referring to the unity underlying the phenomenal universe, the ground of all existence; God becomes truth, love, justice. God is I, inasmuch as I am human."[104]

---

[99]Fromm: *You shall be as gods*, 36f.

[100]Fromm: "Beyond Egotistical Religion" (lecture in 1957).

[101]Fromm: *Psychoanalysis and Religion*, 116f. Fromm saw the intolerance of a religion as a form of group narcissism. And while individual narcissism is considered to be abnormal, group narcissism is not. "That millions of adherents to a religion can claim that they are the only possessors of the truth, that their religion is the only way to salvation, is considered to be perfectly normal." (Fromm: *Greatness and Limitations of Freud's Thought*, 52. Cf. Fromm: *The Heart of Man*, 85f.)

[102]Fromm: *The Dogma of Christ*, 137. Cf. Fromm: *Psychoanalysis and Zen Buddhism*, 94; Fromm: "Einige post-marxsche und post-freudsche Gedanken über Religion und Religiosität" *Concilium* 8 (1972), 473.

[103]Fromm: *On Being Human*, 118.

[104]Fromm: *The Art of Loving*, 70.

Another theme in Maimonides' thinking that occupied Fromm was his eschatology. In order to show that socialism is the secular expression of prophetic messianism, Fromm quotes Maimonides' characterization of the messianic time, which he then compares with Marx's description of the realm of freedom in the third volume of *Capital*.[105] In the Jewish discussion of whether the messianic age will be the result of man's progress or of man's deterioration, and whether it will be a historical or an apocalyptical event (see 4.6.2.), Maimonides is of the opinion that the messianic age is a historical utopia, containing a new form of living which includes all men. So is Fromm, but not Scholem, who viewed the messianic age as an apocalyptic utopia, a notion which Fromm argues against.[106]

Maimonides, then, is for Fromm the brilliant master of negative theology and an important witness to the progressive view of the messianic age. Only once does Fromm mention Maimonides in a non-favorable light. Maimonides' "Thirteen articles of faith" were never accepted or dogmatized in Judaism, a fact that shows the subordinate role of dogmas in Judaism.[107] One of Maimonides' articles of faith was the belief in the unalterability of the Torah, something that historically is not true, because historical Judaism changed several commandments in the Torah, as Fromm so emphatically noted in his doctoral dissertation (see 3.2.).

3.4.2. Spinoza

The Jewish philosopher Baruch de Spinoza (1632-77) was extremely important for Fromm.[108] After Freud and Marx, Spinoza is the author he quotes or refers to most frequently. An analysis of how Spinoza influenced Fromm would go far beyond the scope of this study. Therefore we will here just very briefly mention in what fields this influence is visible, and look closer at the influence on his to religious thought.

Fromm related how important Spinoza, Marx and Bachofen were for him in his youth. "With them I felt at home. In them I found a synthesis between the things

---

[105]Fromm: *To have or to be?*, 155-157; Fromm: "Konsumreligion" *Neues Forum* 301/302 (1979), 13. Cf. Fromm: *On Being Human*, 141-143.
[106]Fromm: *On Being Human*, 142f. Frommm presented the same criticism of Scholem's interpretation of Maimonides' concept of the messianic age in a letter to Steven S. Schwarzschild 11.10 1974, in which he states that Scholem is blind to the fact that Maimonides does not express an apocalyptic vision of the Messiah, but a "radical socialist Utopia".
[107]Fromm: *Das jüdische Gesetz*, 27f.; Fromm: *You shall be as gods*, 40f.
[108]Knapp writes that Aristotle, Spinoza and Meister Eckhart were "the stalwarts of his [Fromm's] eclectic philosophy." (Knapp: *The Art of Living*, xx)

of the past that were still alive for me and the things of the modern world that I loved."[109] Spinoza has a central role in Fromm's description of the development of the humanistic idea,[110] and Fromm praises him as one who lived his ideas[111] and as one of the great non-idolaters.[112] Spinoza's teaching is compared to that of the Buddha.[113]

One aspect of Spinoza's thinking that is very central for Fromm is Spinoza as a psychologist. Fromm called him "the founder of modern scientific psychology".[114] With his concept of existential needs Fromm has the same approach to psychology as Spinoza, in that he begins with a concept of human nature.[115] Spinoza's most important psychological discovery was the dimension of the unconscious[116], and on it he based his systematic analysis of activity and passivity, something that was very important for Fromm.[117] Spinoza's position on the issue of free will and determinism is the same as Fromm's, one that Fromm calls "alternativism".[118] And Spinoza was, according to Fromm, the first to express the concept of "normal insanity" or the "pathology of normality", a

---

[109]Fromm: *For the Love of Life*, 99.
[110]See, e.g., Fromm: *The Heart of Man*, 83; Fromm: *Marx's Concept of Man*, v; Fromm: "Foreword". In: Marx: *Selected Writings*, xiv.
[111]Fromm: *On Disobedience*, 28.
[112]Fromm: *The Revision of Psychoanalysis*, 52.
[113]Fromm: *Greatness and Limitations of Freud's Thought*, ixf.
[114]Fromm: *To have or to be?*, 93. Similarly, although in other words, Fromm: "Die Grundpositionen der Psychoanalyse" *GA VIII*, 36f.; Fromm: *Beyond the Chains of Illusion*, 28; Fromm: *Sigmund Freud's Mission*, 116; Fromm: "Humanism and Psychoanalysis" *Cont Psycha* 1 (1964), 71; Fromm: *The Heart of Man*, 71.
[115]Burston: *The Legacy of Erich Fromm*: 84. For many years in the USA Fromm lectured on Spinoza's *Ethics*, focusing on the psychological statements in books 3-5. (Funk: *Mut zum Menschen*, 259 n. 182)
[116]Fromm: *Man for Himself*, 33; Fromm: *Marx's Concept of Man*, 20f.; Fromm: "Psychoanalysis". In: Newman (Ed.): *What is Science?*, 364; Fromm: "Einführung in Schultz: Psychologie für Nichtpsychologen" *GA VIII*, 74; Fromm: *The Crisis of Psychoanalysis*, 36; Fromm: *Beyond the Chains of Illusion*, 101: Fromm - Xirau: "Introduction". In: Fromm - Xirau (Eds.): *The Nature of Man*, 22: Fromm: *To have or to be?*, 93.
[117]Fromm: *To have or to be?*, 93-96; Fromm - Maccoby: *Social Character in a Mexican Village*, 73; Fromm: "Die Grundpositionen der Psychoanalyse" *GAA VIII*, 41f.; Fromm: *Beyond the Chains of Illusion*, 68.
[118]Fromm: *The Heart of Man*, 125f., 143-147; Fromm: *The Crisis of Psychoanalysis*, 38; Fromm: "Humanism and Psychoanalysis" *Cont Psycha* 1 (1964), 70f. On this issue Fromm is in opposition to the major trend in Spinoza research that holds the philosopher to be a determinist. (See, e.g., Feldman: "Spinoza". In: Frank - Leaman (Eds.): *History of Jewish Philosophy*, 612-635) Fromm is aware of this fact and acknowledges that Spinoza made deterministic statements, but he still claims that the best definition of Spinoza's view is alternativism. (Fromm: *The Heart of Man*, 143-147)

concept very central for Fromm.[119] Reading Spinoza is much better psychotherapy than many others, Fromm stated.[120]

Spinoza was also important for Fromm as an ethicist. In his books on ethics, *Man for Himself*, Spinoza plays an important part. Spinoza's *Ethics* is, Fromm writes, a striking example of biophilic morality, occupied with life and good, not dwelling on remorse and guilt.[121] Fromm's idea of good and evil corresponded "essentially to the one expressed by Spinoza".[122] The biophilic ethics of Spinoza is seen in the importance he attributes to joy.[123] And Spinoza's statement about death was music to Fromm's ears: "A free man thinks of death least of all things; and his wisdom is a meditation not of death but of life."[124]

But Spinoza was not only an eminent psychologist and ethicist, he was also a profound religious thinker. Fromm saw Spinoza as a representative of humanistic religion whose concept of God has no trace of authoritarianism, "in fact, God is identical with the totality of the universe."[125] The human reality underlying the teachings of Spinoza is essentially the same as that of the Buddha, Jesus, Socrates, and other great teachers of mankind (see 2.1.).[126] Fromm also points out the affinity between Spinoza's pantheism and mysticism.[127]

Spinoza's humanistic religion is in fact, in Fromm's opinion, non-theistic. Spinoza tried to give the symbol God a new meaning, but what he was really saying was that there is no God in the sense of the Judaeo-Christian tradition. "He was still so close to the spiritual atmosphere in which the symbol God seemed indispensable that he was not aware of the fact that he was negating the existence of God in the terms of his new definition."[128]

---

[119]Fromm: *The Anatomy of Human Destructiveness*, 356. Cf. Fromm: *The Sane Society*, 16; Fromm: *Man for Himself*, 237f.; Fromm: *To have or to be?*, 95.
[120]Fromm: Interview with Heiner Gautschy in 1979.
[121]Fromm: *The Heart of Man*, 47f.
[122]op.cit., 148f.
[123]Fromm: *Man for Himself*, 176f.; Fromm: *Psychoanalysis and Religion*, 47; Fromm: "Essay". In: *Summerhill: For and Against*, 254; Fromm: *To have or to be?*, 119; Fromm: *For the Love of Life*, 146; Fromm: *Die Pathologie der Normalität*, 55.
[124]Fromm: *War Within Man*, 15; Fromm: *The Heart of Man*, 47f.; Fromm: "Essay". In: *Summerhill: For and Against*, 254. Cf. Fromm: *Man for Himself*, 42; Fromm: *To have or to be?*, 127.
[125]Fromm: *Psychoanalysis and Religion*, 41.
[126]op.cit., 63, 76.
[127]op.cit., 93f. n.9.
[128]Fromm: *Psychoanalysis and Religion*,114. Cf. Fromm: *May Man Prevail?*, 124f.

According to Fromm, the motif of a godless, non-theistic religiosity was heard faintly in Meister Eckhart, "became louder in Spinoza, and sounded in full strength in the radical humanism of Marx."[129] Spinoza gave precedence to ethics and shifted the center of religion from God to man. His aim was the optimal freedom of man through developing generosity and fortitude, all-embracing love and strong courage. By equating God with nature (Deus sive natura) he denied the traditional concept of God more radically and openly than Meister Eckhart was able to do. Spinoza's influence on philosophy, e.g. on Goethe, Hegel and Marx, was great, but not on the development of religious thought as such. Branded a heretic by the Jewish community in Amsterdam, he had no home in any religion.[130]

In sum, although Spinoza is an important thinker for Fromm, the religious thought of the great philosopher is seldom the focal point. As a link in the development of non-theistic religiosity from Meister Eckhart to Marx he is mentioned and praised. Otherwise the references and quotations are from Spinoza's *Ethics* and not from his *Tractatus theologico-politicus*, where he deals with biblical and Jewish issues. This means that Fromm never commented on or took part in the Jewish debate about Spinoza's attitude to Judaism. Hermann Cohen - another Jewish philosopher who influenced Fromm (see next chapter) - delivered a harsh critique of Spinoza's treatment of Judaism in *Tractatus theologico-politicus*. According to Cohen, Spinoza intentionally falsified Jewish thought, showed direct hatred of his own religion and a preference for Christianity. Spinoza was thus a misfortune for the Jews, an accuser of Judaism before the Christian world.[131] Fromm should have been familiar with this critique, but he never commented on it.

3.4.3. Hermann Cohen

The Neo-Kantian Hermann Cohen (1842-1918) was a well-known and respected philosopher in Germany. Whether Fromm met him personally is not known, but Fromm's teacher, Rabbi Nobel, was a student and good friend of Cohen. So from his early years Fromm was well acquainted with the ideas of Cohen and he already acknowledges the fruitful influence of Cohen in his doctoral dissertation.[132]

---

[129]Fromm: *On Being Human*, 117, cf. 139.
[130]op.cit., 136f.
[131]Cohen: *Jüdische Schriften III*, 290-372.
[132]Fromm: *Das jüdische Gesetz*, 18.

Cohen was a prominent Kantian, founder of the Marburg School of philosphy and responsible for a revival of Kant's thought. At the end of his life he became more interested in Judaism and in his most famous book, *Die Religion der Vernunft aus den Quellen des Judentums* (published posthumously in 1919), he tries to show that an idealized, rational faith can be constructed from Jewish sources.[133]

Cohen's ethical monotheism resembles the religious ideas of Fromm to a great extent. As for Cohen, the central thing for Fromm was the religion of reason and love.[134] In *You shall be as gods* he states that his method of interpreting the Bible has been strongly influenced by the method used by Cohen in his "great opus".[135] This means that whereas Cohen looked for the "Religion of Reason" in the Jewish tradition, Fromm looked for the seeds of radical humanism, a method for which he has been heavily criticized (see 4.9.). Cohen was also - like Fromm - a dedicated opponent of Zionism.[136]

Fromm refers to Cohen as a man who has emphasized that socialism is a secular expression of prophetic messianism[137] and who has pointed out that the qualities of God have been transformed into norms for human action.[138] And in his writings on the Talmudic concept of the Noachites (see 4.6.1.) he says Cohen has handled this subject "masterfully".[139] But the concept of Cohen most important for Fromm is the idea of love for one's neighbor, and especially the stranger.

There are two different interpretations of what is meant by the Old Testament commandment to love one's neighbor. According to one, the word "neighbor" (Hebrew *rea*) refers only to a fellow national; according to the other, it refers to any other human being. Although Fromm recognizes that Cohen has argued for the latter interpretation with "great ingenuity and scholarship", he is inclined to regard the first interpretation as more probable. But although this well-known commandment refers only to fellow nationals, the Old Testament also commands love for the stranger (Hebrew *ger*). This time Fromm agrees with Cohen in believing that *ger* refers to the stranger who does not participate in the same

---

[133]For a good introduction to the Jewish thought of Cohen, see Seeskin: "Jewish neo-Kantianism: Hermann Cohen". In: Frank - Leaman (Eds.): *History of Jewish Philosophy*, 786-798.

[134]For a brief exposition of the similarities and differences between Fromm and Cohen, see Funk: *Mut zum Menschen*, 245f.

[135]Fromm: *You shall be as gods*, 13.

[136]See, e.g., Cohen: *Jüdische Schriften II*, 319-340.

[137]Fromm: *To have or to be?*, 155; Fromm: *On Being Human*, 143.

[138]Fromm: *You shall be as gods*, 66f.

[139]op.cit., 52 n.

religion and not only to converts, as some have argued.[140] Cohen's insistence that one discovers the human being in the stranger, and that by having compassion for the stranger, man develops his capacity to love, found full agreement with Fromm.[141]

3.4.4. Martin Buber

Fromm met the great philosopher Martin Buber (1878-1965) at the Freie Jüdische Lehrhaus in Frankfurt and also had dealings with him later in life. He shared with Buber an interest in Hasidism and, as we have seen (3.2.3.), he made use of and referred to Buber's works on Hasidism in his doctoral disseratation. But although he later in life stated that Buber had done most to bring Hasidic literature to the attention of the Western reader,[142] he himself was not dependent on Buber for his knowledge of Hasidism. He had direct access to the Hasidic sources through his teacher Rabinkow.[143]

Buber is perhaps best known for his "I - Thou" - philosophy. Although Fromm also emphasized the need to establish authentic relations with other people and with the surrounding environment, he very seldom referred to Buber's "I - Thou" - philosophy.[144]

As a matter of fact, there are several similarities between Fromm and Buber in their lives and ideas. Both were Jews with a secular German education, both were interested in mysticism, both were socialists, both worked for a binational solution in the Palestine conflict (see 3.6.). But there are also some significant differences. Buber was more than twenty years older, already famous when Fromm was a young student. Buber came from a secularized family and approached Judaism through Zionism and Hasidism. His socialism was not as Marxist as Fromm's, he was closer to the anarchist tradition through his friend Gustav Landauer. He disliked Freud and psychoanalysis. And although Fromm

---

[140]op.cit., 182f.

[141]Fromm: *The Art of Loving*, 48; Fromm: *The Heart of Man*, 89.

[142]Fromm: *You shall be as gods*, 148 n.

[143]It has been suggested that Fromm's choice of subject for his doctoral dissertation was influenced by Rabinkow and Buber. (Tarr - Marcus: "Erich Fromm und das Judentum". In: Kessler - Funk (Hrsg.): *Erich Fromm und die Frankfurter Schule*, 217)

[144]In "The Philosophy Basic to Freud's Psychoanalysis" *Past Psych* 13 (1962), 30, Fromm states that in therapy the relation between the analyst and the client should be an "I - Thou" - relation and he also mentions the name of Buber. In *Escape from Freedom*, 26, he also writes about the "I - thou" - dichotomy, but without mentioning Buber.

and Buber agreed on the issue of the Israeli-Arab conflict, Buber was a Zionist and Fromm an anti-Zionist.

Fromm explicitly denied that he was influenced by Buber. "I knew Martin Buber when I was about 18 years old and living in Frankfurt, but I do not think that I was influenced in my thinking by him."[145] But he not only denied any influence from Buber, he also stated that there was something about Buber that he could not accept. After the publication of Buber's correspondence Fromm wrote in a letter: "As to Buber's correspondence, I would have been so happy to report to you that it changed my impression of him as a person. I can say truthfully that I was greatly impressed by his learnedness, brilliance and unflagging pursuit of his ideas, but my impression of him as a person has not really changed."[146]

One feels inclined to explain the fact that Fromm denied the influence of Buber by the antipathy he felt for Buber as a person. It is probably also this antipathy that explains why he sometimes quite unnecessarily polemizes with or criticizes Buber.[147] Despite the tension between Buber and Fromm on the personal level, it is evident that Fromm was influenced by Buber in many respects. Knapp has claimed that Fromm's focus on the interaction of human beings within a specific community can largely be traced to the influence of Buber on the young Fromm.[148]

3.5. Jewish mysticism

Although Fromm was a "non-theistic mystic", he did not deal very much with Jewish mysticism in his writings. It appears on the side of Christian and sometimes even Islamic mysticism in statements on a very general level.[149] Hasidism - in which Fromm showed a great interest (see 3.2.3.) - can be seen as a

---

[145]Letter Fromm - Betz 1.9 1969. In: Betz: *An Analysis of the Prophetic Character of the Dialectical Rhetoric of Erich Fromm*, 330.
[146]Letter Fromm - Simon 23.12 1974.
[147]In *The Art of Listening*, 101, Fromm polemizes against a statement by Buber on Adolf Eichmann. And in a letter to Norman Thomas 18.7 1957 he quite sourly criticizes Buber for not showing any interest in a campaign for settling the problem of the Arab refugees from Israel (see 3.6.).
[148]Knapp: *The Art of Living*, 14.
[149]Fromm: *Psychoanalysis and Religion*, 89, 93 n.9; Fromm: *You shall be as gods*, 57; Fromm: *On Disobedience*, 52f.; Fromm: "Die psychologischen und geistigen Probleme des Überflusses" *GA V*, 327.

mystic movement within Judaism, but we are here focusing on the traditional kabbalistic mysticism.

Fromm's main point in his writings about mysticism (see 2.7.) is that many mystics, even within the monotheistic religions, have been non-theists or at least have come close to non-theism. This is also true of Jewish mysticism. Just as for Meister Eckhart God is "The absolute Nothing", the ultimate reality for the Kabbalah is the "En Sof", the Endless One.[150]

The only subject concerning Jewish mysticism that Fromm comments on more than in passing in his books is its relation to messianism. According to Fromm, the appearance of Zohar, the most important Jewish mystical work, contributed much to fanning messianic expectations. "Jewish mysticism became one of the strongest inspirations for messianic faith and often contributed to the appearance of false messiahs, though it also led to the most original development in postmedieval Jewish history: Hasidism."[151]

In a letter Fromm once made a comment on the mother concept, which "has been eliminated in the Jewish tradition and been replaced completely by the concept of a God-father" but that nevertheless has "found its way back, especially in the mystical tradition in many more or less implicit ways."[152] Unfortunately Fromm does not say how the mother concept is expressed in Jewish mysticism. He was probably thinking of the speculations about the figure of Wisdom (Hebrew *chokma*), which is female.

In sum, the mystic Fromm did not use the sources of Jewish mysticism. Meister Eckhart and Zen Buddhism were more interesting and fruitful for him than the mysticism of his own tradition.

---

[150]Fromm: *The Art of Loving*, 77. "En Sof" represents the impersonal character of the hidden God in Jewish mysticism. It has been interpreted in many different ways, both orthodox and hetereodox. (Scholem: *Major Trends in Jewish Mysticism*, 12)

[151]Fromm: *You shall be as gods*, 145.

[152]Letter Fromm - Suzuki 3.12 1958. Fromm adds that the maternal feature can also be found in the Talmudic tradition that talks about God sitting on the throne of justice and the throne of mercy, representing tha fatherly and the motherly concepts. Many years earlier he mentioned the idea of the holy land flowing with milk and honey as an expression of the maternal principle. (Fromm: "Die sozialpsychologische Bedeutung der Mutterrechtstheorie" *GA I*, 106 n.15.) And in *The Sane Society*, 48 n.17, he stated that in Judaism and Christianity, especially in mysticism, there is a polarity between the fatherly and the motherly function of God.

3.6. Zionism and the State of Israel

According to Steven S. Schwarzschild - who knew him very well - Fromm was an opponent of political Zionism "on Jewish, socialist and ethical grounds."[153] But this was not always so. In his youth Fromm was an ardent Zionist.

In old age Fromm once said about his Zionist past. "... I had a period at the age of 15-16 when I was a Zionist. I joined the Zionist youth movement and stayed there for some time. One of the few things that I am really still proud of was that after a few years, I might have been 18 or 19 years old at that time, I disliked the Jewish nationalism so much that I made a speech at the meeting of that whole group which was called 'Blue-White' and said: 'This Jewish nationalism is not a bit better than the National-Socialism.' Now, that took me some courage to say and afterwards I left."[154]

This is a good story, but it is not true. Fromm's old mind might have created the whole story, or - if the event described really did happen - it happened several years later than Fromm claims. At the age of 18-19, i.e. in 1918-19, Fromm was still an active Zionist and any comparison with National Socialism was impossible, because the National Socialist Party in Germany (NSDAP) was not founded until 1919, and took this name in 1920.

Young Fromm - maybe at the age of 15-16, as he stated - joined the Zionist youth organization KJV (Kartell Jüdischer Verbindungen). The local organization in Frankfurt, called V.J.St. (Verein Jüdischer Studenten) Saronia, split up in 1919 and another organization, called V.J.St. Achduth, was founded. Fromm was among the leaders of Achduth. Among other things he lead a working group on the history of Zionism. All this is told in a report written by Fromm in the magazine of the KJV in May 1919.[155]

As late as December 1922 Fromm - together with four other young persons, including Ernst Simon and Leo Löwenthal - published an essay in a Zionist newspaper. Although the essay is very critical of the present state of the Zionist movement, it is written from a Zionist standpoint and the writers state that they are Zionists. Many features in the essay lead us to believe that Fromm was very active in the writing of it. Thus many ideas that are central for Fromm - e.g. the

---

[153]Schwarzschild: "Remembering Erich Fromm" *The Jewish Spectator* (Fall 1980), 29.
[154]Interview with Gerard Khoury in 1979.
[155]Fromm: "V.J.St. Achduth, Frankfurt a.M." *Der Jüdische Student* XIV Heft 3 (Mai 1919), 107.

subordinate role of dogmas in Judaism and the prohibition on the use of God's name - appear in the text, as well as a comparison with Karaism and Reform Judaism, two movements Fromm was studying at about this time for his doctoral work.[156]

It is difficult to fix the moment of Fromm's departure from Zionism. It cannot have been before 1923, but probably not very long after. It is possible that the disassociation from Zionism was a process that correlated with his moving away from the Jewish religion, but more probably it happened before that as a result of the influence of the universalistic interpretation of Judaism by Cohen and Rabinkow, as Funk has stated.[157]

The reasons for Fromm's ceasing to be a Zionist are easier to determine. His experiences during the First World War paved the way for a sceptical attitude to nationalism that later grew into a convinced anti-nationalism. He called the First World War "the event that determined more than anything else my development".[158] The war created in him a curiosity about how all this was possible, and also founded his commitment to peace and hostility towards nationalism.[159] Later in life he has described nationalism as an escape from isolation and feelings of inferiority,[160] as an expression of group narcissism,[161] as a form of incestuous fixation,[162] and as idolatry.[163] "Nationalism is our form of incest, is our idolatry, is our insanity."[164]

Of the persons that influenced the young Fromm Nobel was an active Zionist.[165] In Rabinkow's case it is more difficult to define his attitude to Zionism exactly, because he left almost nothing written for posterity. However, his universalistic

---

[156]Fromm - Goithein - Löwenthal - Simon - Michaelis: "Ein prinzipielles Wort zur Erziehungs-frage" *Juedische Rundschau* No. 103/104 23.12 1922.

[157]Funk: *Erich Fromm*, 50f. Burston (*The Legacy of Erich Fromm*,12) writes that Fromm "repudiated Zionism in 1927", but without mentioning what he based this claim on.

[158]Fromm: *Beyond the Chains of Illusion*, 6.

[159]op.cit., 6-8; Fromm: *For the Love of Life*, 100.

[160]Fromm: *Escape from Freedom*, 20, 121.

[161]Fromm: *The Heart of Man*, 85-87, 90-92; Fromm: *On Disobedience*, 16; Fromm: *The Anatomy of Human Destructiveness*, 203f., 212; Fromm: *Greatness and Limitations of Freud's Thought*, 52f.; Fromm: *The Art of Listening*, 184; Fromm: *Die Pathologie der Normalität*, 118-120; Fromm: *Gesellschaft und Seele*, 80f.

[162]Fromm: *Psychoanalysis and Religion*, 81; Fromm: *The Heart of Man*, 98f..

[163]Fromm: "Foreword". In: Bellamy: *Looking Backwards*, v n.1; Fromm: *The Revolution of Hope*, 136; Fromm: *On Being Human*, 71.

[164]Fromm: *The Sane Society*, 58.

[165]Bühler: *Erziehung zur Tradition - Erziehung zum Widerstand*, 28.

tendencies indicate that he was sceptical about Zionism.[166] That Fromm later in life praised him so wholeheartedly is a sign that he cannot have been an active Zionist.

In his books Fromm wrote almost nothing about Zionism and the State of Israel. It was in his political activity and his personal letters that his convictions about political Zionism were expressed. In his books he mentioned Zionism only once, stating that Freud's disciple Eitington had some sympathy for Zionism,[167] but in *You shall be as gods* he presents an interesting discussion of nationalism versus universalism within Judaism.

Fromm acknowledges that there is a strong nationalistic tradition within Judaism with its claim to be "the chosen people", God's favorite son. But how could it be otherwise? For a people that has been so severely persecuted it is natural to develop a hatred of its oppressors and a reactive nationalistic pride and clannishness to compensate for its chronic humiliations. But the important thing is that this element was balanced by its very opposite, the principle of universalism. The universalism in the Jewish tradition is expressed in the biblical teaching that all mankind descends from *one* man and *one* woman, in the covenant with Noah that is a covenant with the entire human race and the animal kingdom, in the Old Testament commandment to love the stranger, in the universalism of the prophets, and in many Talmudic statements. During persecutions the nationalistic and xenophobic spirit often prevailed over the universalistic, but as long as the prophetic teachings remained alive, universalism was not forgotten. One result of this was that with the emanciaption of the Jews in the 19th century, Jewish thinkers were among the most radical representatives of internationalism and humanism.[168]

The first time Fromm actively interfered in the political process concerning the State of Israel was in 1948, shortly before Israel's declaration of independence. In March he took the initiative to publish an appeal in the USA in support of Martin Buber, Judah L. Magnes and David W. Senator, who had in Jerusalem appealed for a peaceful solution to the Jewish-Arab conflict. After much active work and after the original text had been revised several times, the appeal was published in the *New York Times* on 18th April and signed by Leo Baeck and Albert

---

[166]op.cit., 30. According to Simon ("Reminiscences of Shlomo Barukh Rabinkow". In: Jung (Ed.): *Sages and Saints*, 119), Rabinkow's relationship with the Zionist movement was "problematic", while another of his students, Nahum Goldmann, claimed ("Reminiscences of Shlomo Barukh Rabinkow". In: op.cit., 106) that Rabinkow was "an ardent Zionist".
[167]Fromm: *Sigmund Freud's Mission*, 105.
[168]Fromm: *You shall be as gods*, 81-85.

Einstein.[169] According to Fromm - who was optimistic about the impact of this appeal - this could be the first step of moral support that "might contribute to rescue the Yishuv".[170]

The appeal condemned the extremists on both sides and asked for immediate efforts to prevent war and foster cooperation. Those who now seek peace, the appeal stated, are a minority but they speak in the name of the principles that "have been the most significant contribution of the Jewish people to humanity". The Jewish settlement in Palestine must be founded on a peaceful and democratic basis "in accordance with the fundamental spiritual and moral principles inherent in the Jewish tradition and essential for Jewish hope."[171]

The appeal was not successful. A month later Israel was declared a Jewish state and the first Jewish-Arab war broke out. The dream of Buber and other idealists of a binational state was shattered.

The next time Fromm interfered in Israeli politics was in 1957. For some months he actively advocated a plan - not made by himself, but strongly supported by him - to settle the problem of the Arab refugees from Israel. The plan was that "the Israeli government should declare unilaterally and without conditions: 1. That it recognizes in principle the right of the Arab refugees to return. 2. That in view of the fact that this is not possible, it offers the second-best, namely full restitution... 3. That they will, however, admit a number which is practically feasible, let us say 100,000 refugees, into the State of Israel."[172]

Fromm considered this plan a good, though not the best, solution to a big problem. He spoke about it with Martin Buber and Nahum Goldmann, the head of the World Zionist Organization and of the Jewish Agency and a friend of Fromm from his Frankfurt days. Buber's response was a disappointment, but Goldmann reacted with sympathy and promised to discuss the plan with the Israeli Prime Minister David Ben-Gurion.[173] Together with Dean James A. Pike Fromm also

---

[169]See Funk's decription of this process in Fromm: *Ethik und Politik*, 227f. Three versions of the appeal are published in German translation in op.cit., 228-235. The original English versions can be found at the Erich Fromm Archives in Tübingen.

[170]Letter Fromm - Strauss 13.4 1948. "Yishuv" is a name for the Jewish community in Palestine before the State of Israel was declared.

[171]Fromm & al.: Appeal for cooperation between Jews and Arabs (different versions) 1948.

[172]Letter Fromm - Thomas 18.7 1957.

[173]ibid.; Letter Fromm - Pike 13.6 1957.

planned to form a committee of Jews and non-Jews to work for the implementation of the plan.[174]

Fromm himself would have preferred all 800,000 Arab refugees to be allowed to return. This would have meant that Israel would have become a binational state, as Judah L. Magnes, Martin Buber and the rest of the Ihud party wanted. For Fromm the binational solution was "the only reasonable"[175] one and Ihud represented "the only ray of light in the State of Israel".[176] But he recognized that to allow all refugees to return was not politically possibleand thus advocated the second-best solution, this plan of restitution.

This plan resulted in nothing. But for Fromm it was important that Jews protested against the policy of Israel, because that would make it easier for non-Jews to do the same without the fear of being accused of anti-Semitism, "an accusation which the Zionists so readily produce."[177] Fromm was a member of the Editorial Advisory Board of the Jewish Newsletter, a biweekly magazine that criticized the policy of Israel and the American Jewish tendency to brand any criticism of Israel as disloyalty to Jews.[178]

After these two failures Fromm never again tried to interfere in Israeli politics. But he kept a close watch on what was happening in the Near East and commented on issues concerning Israel, although not publicly. The Six Day War of 1967 prompted him to write an essay on martyrs and heroes in Jewish history that was published posthumously.[179]

Fromm begins his essay by noting that after the war many people, both Jews and non-Jews, were impressed by the Israeli military victory and now knew that the Jews were not cowards. This pride at Jewish heroism was related to the shame many Jews felt for the fact that so many Jews were silently and without resistance killed in the Holocaust (the uprising in the Warsaw ghetto being an exception). Fromm then describes how the Jewish tradition cherishes martyrs, e.g. Rabbi Akiba, killed for their convictions. While heroes seek fame and glory and guarantee physical survival, martyrs have been indispensable for spiritual survival. The Jewish tradition has always been sceptical about heroes like King

---

[174]Letter Fromm - Simon 24.6 1957.
[175]Letter Fromm - Pike 13.6 1957.
[176]Letter Fromm - Thomas 18.7 1957.
[177]Letter Fromm - Pike 23.10 1957.
[178]"A Decade of Non-Conformity. The Jewish Newsletter". Advertisement in *NYTBR* 27.10 1957.
[179]In German translation in Fromm: *Ethik und Politik*, 216-226.

David, who was rebuked for his immoral behavior, the Maccabees (the Book of Maccabees was not accepted into the Bible), and the Zealots. And although the Jewish tradition does not promote martyrdom, it appreciates martyrs. Fromm's conclusion is then that the Jews have a right to admire their military heroes, but when they hold martyrs in contempt, they hold their greatest traditions, and the greatest traditions of mankind, in contempt.[180]

In the 1970's Fromm got into an argument with his old friend Ernst Simon. Simon was a close ally when it came to the policy of the State of Israel, but unlike Fromm, he criticized Israel from a Zionist position (he emigrated to Palestine as early as 1928). In a letter dated 26.12 1976 Simon expresses the irritation he feels at Fromm's at times very aggressive anti-Zionism and anti-Israel position (Anti-israelismus), and his sometimes immense (masslose) critique of Israel. Simon wrote that Fromm had stated that he felt for Israel like for any other little people in the same situation. Does Israel mean no more than that for Fromm? And Fromm made a big mistake, Simon writes, in calling Nasser a humanist socialist, or something like that in one of his books.[181] When Simon informed him that Nasser had used gas in the war in Jemen, Fromm's excuse was that he did not know enough about Nasser. But why does a person like Fromm not check such points before publishing them? And has Fromm publicly corrected his statements, Simon asks.[182]

In his reply Fromm recognizes that he was mistaken in his image of Nasser. "I regret it indeed but is it not also human to err?" On the question of Zionism and the State of Israel Fromm has a different opinion from Simon. "Why have I not the right to my reactions even if they are contrary to yours, without making this a reason of questioning our friendship? ... We both act honorably according to our conscience and our knowledge, and that is the best any man can do." He expresses his hope that their long and warm friendship can withstand these differences, although Simon's emotional, "somewhat fanatical" indignation at his critique of Israel was, in Fromm's opinion, based on a very narcissistic nationalism.[183]

The friendship between Fromm and Simon withstood this outburst and they continued to write friendly letters to each other. Fromm also recognized that the

---

[180]ibid.

[181]Simon's memory is not quite correct here. In *May Man Prevail?*, 15,, Fromm wrote that many countries in the Third World might choose a democratic, decentralized socialism and become allies of the neutral block, as represented by Tito, Nasser and Nehru.

[182]Letter Simon - Fromm 26.12 1976.

[183]Letter Fromm - Simon 7.1 1977.

Zionism of Simon was of a very hopeful nature. "... indeed I would feel very sympathetic towards Israel if yours were the attitude of the majority."[184]

Although Fromm showed a great interest in Israel, he never visited the country.[185] But he followed the events there closely and expressed very strong opinions about them.

Just how suspicious Fromm was of the policy of Israel is shown by his comment at the outbreak of the October War (Jom Kippur War) in 1973. "Since two days we have the new war in the Near East, which it would seem the Egyptians have started, although I cannot help having a slight doubt even here, considering past Israeli behavior. At any rate I have the impression that Dayan, who knew as he had said himself, of the coming attack for days, intentionally lured the Egyptians into the interior in order to destroy a large force of soldiers and weapons. With this he has a new basis for taking the position officially that he will not return any of the occupied land, and secure his own victory at the coming elections as the saviour of the fatherland."[186]

In his critique of Israel Fromm even committed the "ultimate sin": he compared Israel's acts to those of the Nazis. Writing about the principle of retaliation, he states: "Actually when the Nazis destroyed Lidice as a retaliation of the murder of one of their leaders, the world was indignant. What else are the bombings of the camps of Arab refugees but small Lidices based on the same spirit of revenge and alleged intimidation, of which of course the opposite is true."[187]

Frommm deals with the issue of terrorism by claiming that the Jewish terrorism of Stern and Irgun in 1947 was "in intensity and extent larger than the terror of the Arabs". And having declared that he was opposed to this terror then as much as he is opposed to the Palestinian terrorism now, he adds: "Those who know the situation[,] however, say that the Arafat group itself has never approved of terror against innocent bystanders but has applied it only to military or similar kinds of installations."[188]

---

[184]Letter Fromm - Simon 28.2 1977.
[185]Personal communication from Rainer Funk 12.4 1997.
[186]Letter Fromm - Darmstadter 9.10 1973. Fromm was mistaken in his speculations about the future. Although Israel was again victorious in this war, it suffered heavy losses and the discontent with this was one reason for the transfer of power in the 1977 elections.
[187]Letter Fromm - Darmstadter 16.12 1974.
[188]ibid. This was written before Begin - once a member of one of the Jewish terrorist groups - became Israeli Prime Minister.

One terrorist attack is discussed by Fromm somewhat further. A Palestinian group took children as hostages, since they calculated that, since it was a matter of children, the Israeli government would give in to their demands. But Dayan did publicize the kidnappers' letter, refused the help offered by the French Ambassador, and ordered an attack in which many were killed. This was for Fromm a serious violation of the Jewish law that one should do anything to save the lives of children, and it was a amnifestation of the way political life in Israel had killed real religious life.[189]

As we noted at the beginning of this chapter, Fromm's basic anti-Zionism was an expression of his opposition to any kind of nationalism. But why was he so strongly opposed to the policy of the State of Israel?

First of all, Fromm criticized Israel for ethical reasons. He felt very strongly that the Arab population of Palestine was suffering an injustice. He explained his efforts on behalf of the Arab refugees in 1957 as being an interest "in the principle of justice to the Arabs, and at the same time of peace in the Middle East".[190] The same empathy for the Arabs is expressed in another statement: "I think that the whole position of a state, whose only moral justification is to find a home for homeless people, and who does so by depriving just as many other people of their homes is untennable [sic] morally, and truly stupid politically."[191]

Secondly, Fromm saw the conflict in the Near East from the perspective of world politics. For him the State of Israel was "an outpost of American imperialism in the Near East... My whole attitude toward Israel and the Arabs cannot be separated from the analysis of the whole world situation of the strength of American and European imperialism and their last attempts to keep up their traditional role of superiority over the non-industrialized parts of the world. I look at political events in the Near East from the standpoint of this total struggle and indeed I feel in no way identified with Israel."[192] Shortly after the end of the Vietnam War he wrote that this war was "the most drastic symbol for the end of the white man's exploitation of the non-industrial world, which happens, or happened, to be at the same time people of different color." This racial prejudice is, according to Fromm, the reason for the pro-Israeli opinion in the USA, and is also revealed in the Israeli arrogance towards the Arabs and the oriental Jews.

---

[189]Letter Fromm - Darmstadter 27.1 1975.
[190]Letter Fromm - Thomas 18.7 1957.
[191]ibid.
[192]Letter Fromm - Simon 7.1 1977.

"The gooks in South East Asia, as well as the gooks in the Near East or anywhere else - they should not dare to defy the white man's weapons."[193]

Thirdly, Fromm criticized Israel for Jewish reasons. In *You shall be as gods* he writes that from a humanist standpoint the tragedy of the Jews, that they lost their state and were forced into *diaspora*, turned out to be a blessing, in that from their despised and marginalized position they developed and upheld a tradition of humanism.[194] Although he does not explicitly say this here, it is easy to interpret that the opposite is also true, i.e. that possession of a state, of power and influence can be a threat to the capacity to develop the tradition of humanism.

This was in fact what Fromm thought was happening in Israel. "It is just a terrible thought and feeling that the spirit of the Prophets is being killed by those who claim they are fulfilling the messianic vision, and even more terrible to think that the great idea of the eventual return of Israel to their land might be one of the factors which, through intensifying and prolonging the cold war, might lead to the destruction of the human race. What contempt for the greatness of the Jewish spirit, from the Prophets on to those who went to their death not fighting but with faith, emanates from these new heroes of violence and power."[195] And in another letter: "It is a sad thing to see how a nation which for 2,000 years was characterized by moral and pacifist ideals, changes its tune within a generation, if the opportunity arises."[196]

Fromm deeply believed that the lesson to be learned from Jewish history was that it was better to be powerless but with an unbroken spirit of humanism and universalism than to build one's security on power like all other nations. This was the position of world Jewry until the success of political Zionism. "The power of Hitler and the trauma of the Holocaust have so deeply affected later Jews that most of them surrendered spiritually and believed they had found an answer to their existence in founding a state - which, however, lacks none of the evils inherent more or less in all states, precisely because they are based on powers."[197]

---

[193]Letter Fromm - Schwarzschild 6.6 1975. Quoted from Schwarzschild: "Remembering Erich Fromm" *The Jewish Spectator* (Fall 1980), 32.
[194]Fromm: *You shall be as gods*, 15.
[195]Letter Fromm - Schwarzschild January 1970. Quoted from Schwarzschild: "Remembering Erich Fromm" *The Jewish Spectator* (Fall 1980), 32.
[196]Letter Fromm - Thomas 18.7 1957.
[197]Fromm: *On Being Human*, 108.

This is the reason why Fromm believed that political Zionism was a false Messiah.[198] Other false Messiahs have caused disaster for the Jews, and political Zionism has also been destructive for Judaism in that its true nature has been so completely changed and Israel has become like any other nation. Fromm recalls that Scholem once told him that the greatest blunder of the Jews was not to have built a state at the time of Sabbathai Zwi. Fromm's comment: "Maybe if they had, the Jews would have disappeared from the historical record already some time ago."[199] A state of their own is not - as is alleged - a guarantee for the survival of the Jewish people; on the contrary, it is a threat.

One person who spoke out against Zionism from a religious Jewish position was Rabbi Aaron Samuel Tamaret. He opposed Zionism not from the traditional orthodox standpoint - that one should just wait for the Messiah to restore Israel - but from a very radical humanistic standpoint, criticizing Zionism for building its project on violence and power. After the magazine *Judaism* had published excerpts from his writings[200], Fromm published an enthusiastic comment in the next issue. Rabbi Tamaret has applied "the principles of prophetic Judaism to the scene of contemporary politics". Unlike the Zionists and the leaders of Israel, he has done so in the spirit of the Jewish religious tradition in that he has opposed nationalism and war. "In a time when politics has become completely secularized and separated from the values which characterize Jewish religious thoughts, Rabbi Tamaret's writings are of great significance; they should give new strength to all who fight against idols, especially the idols of nationalism and war."[201]

I think Schwarzschild is perfectly right when he writes about Fromm: "His biting critique of contemporary Jewish politics was motivated by total identification with the Jewish people and with what he believed (I think, rightly) to be its highest values."[202]

---

[198]Letter Fromm - Darmstadter 27.1 1975.

[199]Ibid.

[200]Tamaret: "Politics and Passion: An Inquiry into the Evils of our Time" *Judaism* 12 (Winter 1963), 36-56. Rabbi Tamaret was an orthodox East European rabbi who participated in the Fourth Zionist Congress in 1900 but was disappointed and became a strong opponent of Zionism. In the excerpts from his writings he emphasizes the moral mission of the Jews and criticizes nationalism and war.

[201]Fromm: "Religious Humanism and Politics" *Judaism* 12 (Spring 1963), 223f. As other examples of Jews who have in our own time successfully applied religious principles to politics Fromm mentions Nathan Chofshi and Rabbi Benjamin, journalist and member of Ihud.

[202]Schwarzschild: "Remembering Erich Fromm" *The Jewish Spectator* (Fall 1980), 31.

3.7. Anti-Semitism

As we have already seen Fromm claimed that the accusation of anti-Semitism was a weapon eagerly used by the Zionists to brand any critique they disliked. Otherwise he hardly discussed the subject of anti-Semitism, and only in occasional comments.

What Fromm's own experiences of anti-Semitism were is impossible to know. He writes that as a small boy he experienced "small episodes of anti-Semitism",[203] but he does not say what these episodes were. The circles in which he was active later in life - the Frankfurt School, psychoanalysts, and socialists - had many Jews, so he was no different there from the others. But in the wider context he was different as a Jew. He saw the enormous growth of anti-Semitism in Germany in the interwar period, and this forced him - like so many others - into exile, something that turned out to be their salvation.

Despite this experience, Fromm almost totally ignores the problem of anti-Semitism. In describing the personalities of Himmler and Hitler he does mention their anti-Semitism, but it is not a central feature of the discussion.[204] He also mentions anti-Semitism in connection with Freud,[205] but although he devoted a large book to the study of human evil, he only mentioned anti-Semitism in passing.[206]

We can of course speculate about why he was so silent about anti-Semitism in general and the Nazi genocide in particular, but I cannot see the benefit of such speculation. The evil of Hitler is evident to all; we do not have to emphasize his anti-Semitism to prove that. One clear consequence of the Nazi terror for Fromm was his immense fear of German rearmament.[207]

But the relation between Germans and Jews has not always been tragic. In a letter to Ernst Simon in 1977 Fromm mentions that the mixture of German and Jewish culture has been an unusually productive synthesis - he mentions Marx, Freud,

---

[203]Fromm: *Beyond the Chains of Illusion*, 5.
[204]Fromm: *The Anatomy of Human Destructiveness*, 312, 314, 395, 398-400.
[205]Fromm: *Sigmund Freud's Mission*, 49, 74.
[206]Fromm: *The Anatomy of Human Destructiveness*, 273. In *Gesellschaft und Seele*, 129, anti-Semitism is mentioned together with nationalism as an expression of fanaticism.
[207]One of his articles on this subject has the striking title "Is Germany on the March Again?" *War/Peace Report* 6 (March 1966), 3f.

and Einstein as examples of this - and asks if Simon has any explanation why this is so.[208] His own thoughts on this subject have been published posthumously.[209]

In these "Remarks on the Relations between Germans and Jews" Fromm starts by mentioning the three German-Jewish geniuses Marx, Freud, and Einstein. "Inasmuch as no genius is a flower growing in the desert, but needs a soil that permits and furthers its growth, we must assume that this extraordinary productivity of the German-Jewish cultural marriage has its roots in a deep affinity between the Jewish and the German cultures. This affinity is more difficult to grasp today, after we have witnessed the ferocity of anti-Jewish feelings in that part of the German population in which Nazism took its hold. Yet the Jews and the Germans must share some essential qualities that make the fruitfulness of their relationship explainable."[210]

Fromm's suggestion is, then, that it is lack of power that is the basis for the deep affinity between the German and the Jewish spirits. Until about 1871 Germany was a powerless nation, a "people of poets and thinkers". It then began to expand in power and might, but the Jewish minority still represented the humanistic and anti-power standpoint of their own and of the earlier German culture, so beautifully expressed by Goethe. Marx, Freud, and Einstein all had their roots in this same old German-Jewish cultural intermarriage of the first hundred years of their co-existence. The Jews had, of course, been living in Germany for longer than this, but not as part of German culture.[211]

In his discussion of this subject Fromm also makes an interesting remark on the reasons for the anti-Semitism of the Nazis. The intensity of the Nazi hatred of the Jews can be understood via the anti-power standpoint of the Jews. The Nazis, who worshipped power and force, could not stand the Jewish standpoint and therefore they considered - not entirely wrongly - the Jews a threat. "In fact, the Jews were always a danger, and not only for Germany, because *they proved that a people could survive through two thousand years without having any power.*" Thus they discredited the general belief that power and force are necessary conditions for national survival.[212]

---

[208]Letter Fromm - Simon 24.10 1977.
[209]Fromm: *On Being Human*, 105-110.
[210]op.cit., 106f.
[211]op.cit., 107-110.
[212]op.cit., 107f.

Fromm's claim that it was the anti-power standpoint of the Jews that was so dangerous in the eyes of the power-fixated Nazis is interesting, but also problematic. This idea is influenced - or perhaps even determined - by Fromm's idea that it is good for the Jews not to have power and might. The Zionists drew the opposite conclusion, that it would be best for the Jews to have political power in a state of their own. Being powerless had made the Jews the perfect scapegoat. Maybe this is one of the reasons for Fromm's silence about anti-Semitism, that it was an argument for Zionism. The Zionists could claim that if there had been a Jewish state and if the European Jews had emigrated to it in the interwar period, the Holocaust would never have happened. Being powerless might generate beautiful philosophy and sweet poetry, but the possession of power guarantees security. This was the opinion of the majority of Jews after the Holocaust.

Fromm's idea seems to have been that the Jews should be different. If all other people were nationalistic, the Jews should be universalistic. If all other nations based their existence on power, the Jews should not. Many socialist Zionists had a similar vision, though one connected with Zionism. They thought that it was not enough to have a state for Jews, but a Jewish state, built on the Jewish tradition. This state would be different, better, and thus stand as a model for the rest of the world.[213] When the Jewish state came into existence, many circumstances - which we cannot deal with here - caused the ruling socialist Zionists to choose a *Realpolitik* that undermined and finally destroyed these visions of a socialist model state, totally different than other states.[214]

3.8. The Judaism of Erich Fromm

We have seen that Fromm was influenced for life by his Jewish background, that he was influenced by different Jewish thinkers, and that he gave very sympathic verdicts on the Torah, the Talmud, and Jewish mysticism, but that he strongly opposed political Zionism and criticized the policy of Israel. Let us now turn to his statements about his own Judaism.

---

[213]In 1862 the Proto-Zionist Moses Hess already declared that the Jewish state would play a decisive role as a model for the socialist transformation of the world. Ahad Ha'am, Judah L. Magnes, Martin Buber, and many others criticized the leading Zionists for betraying the original ideal and making the Jewish state into a state like all others. See, e.g., Hertzberg (Ed.): *The Zionist Idea*, 116-139 (Hess), 248-277 (Ahad Ha'am), 440-465 (Magnes and Buber).
[214]This process has been excellently described in a recent Swedish book, Rosenberg: *Det förlorade landet* (The Lost Country).

On receiving Judaistic books from Leo Jung, a famous orthodox rabbi, Fromm thanked for this gift in a letter, expressing his "intense interest" in them. And he added: "I am deeply rooted in that tradition which you present so beautifully..."[215]

But Fromm was not only interested and rooted in the Jewish tradition. He identified with it. Once he stated, "I am speaking as a Jew who loves the Jewish tradition."[216] Another time he stated that "I am still strongly rooted in this tradition which I love in spite of the fact that I have separated myself from all its practice and even from any participation in Jewish religion or any other form of Jewish life."[217] And to his old friend, Ernst Simon, with whom he had studied the Talmud and Judaica since they were teenagers, he wrote: "If you say I have turned away from the Jewish tradition, this is true and not true, depending what is meant by the sentence. If you say I have turned away from the life of a praticing Jew which I led until the end of my twenties, you are of course perfectly right, but my interest in and love for the Jewish tradition has never died and nobody can talk to me for any length of time who will not hear a Talmudic or Hasidic story."[218]

Some time in the 1970's Fromm wrote on ten scraps of paper a text he headed "Mein Judentum" (the text is in English although the title is in German). The text was perhaps intended as a guideline for a radio speech.[219] In it he states that he cannot speak of "my Judaism" in that he does not belong to any religious organization. But if anyone suspects that he wants to hide his Jewishness, "he must consider that such an attempt would be rather ridiculous considering the shape of my face and my nose. But if he knows me and my work, he will have also no reason to believe that I want to hide my Jewish origins."[220]

As a child, Fromm writes, he was proud to be a Jew, a member of "God's chosen people". Today he condemns this pride as being nationalistic and narcissistic. But then Fromm was proud of his Jewishness, not only because he came from a rabbinical family, but because there was practically no criminality or alcoholism in the Jewish community he knew.[221] The text ends very abruptly and it is evident that Fromm was not able to finish it.

---

[215]Letter Fromm - Jung 7.10 1970.
[216]Quoted by Darmstadter in his letter to Fromm 9.10 1967.
[217]Letter Fromm - Merton 7.2 1966.
[218]Letter Fromm - Simon 7.1 1977.
[219]Personal communication from Rainer Funk 12.4 1997.
[220]Fromm: "Mein Judentum" (manuscript from the 1970's).
[221]Ibid.

Fromm recognized two tendencies within Judaism, a nationalistic and a universalistic. He opposed the nationalistic tendency, expressed in the Zionist movement, as he opposed all other forms of nationalism, whereas he loved and identified with the universalistic tendency in Judaism. He saw it as an extremely important contribution to the development of mankind, and he wanted to be part of it and develop it further. Not only did Erich Fromm have a genuinely Jewish nose; he also had a genuinely Jewish soul.

4. Fromm and the Bible

4.1. View of the Bible

Fromm was brought up with the Bible. He read it; he loved it; he was influenced by it for the rest of his life.

In his seventies Fromm said in an interview: "There have been three, four, five books in my life that have made me what I am. First of all come the books of the prophets. Notice that I do not say the 'Old Testament'. When I was young, I did not detest the military accounts of the conquest of Canaan as much as I do now. But even then I didn't like them, and I doubt that I read them more than once or twice. But the prophetic books and the psalms, especially the prophetic books, were and still are an inexhaustible source of vitality for me."[1] And when, a short time before his death, he was asked what basic values should guide us, his answer was: Read the Bible![2]

That Fromm was familiar with and influenced by the Bible can also be seen from the fact that he frequently quoted it and used biblical expressions, not only when dealing with religious topics but also in other contexts. But what did he really think of the Bible?

First of all, the Bible - by which we here mean the Jewish Bible, i.e. the Old Testament - was for Fromm a revolutionary book, dealing with and aiming at the liberation of man, a book with a vision that is still valid and awaiting realization, a book that expresses the genius of a people struggling for life and freedom throughout many generations. It is not the "word of God"; it is a book written by men, but "an extraordinary book, expressing many norms and principles that have maintained their validity throughout thousands of years."[3]

How should the Bible be studied and understood? Fromm first gives an interesting epistemological comment. Because it is a revolutionary book, perhaps it can be better understood today in a time of revolution and by those who "are

---

[1] Fromm: *For the Love of Life*, 101. In a letter to Thomas Merton 7.2 1966 Fromm wrote about his writing of *You shall be as gods*: "It may sound presumptuous that I should write a book on the Old Testament, because I am not an Old Testament scholar; but nevertheless I have studied it since I was a child..." Merton's comment to this was: "...I am sure that is just what the Old Testament needs: a radical interpretation." (Letter Merton-Fromm 13.10 1966)
[2] Fromm: Interview with Guido Ferrari 8.3 1980.
[3] Fromm: *You shall be as gods*, 7.

least fettered by tradition and most aware of the radical nature of the process of liberation going on at the present time."[4] With this statement Fromm comes close to Christian liberation theology, which has criticized the common assumption of a universal or class-neutral meaning to the Bible, and also in its understanding of the Bible has made an option for the poor fighting for their liberation.[5]

Fromm further treats the Bible as *one* book, although it was written by several authors. According to him, the editorship of the biblical books was, "in a broad sense, a work of authorship."[6] But the Bible can also be viewed as one book because "it has been read and understood as one book for the last two thousand years."[7] Fromm only occasionally discusses historical-critical issues, although it is evident that he was familiar with them.[8] In his book about the Bible, *You shall be as gods*, his purpose is to understand the biblical text, not to give a historical analysis. In his interpretation of the Bible he also takes the later Jewish tradition into consideration saying that he found inspiration and encouragement for this he in Hermann Cohen and his method of analysis in *Die Religion der Vernunft aus den Quellen des Judentums*.[9]

Fromm's interpretation of the Bible is, in his own words, that of radical humanism. According to him, radical humanist thought is the main stream of evolution in the Bible and the Jewish tradition. The conservative-nationalistic pattern also to be found in the Bible is a relic of older times.[10] Judaism was able to develop a radical humanism because the Jews were a small, powerless nation without might and splendor. The suffering of the Jews also gave rise to national resentment, clannishness, and arrogance, but above all to a longing for liberation and a vision of peace and justice. "What from a mundane standpoint was the tragedy of the Jews - the loss of their country and their state - from the humanist

---

[4]ibid.
[5]"... the most adequate 'ownership' of the Bible, the most adequate 'pertinency' for rereading the kerygma of the Bible, is with the poor. That kerygma belongs to them 'preferentially' - first and foremost." (Croatto: *Biblical Hermeneutics*, 63)
[6]Fromm: *You shall be as gods*, 8.
[7]ibid.
[8]He already referred in *Das jüdische Gesetz* to a work by Wellhausen, a famous historical-critical exegete (p.21), and in *You shall be as gods* he mentions the Pentateuchal sources J, E, and P, according to the classical four-source-theory of Old Testament exegesis (p.8, 26n.). That Fromm was not so precise on historic-critical issues is shown by the fact that in quoting from the latter part of the Book of Isaiah he sometimes refers to Isaiah and sometimes to Second Isaiah. (Fromm: *The Dogma of Christ*, 146; Fromm: *You shall be as gods*, 44f., 124, 127, 130.)
[9]Fromm: *You shall be as gods*, 13.
[10]op.cit., 12.

standpoint was their greatest blessing: being among the suffering and despised, they were able to develop and uphold a tradition of humanism."[11]

4.2. Creation

As has already been stated, Fromm was heavily influenced by Bachofen's theory of the difference between patriarchal and matriarchal societies. From this perspective he studied the first stories of the Bible, especially the Story of Creation. He made brief comments on this in some of his works,[12] but wrote the most detailed and thorough study of this issue in 1933 already, a study that was published posthumously.[13]

The Old Testament is, Fromm claims, written in the spirit of patriarchalism, it is "der Triumphgesang der siegreichen Männerreligion, ein Siegeslied der Vernichtung der matriarkalischen Reste in Religion und Gesellschaft."[14] This can be seen from the Stories of Creation. In real life women have one essential advantage over men: they can give birth to new life. But in religious myths this has been changed. In the second Story of Creation it is not the woman who gives birth to the man, but the opposite, the woman is created from a rib of the man. And the expression of the male capacity to create is the central position occupied by the word. In the first story God creates by his word, in the second man gives name to all the animals. Creation by thought is the male substitute for the female womb.[15]

But not all matriarchal characteristics have been eliminated from the story. This is evident if one compares it with the Babylonian Story of Creation (Enuma Elish), which Fromm analyzes in detail. In it the goddess Tiamat is the focal point. After many intrigues she is finally defeated by her sons under the leadership of Marduk, who as sole ruler of the world then creates man. The struggle between Tiamat and Marduk is a symbolic expression of the struggle between the sexes.[16] As Fromm

---

[11]op.cit., 15.
[12]Fromm: *The Forgotten Language*, 231-235; Fromm: *The Sane Society*, 53f.; Fromm: "Man - Woman". In: Hughes (Ed.): *The People in Your Life*, 5f.; Fromm: *The Dogma of Christ*, 88f.; Fromm: *The Anatomy of Human Destructiveness*, 164; Fromm: *For the Love of Life*, 146.
[13]Fromm: "Die männliche Schöpfung". In: Fromm: *Liebe, Sexualität, Matriarkat*, 68-94.
[14]op.cit., 72f. As was seen in 4.1. Fromm later in life, while not denying the regressive elements, placed more stress on the progressive features of the Old Testament.
[15]op.cit., 73-75, 94.
[16]op.cit., 77-88.

later put it: "History doesn't begin as Freud thought, with the rebellion against the Father, but with the fight of the sons against the Great Mother."[17]

The biblical story begins where the Babylonian story ends. There is no description in Genesis of any fight between a female goddess and a male god; the latter is the sole ruler of the world from the very beginning. But there are relics in the biblicall text of the older concepts explicit in the Babylonian version. The "abyss", the "deep" of Gen. 1:2 (Hebrew *tehom*) is reminiscent of the first mother Tiamat. "There are good reasons to assume that 'Tehom' of the biblical text is the Tiamat of the Babylonian text."[18] And when as a punishment for man's disobedience God states that man shall rule over woman (Gen. 3:16), it indicates that there was once a time when this was not so.[19]

4.3. The "Fall"

The bibilical story of Adam and Eve eating the forbidden fruit (Gen. 3) - the story known in the nChristian tradition as the Fall - was of great interest to Fromm. His interpretation of this story is very different from the traditional Jewish or Christian ones. "Not one of the Biblical commentators would say that this story is an act of bravery, the reward of which was differentiation between good and evil, but Fromm does."[20]

The act of Adam and Eve was, first of all, an act of disobedience. Fromm the peace activist often used the following expression: "Human history began with an act of disobedience, and it is not unlikely that it will be terminated by an act of obedience."[21] As can be seen from this statement, Fromm thinks that the act of Adam and Eve was the starting point of human history. While theology has traditionally seen the "fall" of man as something bad and tragic, Fromm turns

---

[17]Fromm: Interview with Gerard Khoury in 1979.
[18]ibid. Biblical sholars today do not normally think that the Hebrew *tehom* is ethymologically derived from the Babylonian Tiamat, but the concept of *tehom* is considered to have preserved its mythical characteristics and can therefore be compared with Tiamat. (See, e.g., Waschke: tehom *ThWAT VIII*, 563-571)
[19]Fromm: "Die männliche Schöpfung". In: Fromm: *Liebe, Sexualität, Matriarkat*, 88.
[20]Shapira: "Fromm and Judaism". In: Eletti (Ed.): *Incontro con Erich Fromm*, 232.
[21]Fromm: *On Disobedience*, 1. The same idea is also expressed in slightly different words in op.cit., 33; Fromm: *Beyond the Chains of Illusion*, 167; Fromm: *The Dogma of Christ*, 113. The disobedience of Adam and Eve is in all these passages compared to that of Prometheus, who according to Greek mythology was disobedient and rebellious, and it was through his disobedience that human history began.

everything upside down. It was not a "fall of man"; on the contrary, it was his awakening and the beginning of his rise.[22]

At the center of Fromm's interpretation of Gen. 3 stands verse 5, the words of the serpent that through eating the forbidden fruit man will be as God knowing good and evil. When Adam and Eve had eaten the fruit, the Bible says that their eyes were opened (v.7). The serpent was right, man was awakened from his ignorance and was now able to see the truth. Man became *as* God. But man was not God, mortality distinguished him from God (v. 22). To prevent man from becoming God, God expelled Adam and Eve from Paradise. This is, according to Fromm, an archaic part of the text. The message is nevertheless evident: man can become like God, can imitate God (imitatio Dei).[23]

Fromm finds further evidence for the claim that the Bible teaches that man can be like God in the statement of God, "You shall be holy; for I the Lord your God am holy" (Lev. 19:2b), and in the teaching of the prophets that man should practice the main qualities of God: justice and love. Following his conviction that man can know nothing of God's essence, only of God's actions (see 3.4.), Fromm claims that to imitate God's actions by practicing love and justice also means to know God and to become like God.[24] But according to Fromm there are also rabbinical statements that imply that the difference between God and man can be eliminated (he quotes Sanhedrin 65b and 38b).[25]

The act of Adam and Eve was, however, not only a step towards becoming like God, it was also an act of freedom. In the beginning Adam and Eve were bound

---

[22]Fromm: *You shall be as gods*, 70f. A very original interpretation of this story - and one that to some extent resembles Fromm's - has been presented by Bloch. (Bloch: *Das Prinzip Hoffnung*, 1496-1498; Bloch: *Atheismus im Christenthum*, 60, 116f.)

[23]op.cit., 64f. Fromm's interpretation of this story resembles the one made by Cyrus H. Gordon, expert on the Ancient Near East, although Gordon does not expound on it as much as Fromm. Anyway Gordon claims that the story "is not so much an account of the 'Fall of Man' but rather of the rise of man halfway to divinity. He obtained one of the two prerogatives or characteristics of the gods: intelligence; but he was checked by God from obtaining immortality, which would have made man quite divine." (Gordon: *Introduction to Old Testament Times*, 23f.) Fromm was most probably not aware of Gordon's interpretation, although it had appeared earlier.

[24]The idea that God is experienced through action and not by reasoning is also expressed in the saying of Jesus: "Whoever has the will to do the will of God shall know whether my teaching comes from him or is merely my own." (John.7:17). (Dellbrügge: "Impressionen eines Theologen beim Lesen Erich Fromms". In: Evangelisches Studienzentrum Heilig Geist (Hrsg.): *Erich Fromm und der christliche Glaube*, 94)

[25]Fromm: *You shall be as gods*, 65-70.

to blood and soil, something that Fromm calls incestuous fixation (where incestuous primarily means not a sexual but an affective fixation). But through their act of disobedience their eyes were opened, the original harmony with nature was broken, the process of man's individuation and through it human history began. The Bible also teaches the importance of cutting the bond to father and mother in other passages (e.g. in Gen.2:24, and in the commandment to Abraham to leave his father's house).[26]

Although man's emancipation from the primary ties of incestuous attachment started with an act of disobedience, disobedience is not a value in itself. On the contrary, the Bible teaches the importance of obedience to God. For Fromm this means obeying reason, conscience, law, moral and spiritual principles - the opposite to incestuous fixation. At this stage of history obeying God and his laws was the only way to help man liberate himself from the incestuous ties to nature and clan. The ultimate consequence of man's liberation is his freedom *from* God. Fromm discerns in the Talmud and in the Hasidic tradition (see 3.2.3.) a trend to make man completely autonomous, even to the point where he will be free from God or, at least, where he can deal with God on terms of equality.[27]

In sum, Adam and Eve's disobedience was the condition for man's self-awareness, for his capacity to choose, and thus his first step towards freedom. It was *not* a sin; nowhere in the Old Testament is there even a hint that this disobedience corrupted man, as Christianity teaches (the doctrine of original sin). The prophets interpreted man's first "sin" in an entirely different way from that of "original sin" as developed by the church, especially in the Augustinian tradition and even exaggerated by the Reformation.[28]

Although Fromm states that the Old Testament does not call the act of Adam and Eve a sin, on other occasions he discussed different concepts of sin with the story of the Fall as a starting point. The statement that having eaten the fruit Adam and Eve noticed that "they were naked and felt ashamed has often been interpreted moralistically ("Of course they felt ashamed when they saw each other naked"). In Fromm's opinion this is not the point of the story. That "their eyes opened" means that they left their prehuman state of ignorance and became aware of reality and experienced each other as separate individuals. It was this experience of being separate that made them feel ashamed. Separateness can be overcome by

---

[26]op.cit., 70f. Cf. Fromm: *Beyond the Chains of Illusions*, 167; Fromm: *On Disobedience*, 1f.; Fromm: *The Dogma of Christ*, 114.
[27]Fromm: *You shall be as gods*, 72-81.
[28]Fromm: *The Heart of Man*, 19f.; Fromm: *You shall be as gods*, 121f., 159.

love. But Adam and Eve did not love each other. This can easily be seen from the fact that they did not protect each other,;on the contrary Adam blamed Eve (Gen. 3:12). In Fromm's opinion, the sin of Adam and Eve was that they faced each other as separate, isolated, selfish human beings unable to overcome their separation in the act of loving union.[29]

This interpretation of the story of the Fall corresponds to the humanistic concept - or the concept of the being mode - of sin as unresolved estrangement that can be overcome by the full unfolding of reason and love. But because the story is, in Fromm's opinion, a blending of authoritarian and liberating elements, it can also be interpreted according to the authoritarian concept - or the concept of the having mode - of sin as disobedience that can be overcome by repentance that leads to punishment that leads to renewed submission.[30]

The estrangement man feels is caused by the fact that the complete prehuman harmony with nature is broken. Man becomes cursed by God. Enmity and struggle are proclaimed between man and animal (Gen. 3:15), between man and the soil (v. 17-19), between man and woman (v.16b), and between woman and her own natural function (v.16a). The aim of man - later forecefully proclaimed by the prophets - is to overcome this separateness, to replace enmity and struggle with peace.[31]

So far we have seen what the story of the Fall tells about man, but it also tells something about God. According to Fromm, the beginning of the Old Testament is written in the spirit of authoritarian religion. God is depicted as an absolute ruler who arbitrarily declares prohibitions and who jealously fears man's becoming an equal. To stop this from happening, he expels Adam and Eve from the Garden of Eden and puts an angel to see that they do not enter again. Only later in the Old Testament does the picture of God change.[32]

Flückiger has called the Story of the Fall a key passage in Fromm's whole thinking. He also claims that Fromm's own personal experience is reflected in his treatment of this story. Fromm defends the disobedience of Adam and Eve

---

[29]Fromm: *To have or to be?*, 122f. A similar discussion of how separateness causes guilt - but without the use of the word "sin" - can be found in Fromm: *The Art of Loving*, 8f.

[30]Fromm: *To have or to be?*, 124f. In *Man for Himself*, 12, Fromm refers to the story of the Fall as an example of authoritarian ethics where sin is disobedience.

[31]Fromm: *The Forgotten Language*, 246f.; Fromm: *The Dogma of Christ*, 141f. Cf. Fromm: *Die Pathologie der Normalität*, 90.

[32]Fromm: *Psychoanalysis and Religion*, 42f.

because he himself was disobedient to his own religious tradition.[33] Flückiger further gives three examples of how Fromm's treatment of this story is exegetically untenable:[34]

1) The dichotomy between being a part of nature and transcending nature that Fromm claims was the result of the "fall" was, according to the Bible, there already from the beginning. But Flückiger does not explain what the statement "their eyes were opened" (Gen. 3:7) after they had eaten the forbidden fruit means. Something happened when they disobeyed; the Bible is very clear about that. Fromm's theory that it was the beginning of man's alienation from nature is no worse than any other, and certainly better than Flückiger's, who does not present any theory at all.

2) Fromm's claim that the serpent was right in saying that man will not die from the forbidden fruit is not correct, because through this disobedience man became mortal, though he did not die at once. But Fromm's point is that the serpent was right not as to dying or living, but as to the result of eating the forbidden fruit, becoming as God knowing good and evil. In the text even God acknowledges that this has happened (Gen. 3:22). Immortality would have meant being God, knowing good and evil meant being *like* God. The serpent was right about that.

3) Fromm's statement that God denied man the possibility to become immortal and therefore expelled him from Paradise out of jealousy is not correct. Nowhere in the biblical text is anything said of God's jealousy. God had given Adam everything, Flückiger states. But God had not given Adam everything. He got knowledge of good and evil after disobeyimg, and immortality not at all. And although the Bible does not explicitly mention jealousy, Gen. 3:22-24 depicts a God who jealously defends his own divine monopoly.

4.4. The divine name

According to Fromm, the biblical concept of God passed through amny stages in its development. The first concept was formed according to the political and social concepts of a tribal chief or king, and God was seen as a supreme ruler.

---

[33]Flückiger: "Funktion und Wesen der Religion nach Erich Fromm" *Theologische Beiträge* 16 (1985), 219. Similarly Shapira: "Erich Fromm and Judaism". In: Eletti (Ed.): *Incontro con Erich Fromm*, 232: "He found that the first beings also did what he did; they revolted against the Creator."
[34]Flückiger: "Funktion und Wesen der Religion nach Erich Fromm" *Theologische Beiträge* 16 (1985), 221f.

This is evident in the first stories of the Bible, where God acts as a supreme ruler who does whatever he likes. The first important change comes when God concludes a covenant with Noah and his descendants (Gen. 9:11). "With the conclusion of the covenant, God ceases to be the absolute ruler. He and man have become partners in a treaty. God is transformed from an 'absolute' into a 'constitutional' monarch. He is bound, as man is bound, to the conditions of the constitution. God has lost his freedom to be arbitrary, and man has gained the freedom of being able to challenge God in the name of God's own promises, of the principles laid down in the covenant."[35]

The next decisive change comes with God's revelation to Moses. Here God reveals himself as the God of history rather than the God of nature. But what is more important is the idea of a nameless God, which is the full expression of the distinction between God and idols. An idol has a name, because all things have names. When Moses argues that he must tell the Hebrews the name of God, God makes a concession and says the famous words: "I am who I am" (EHYEH asher EHYEH) (Ex. 3:14). 'Ehyeh' is the first person singular of the imperfect tense of the Hebrew verb 'to be'. Unlike the perfect tense, the imperfect tense indicates that the action is not complete and is going on. God's being "is not completed like that of a thing, but is a living process, a becoming; only a thing, that is, that which has reached its final form, can have a name. A free translation of God's answer to Moses would be: 'My name is *Nameless*; tell them that 'Nameless' has sent you.' Only idols have names, because they are things. The 'living' God cannot have a name. In the name of *Ehyeh* we find an ironical compromise between God's concession to the ignorance of the people and his insistence that he must be a nameless God."[36]

This is the basis for the later idea that God's name can not be uttered and for the commandment not to make any images of God. No representations of God were tolerated, nor any representation of sound, i.e. a name, nor any representation of stone or wood. You can talk *to* God, but not *about* God lest God be transformed

---

[35]Fromm: *You shall be as gods*, 25, see 17-28. Cf. Fromm: *Psychoanalysis and Religion*, 43-45; Fromm: *The Art of Loving*, 68f.

[36]Fromm: *You shall be as gods*, 31, see 28-31, cf. 95f. While in *You shall be as gods* Fromm gives the translation of *ehyeh asher ehyeh* as "I AM WHO I AM", in *The Art of Loving*, 69, he translates it "I am becoming that which I am becoming", and in *Psychoanalysis and Religion*, 115f., "I AM THAT I AM" or "I am being that I am being". Despite the different translations, in all three books he draws the same conclusion, that the real meaning of this statement is that "my name is nameless".

into an idol. A theological application of this is the negative theology of Maimonides (see 3.4.1.).[37]

Flückiger has criticized Fromm's concept of a nameless God by stating that in the Old Testament Yahweh was always considered to be a real name.[38] That is true, but if one does not take the Bible to be the literal word of God, it is not only possible but also probable that we understand it better today than thousands of years ago. And Fromm's interpretation stands in a long Jewish tradition with the prohibition against using God's name and Maimonides' negative theology as the main witnesses.

The story about God revealing his name to Moses is a difficult one. The answer about God's name is mysterious, and Fromm's claim that it has to be understood that God in fact has no name is an interesting interpretation. But the play on the verb "to be" can also be interpreted to mean that God *will be there* or *will be present*, and can thus be connected with God's statement "I will be with you" in v. 12. This is how Buber interpreted this passage.[39] Fromm does not discuss any alternative interpretation; he just presents his own, connected with the anti-idolatry standpoint which he considers to be the main message of the Old Testament (see 4.6.1.).

4.5. The history of Israel

Although Fromm's biblical interest was mostly directed at the story of the "fall" and the message of the prophets, he also interprets the history of Israel - as described in the books of the Old Testament - in a fascinating way.

In Fromm's interpretation one of the main themes of the Old Testament is: "leave what you have, free yourself from all fetters: *be!*"[40] Hebrew history starts with Abraham, who left all he had to go to the unknown. But his descendants clung to the soil and possessions and thus became slaves and idol worshippers.[41] The message of the story of Abraham's leaving his home is that man must cut the primary ties that bind him to his land and his folk. Fromm finds the same message

---

[37]Fromm: *You shall be as gods*, 31-37.
[38]Flückiger: "Funktion und Wesen der Religion nach Erich Fromm" *Theologische Beiträge* 16 (1985), 209.
[39]Buber: *Werke 2*, 62f., cf. 267. Many others have supported this interpretation, e.g. Croatto (*Biblical Hermeneutics*, 52).
[40]Fromm: *To have or to be?*, 48.
[41]ibid.

in the story of Abraham's sacrifice of Isaac. Although he states that the traditional interpretations - that it is a test of Abraham's obedience and that the story shows God's disapproval of human sacrifice - are probably correct, he argues that the text suggests yet another interpretation, i.e. that man must be ready to cut all ties of blood and be completely free from incestuous fixation. To support this theory - which he himself calls a "tentative suggestion" - he emphasizes that certain formulations in the commandment to sacrifice Isaac (Gen. 22:2-3) are identical with formulations in the commandment to Abraham to leave his country (Gen. 12:1). This implies that they both have the same message: cut all ties of blood, in the first commandment those with father and mother, in the second those with the beloved son.[42]

The same pattern is repeated in the story of Moses. He, too, had to leave his home in order to become a revolutionary leader. Fromm analyzes the story of the exodus in detail and sums up the essential features of the story: The possibility of liberation exists only because man suffers, but his suffering does not give him wisdom on how to liberate himself, it only creates a wish that the suffering may stop. God understands the suffering, however, and sends his messenger. But neither the people nor Pharaoh understand the language of freedom or of reason, only the language of force (the miracles).[43]

Moses liberated the people and lead them to the desert, the symbol of the unfettered, nonpropertied life.[44] But the people escaped from freedom, they feared the uncertainty of the propertyless desert life and yearned for the "fleshpots of Egypt", i.e. the well-regulated and set existence they had enjoyed in Egypt. Slaves remain slaves at heart, even after they have been freed. God's response to this was a promise to feed them, but with two important conditions: each should gather according to their needs (Ex. 16:17f.), and they were forbidden to save anything till the next morning (Ex. 16:20f.). An excellent example of the non-hoarding attitude and of the Marxist principle: to each according to his needs.[45]

---

[42]Fromm: *You shall be as gods*, 89f. Cf. Fromm: *The Sane Society*, 52f.
[43]op.cit., 106f. Cf. Fromm: "Faith as a Character Trait" *Psychiatry* 5 (1942), 311f.; Fromm: *Man for Himself*, 203f. That Fromm's knowledge of the Bible deepened through the years is shown by the fact that when he wrote about the exodus in *Man for Himself* he talked about "the Jews", but 19 years later in *You shall be as gods* he used the more correct term "the Hebrews".
[44]Viewing the desert as something good is not unique. In Hos. 2:14-33 salvation starts by God leading Israel into the desert. But normally in the Bible the desert is a symbol of sterility, lifelessness, chaos.
[45]Fromm: *To have or to be?*, 48-50; Fromm: *You shall be as gods*, 108-110.

The story of the exodus does not have a happy end. The Hebrews cannot bear to live without having. They demand a visible manifestation of something they can worship: the Golden Calf. The fact that the people could not stand a relatively short absence of their leader without regressing to idol worship made God, for the first time in the story, lose not only his patience but also his hope (Ex. 32:9f.). That Moses - who was also a member of a generation that grew up in idol worship and serfdom - had to die before they entered the new land shows that revolution can succeed only in steps in time. "Suffering produces rebellion; rebellion produces freedom *from* serfdom; freeedom *from* may eventually lead to freedom *to* a new life without idolatry. But since there is no miraculous change of heart, each generation can take only one step. Those who have suffered and started the revolution cannot go beyond the limits their past sets for them. Only those who have not been born in slavery may succeed in achieving the promised land."[46]

The next generation entered the new land, exterminated their enemies, worshipped idols, and transformed their democratic tribal life into that of Oriental despotism. The revolution failed and the whole people and their story would perhaps have been forgotten had not new revolutionary thinkers and visionaries emerged, i.e. the prophets. The prophets announced that the people had to be expelled again from the land they had been incestuously fixated to and incapable of living in as free people. Only through experiencing a new desert could they be ready for the realization of the messianic vision.[47]

4.6. The prophets

As noted above (see 4.1.) Fromm's favorite books in the Bible were the prophets. The Hebrew prophets frequently figure in his lists of great humanistic teachers, along with the Buddha, Socrates, Jesus, and others (see 2.1.). Fromm professed that "the prophetic writings are to me unique in their spirit but also in their language and style, and there is almost nothing in literature which moves me as

---

[46]Fromm: *You shall be as gods*, 113. Here one can see a criticism of Marx's erroneous belief that it was possible to build a good society in a short time, a criticism that Fromm explicitly expressed in *The Sane Society*, 264f.
[47]Fromm: *To have or to be?*, 52f.; Fromm: *You shall be as gods*, 114f. Cf. Fromm: *The Sane Society*, 52f.; Fromm: *Psychoanalysis and Religion*, 84f.

much as the writings of some of the great prophets."[48] And further: "I often think in terms of sentences you find in the Prophets."[49]

Fromm has an interesting view of what a prophet is. In an essay written in honor of Bertrand Russell, he makes a distinction between prophets and priests. Prophets are persons who announce ideas and at the same time live them, while priests are those who administer these ideas. In the hands of priests the original idea of the prophet loses its vitality and becomes a formula.[50] Fromm also claims that the Hebrew priesthood was a concession to the ignorance of the people, created when Aaron was appointed by God to be the partner of Moses, after Moses had hesitated about his mission. (Ex. 4:10-17)[51]

Fromm mentions the Buddha, Christ, Socrates, and Spinoza as prophets. But to exemplify the character of prophets, he writes about the Old Testament prophets. "They lived what they preached. They did not seek power, but avoided it. Not even the power of being a prophet. They were not impressed by might, and they spoke the truth even if this led them to imprisonment, ostracism or death. They were not men who set themselves apart and waited to see what would happen. They responded to their fellow men because they felt responsible. What happened to others happened to them. Humanity was not outside, but within them. Precisely because they saw the truth they felt the responsibility to tell it; they did not threaten, but they showed the *alternatives* with which man was confronted. It is not that a prophet wishes to be a prophet; in fact, only the false ones have the ambition to become prophets."[52] That the true prophets did not

---

[48]Letter Fromm - Betz 14.10 1972. In: Betz: *An Analysis of the Prophetic Character and the Dialectical Rhetoric of Erich Fromm*, 331.

[49]Fromm: "Interview with Richard Heffner" *McCalls* 92 (Oct. 1965), 216.

[50]Fromm: *On Disobedience*, 27-29. Cf. Fromm: *You shall be as gods*, 96f.; Fromm: *May Man Prevail?*, 123f.

[51]Fromm: *You shall be as gods*, 96.

[52]Fromm: *On Disobedience*, 27. The conclusion of the essay is that Bertrand Russell is a prophet of our time, who "warns the world of impending doom precisely as the prophets did, because he loves life and all its forms and manifestations." (p. 42) Betz has convincingly argued that Fromm is to be considered a modern prophet, and has backed this claim with a thorough analysis of Fromm's rhetoric. (Betz: *An Analysis of the Prophetic Character of the Dialectical Rhetoric of Erich Fromm*; Betz: *Erich Fromm - Prophet in the Name of Life* (manuscript)) The fact that Fromm himself denied that he was a prophet (Fromm: Interview with Heiner Gautschy) does not mean that he did not function as one. Most prophets do not consider themselves as prophets, starting with Amos (Am. 7:14). Weinrich - who has criticized Fromm from a Christian perspective - also regards him as a prophet, but a false prophet. (Weinrich: "Priester der Liebe, Fragen eines Theologen an die Religionspsychologie von Erich Fromm und Hanna Wolff" *Einwürfe* 1 (1983), 171f.)

want to be prophets is because they were motivated entirely by an inner vision and conviction and not by a narcissistic wish to be leaders. The absence of narcissistic motivation is in Fromm's opinion the chief criterion for the true prophet in the past as well as today.[53]

The prophets are, Fromm argues, the agents of God. God does not intervene in human history directly, he does not change the heart of man. Man has to change himself, to save himself. God's role is to send messengers to warn and guide man. But the decision is always man's own. To support this notion, Fromm quotes the story about how the Hebrews asked Samuel to give them a king. Although Samuel (and God) disliked the request for a king, he had to "hearken to their voice". It was the choice of the people, God did not stop them.[54]

According to Fromm, the prophets had three functions. First, they revealed the truth about God and man and showed man certain goals. They were not foretellers or delphic oracles; they adressed their own time.[55] The prophets do say something about the future, not because any secrets have been revealed to them, but because they see "the forces operating *now* and the consequences of these forces unless they are changed."[56] Secondly, the prophets showed the people the alternatives. The prophets were not determinists, but alternativists. They believed that the people had a real choice. What they did was to show the people the alternatives. Fromm holds that the alternativistic position of the prophets was passed on by the Talmudic and rabbinic tradition, while the apocalyptic literature and early Christianity were characterized by a more deterministic position.[57] Thirdly, the prophets were protesters. They did not just show the alternatives, they warned the people of the wrong alternatives. Having preached and warned, they then let the people choose.[58] The prophets - like the

---

[53]Fromm: *You shall be as gods*, 94 n.
[54]Fromm: *The Dogma of Christ*, 142f. Cf. Fromm: *You shall be as gods*, 115-121, 165, 176-178; Fromm: *The Heart of Man*, 147f. n.18. Fromm acknowledges that the Bible teaches that a person can harden his heart to the point of no return. (Fromm: *The Heart of Man*, 127 n.7) This is what happened with Pharaoh. Although the Bible says that "God hardened Pharoh's heart", it means that God did not intervene when Pharaoh hardened his heart. (Fromm: *You shall be as gods*, 100f., 165. Cf. Fromm: *The Heart of Man*, 136f.; Fromm: *The Dogma of Christ*, 144)
[55]Here Fromm uses a German word play, stating that the prophets were not "*Voraus*sager", but "*Aus*sager" or rather "*Wahr*sager". Fromm: "Die Aktualität der prophetischen Schriften" *GA VI*, 77.
[56]Fromm: *You shall be as gods*, 118f.
[57]Fromm: *The Revolution of Hope*, 17f.
[58]Fromm: "Die Aktualität der prophetischen Schriften" *GA VI*, 77f. Cf. Fromm: *The Heart of Man*, 147f. n.18.

whole of the Old Testament - did not believe that man's nature was inherently evil, and therefore they believed that man was capable of choosing good.[59]

In *You shall be as gods* Fromm adds a fourth function, that the prophets "do not think in terms of individual salvation only, but believe that individual salvation is bound up with the salvation of society."[60] This is not really a function of the prophets comparable to the other three. It is rather a characteristic of the content of their preaching that could be included in the first function, revealing the truth about God and man. The reason why Fromm emphasizes this as a separate function in *You shall be as gods* is probably that the context deals with God as the God of history who wants to establish a just society, a God whose realm is never a purely spiritual one.

Before turning to the message of the prophets let us look at what Fromm wrote about one special prophet, Jonah. The Book of Jonah is different from the other prophetic books in that it does not contain the message of the prophet but just a story about him. According to Fromm "Jonah is different from all other prophets, inasmuch as he is not prompted by compassion and responsibility."[61] Jonah is a critic who is not interested in helping the object of his critique to repent and be saved, while the great prophets, from Isaiah to Marx, were critics who always showed new ways, new alternatives.[62] Jonah is a man of justice but not of mercy, he is a man with a strong sense of order and law, but without love.[63]

According to Fromm - who already stated that the story of Jonah was one of his favorite stories in the Bible when he was young[64] - the story of Jonah tells us something very important about love. Love cannot be divorced from responsibility. "Jonah does not feel responsible for the life of his brothers. He, like Cain, could ask, 'Am I my brother's keeper?'"[65] Another element of love that is so beautifully described in this story is love as active concern for the life and the growth of that which we love. Love and labor are inseparable. "One loves that for which one labors, and one labors for that which one loves."[66]

---

[59]Fromm: *You shall be as gods*, 161f.
[60]op.cit., 117f.
[61]op.cit., 119.
[62]Fromm: *Ethik und Politik*, 42f.
[63]Fromm: *Man for Himself*, 98f.; Fromm: *The Art of Loving*, 26f.; Fromm: *You shall be as gods*, 119.
[64]Fromm: *Beyond the Chains of Illusion*, 5.
[65]Fromm: *Man for Himself*, 99. Cf. Fromm: *The Art of Loving*, 28.
[66]Fromm: *Man for Himself*, 99; Fromm: *The Art of Loving*, 27. Fromm also made an analysis of the symbol language of this story in his book about dreams and myths. (Fromm: *The*

4.6.1. Idolatry

Fromm saw the importance of the Old Testament prophets especially in two concepts, the messianic vision and the rejection of idolatry. Idolatry plays a very central part in his thinking, and he returns to it frequently.

According to Fromm the "war against idolatry is the main religious theme that runs through the Old Testament from the Pentateuch to Isaiah and Jeremiah."[67] The point of the anti-idolatrous teaching is not that one should worship *one* God instead of many. "Monotheism is not a question of arithmetics, not a question of numbers."[68] The difference between worship of God and idolatry is that God is a *living* God, while the idol is a thing, not alive, but dead. (Hos. 14:4, Ps. 135:15, Is. 44:9f., 46:6f.) An idol is further made by man. When a man worships an idol. i.e. the work of his own hands, what he is really doing is worshipping himself, but in an alienated way. Following Feuerbach's idea of religion as a projection, Fromm claims that man transfers his own passions and qualities to the idol, and thus impoverishes himself.[69] The idol is the alienated manifestation of man's own powers, and the way to be in touch with these powers is a submissive attachment to the idol. Therefore idolatry is necessarily incompatible with freedom and independence. "Again and again the prophets characterize idiolatry as self-castigation and self-humiliation, and the worship of God as self-liberation and liberation from others."[70]

Fromm's conviction is that the prohibition of idolatry is more important than the worship of God. He finds this notion in the Jewish tradition, where the Talmud states, "Whoever denies idolatry is as if he fulfilled the whole Torah." (Hullin 5a)[71] Fromm then brings up the Talmudic concept of the Noachites. According to

---

Forgotten Language, 20-23)

[67]Fromm: *You shall be as gods*, 42.

[68]Fromm: "Beyond Egotistical Religion" (lecture in 1957). Cf. Cohen: "Der Gegensatz zwischen dem einzigen Gotte und den Göttern beschränkt sich nun aber nicht auf den Unterschied in der *Anzahl*; er prägt sich auch aus in dem Unterschiede zwischen einer unsichtbaren *Idee* und einem wahrnehmbaren *Bilde*." (Cohen: *Die Religion der Vernunft aus den Quellen des Judentums*, 61)

[69]Fromm does not in this context refer to Feuerbach's idea of projection, but to Freud's idea of transference. Fromm: *On Being Human*, 24.

[70]Fromm: *You shall be as gods*, 46, see 42-46. Cf. Fromm: *Beyond the Chains of Illusions*, 58f.

[71]Michael Maccoby - longtime co-worker of Fromm - reports that he once suggested to Fromm that his religious belief could be seen as consistent with Jewish tradition. Fromm's reply was that the only absolutely essential commandment for a Jew was that which forbids all idolatry. (Maccoby: "The Two Voices of Erich Fromm: The Prophetic and the Analytic"

the Talmud (Sanhedrin 56a), the non-Jews, the sons of Noah or the Noachites, must obey seven commandments. Of these seven commandments only two are religious, both negative, the prohibition of blasphemy and idolatry. According to both the Talmud (Tosefta, Sanhedrin, XIII, 2) and Maimonides (*Mishneh Torah*, XIV, 5, 8), a righteous Gentile, i.e. a person following the seven commandments, will have a portion in the world to come. Fromm's conclusion is thus: "Mankind, for its salvation, does not need to worship God. All it needs is *not* to blaspheme God and *not* to worship idols."[72]

Following his idea of negative theology (see 3.4.1.) Fromm proclaims the absurdity of theology. Instead we need "idology", we must talk about the idols, otherwise we cannot avoid serving them.[73] According to Fromm idolatry has characterized the whole history of mankind up to this day. Once idols were animals, trees, stars, figures of men and women, called Baal, Astarte, and thousands of other names. Although nobody today worships Baal or Astarte, we should not make the mistake of believing that there is no idolatry anymore. The idols today are honor, flag, state, mother, family, fame, production, consumption, and many more.[74] But because the *real* object of man's worship is veiled under the official worship of God, we need an "idology" to unmask the real objects of our worship, the form it takes, the way it is mixed with our official religion, etc.[75]

Fromm called upon all persons of good will - religious as well as non-religious - to join the fight against idolatry. Arguments about God divide, but the negation of idols unites. In 1975 he published "A Non-Christian Humanist Addresses Himself to Humanist Christians" with the subtitle "On the Common Struggle Against Idolatry".[76] And when in 1972 he published an article in the Catholic magazine *Concilium*, he appealed to his readers to join in the struggle against idolatry. He ended his article thus: "Die Aufdeckung der Idole und ihre Bekämpfung ist das

---

Society 32/5, 79.)

[72]Fromm: *You shall be as gods*, 51, see 49-52. Fromm acknowledges (op.cit., 52 n.) his indebtedness to Cohen on the subject of the Noachites. See Cohen: *Die Religion der Vernunft aus den Quellen des Judentums*, 141-144.

[73]Fromm presents a brief contribution to idology in *The Revision of Psychoanalysis*, 42-55, where he analyzes the psychological need for idols, the circumstances that promote idolatry, and the conditions for overcoming idolatry.

[74]The lists of idols that Fromm presents in different works vary somewhat. But they are all connected to phenomena like patriotism, nationalism, consumerism, ideology, and a materialist lifestyle.

[75]Fromm: *You shall be as gods*, 47f. Cf. Fromm: "Einige post-marxsche und post-freudsche Gedanken über Religion und Religiosität" *Concilium* 7 (1972), 475f.

[76]Published in Fromm: *On Being Human*, 96-99.

gemeinsame Band, das christliche und nicht-theistische religiöse Menschen vereint, oder, wie ich meine, vereinen sollte."[77]

Fromm connects the prophetic concept of idolatry with modern psychological and sociological concepts. The struggle against idolatry is, in his opinion, at the same time a struggle against *narcissism*. "In idolatry one partial faculty of man is absolutized and made into an idol. Man then worships himself in an alienated form. The idol in which he submerges becomes the object of his narcissistic passion. The idea of God, on the contrary, is the negation of narcissism because only God - not man - is omniscient and omnipotent."[78]

A more frequent connection made by Fromm is that between idolatry and *alienation*. The term "alienation" can be traced far back in history, but it became a very central concept through the writings of Marx, especially the young Marx.[79] A great admirer of Marx, Fromm used the term extensively. It was, for example, the starting point for his social critique in *The Sane Society*.[80]

Fromm's definition of alienation is "the fact that *man does not experience himself as the active bearer of his own powers and richness, but as an impoverished 'thing', dependent on powers outside of himself, unto which he has projected his living substance*."[81] Although the use of the term "alienation" in this sense is quite new, the phenomenon is much older, Fromm adds. It was first decribed in the Old Testament, where it was called "idolatry". According to Fromm the concept of alienation is perhaps nowhere described in such depth as in the prophetic literature.[82] "Idolatry, in the sense of the Old Testament prophets, is essentially the same concept as that of 'alienation'."[83] Referring to Hos. 14:8 and Ps. 135, he describes how in idolatry man produces an idol by his own work, but how he then worships this product of his own hands as something apart from and against himself. The thing that he has made himself is not experienced as a result

---

[77]Fromm: "Einige post-marxsche und post-freudsche Gedanken über Religion und Religiosität" *Concilium* 7 (1972), 476. Fromm also ended *Psychoanalysis and Religion* (p. 118f.) with an eloquent, emphatic appeal to cease to argue about God and instead to unite in the unmasking of contemporary forms of idolatry. In *The Revolution of Hope* he states (p. 136) that negating and combating idolatry in every form and shape is one of the principles uniting *all* radical humanists.

[78]Fromm: *The Heart of Man*, 89.

[79]See, e.g., Israel: *Alienation*, 11-120.

[80]For a thorough analysis of Fromm's concept of alienation, see Aregger-Moros: *Das Konzept der Entfremdung im geschichtphilosophischen Denken von Erich Fromm*.

[81]Fromm: *The Sane Society*, 124.

[82]Fromm: "Die psychologischen und geistigen Probleme des Überflusses" *GA V*, 327f.

[83]Fromm: *The Revision of Psychoanalysis*, 42. Cf. Fromm: *The Revolution of Hope*, 136.

of his own productive effort. By submitting to this dead thing, man does not experience himself as the center from which living acts radiate. He becomes alienated.[84]

Monotheism is the opposite to idolatry; it is the productive, non-alienated way of life. God is living and infinite, and because man is created in the likeness of God, he is not a dead thing, but the bearer of infinite qualities.[85]

Although Fromm had earlier written about both alienation and idolatry, it is in *The Sane Society* - in the passage referred to above - that he makes the connection between the two for the first time, and announces that the modern concept of alienation is an equivalent of the biblical concept of idolatry. He probably took this idea from Tillich, who had already made the same connection.[86]

Fromm also connected idolatry to his own concept of *necrophilia*. Necrophilia normally means sexual attraction to corpses, but from the 1960's onward Fromm used this term in a broader sense, as love of death. He got the idea of using necrophilia in a broader sense from an episode during the Spanish Civil War, when a fascist officer cried "Long live death", and the Spanish philosopher Miguel Unamuno called it a necrophilious cry.[87]

Fromm's definition of necrophilia in the characterological sense is "*the passionate attraction to all that is dead, decayed, putrid, sickly; it is the passion to*

---

[84]Fromm: *The Sane Society*, 121f.; Fromm: *Marx's Concept of Man*, 44f.; Fromm: "Die Aktualität der prophetischen Schriften" *GA VI*, 78f.; Fromm: *Beyond the Chains of Illusion*, 57f.; Fromm: *On Being Human*, 97.

[85]Fromm: *The Sane Society*, 122, 176; Fromm: *Beyond the Chains of Illusion*, 58.

[86]In a lecture held in 1952 and published the following year Tillich connected idolatry with the Marxist concept of ideology and indirectly also alienation. (Tillich: *Das religiöse Fundament des moralischen Handelns*, 203f.) Fromm acknowledged that Tillich made this connection referring to this passage in *Marx's Concept of Man*, 44 n.1. For a comparison of the thoughts of Fromm and Tillich in general and their views of alienation and estrangement in specific, see Hammond: *Man in Estrangement*.

[87]The episode is described in Fromm: *On Disobedience*, 40; Fromm: *War Within Man*, 7f.; Fromm: *The Heart of Man*, 37f.; Fromm: *The Anatomy of Human Destructiveness*, 330f. and Fromm: *Die Pathologie der Normalität*, 127f. Fromm got to know this episode from Hugh Thomas: *The Spanish Civil War* (see p. 354f.). An interesting detail is that in his quotation from Thomas Fromm changed one word. While in Thomas' version the officer's cry is called "necrophilistic", in Fromm's version it is called "necrophilious". The first time Fromm used the term "necrophilia" and referred to Unamuno was in 1963 (Fromm: *The Dogma of Christ*, 111f.), but he himself states that he started to study the subject in 1961 (Fromm: *The Anatomy of Human Destructiveness*, 331).

transform that which is alive into something unalive; to destroy for the sake of destruction; the exclusive interest in all that is purely mechanical. It is the passion 'to tear apart living structures'."[88] The opposite of necrophilia is biophilia, "the passionate love of life and of all that is alive", the "wish to further growth, whether in a person, a plant, an idea, or a social group."[89]

What has all this to do with idolatry? According to Fromm idolatry is related to necrophilia, because in idolatry man worships a dead thing and is himself transformed into a lifeless object. "Man, trying to be like God, is an open system, approximating himself to God; man, submitting to idols, is a closed system, becoming a thing himself. The idol is lifeless; God is living, The contradiction between idolatry and the recognition of God is, in the last analysis, that between the love of death and the love of life."[90]

Although monotheism is the opposite of idolatry, God can also be made into an idol. Fromm believes that while in humanistic religion God is a symbol of man's own powers, in authoritarian religion he becomes the sole possessor of man's reason and love. Man projects the best he has onto God and himself becomes deprived of these qualities. "Everything he has is now God's and nothing is left in him. *His only access to himself is through God.* In worshipping God he tries to get in touch with that part of himself which he has lost through projection. After having given God all he has, he begs God to return to him some of what originally was his own. But having lost his own he is completely at God's mercy. He necessarily feels like a 'sinner' since he has deprived himself of everything that is good, and it is only through God's mercy or grace that he can regain that which alone makes him human."[91]

Although Fromm does not mention idolatry in this text, it is evident that the projection onto God he refers to is exactly like the projection onto idols he describes in other passages. But he also explicitly states that God can be turned

---

[88]Fromm: *The Anatomy of Human Destructiveness*, 332.
[89]op.cit., 365.
[90]Fromm: *You shall be as gods*, 44. Cf. op.cit., 46;; Fromm: *Ethik und Politik*, 26. In a lecture in 1966 Fromm stated that some Jewish practices of going to services for the dead on certain holidays are an expression of an unnecessary occupation with death and "the purest form of ancestor worship". This was absent from traditional Judaism but entered Jewish life later. When asked about this remark, Fromm apologized for being flippant, and stated that he did not mean that Judaism is a religion of ancestor cult. On the contrary the Kaddish - the traditional Jewish prayer read at the grave - is "one of the most beautiful hymns to God and to life" and it is a characteristic Jewish tradition not to be concerned with death. (Fromm: "Responsibility, Duty and Independence" (lecture 17.5 1966).)
[91]Fromm: *Psychoanalysis and Religion*, 50f.

into an idol.[92] And how could it be otherwise? If belief in God is a projection - as Feuerbach, Marx, Freud, and to a certain extent Fromm believed - then God inevitably becomes an idol.

I find this claim by Fromm very problematic. If one takes his description of how the worship of God becomes idolatry literally - of course it should be -all forms of traditional theism must be seen as idolatry. The only non-idolatrous humanistic form of theism is belief where "God is a symbol of *man's own powers* which he tries to realize in his life, and is not a symbol of force and domination, having *power over man.*"[93] But are all other forms of theism where God is seen not as a symbol only but as a reality, a living transcendent being, *per se* a form of idolatry? Fromm seems to think so. Therefore he can write that "monotheistic religions themselves have, to a large extent, regressed into idolatry",[94] and claim that the Jewish and Christian God was experienced as an idol by most believers,[95] and that God "today" is an idol for one's own love and wisdom.[96] Most explicit on this is his statement in his last book that the concept of truth and the need for disillusionment are less central and radical in the Christian and Jewish traditions than in Buddhism, because they are "tainted with the idea of a God-idol".[97]

Fromm stated that a personal concept of God - viewing God as a person, as in the monotheistic religions - is idolatrous, because "a person is an idol if he is made into a god".[98] To see God as a loving father is idolatry, because a father is a person, and it is - as Freud pointed out - a sign that we are still children in hope and fantasy.[99] By this statement Fromm also makes Jesus - whom he otherwise praises - into a childish idolater, because Jesus talked about God as a loving father. Perhaps Fromm thought that Jesus did so only in a symbolic way, although it has always been believed that he really considered his heavenly Father a real being.

---

[92]op.cit., 118; Fromm: *On Disobedience*, 106; Fromm: *Marx's Concept of Man*, 44 n.2. Fromm: "Einige post-marxsche und post-freudsche Gedanken über Religion und Religiosität" *Concilium* 7 (1972), 476; Fromm: *Beyond the Chains of Illusion*, 155; Fromm: *On Being Human*, 167f.; Fromm: *Gesellschaft und Seele*, 129, 189; Fromm: *To have or to be?*, 42.
[93]Fromm: *Psychoanalysis and Religion*, 37. Cf. op.cit., 49; Fromm: "Psychoanalysis and Zen Buddhism". In: Suzuki - Fromm - de Martino: *Zen Buddhism and Psychoanalysis*, 94; Fromm: *You shall be as gods*, 18f.; Fromm: *The Revolution of Hope*, 85, 140.
[94]Fromm: *The Sane Society*, 122.
[95]Fromm: *The Revision of Psychoanalysis*, 43.
[96]Fromm: *Gesellschaft und Seele*, 123f.
[97]Fromm: *Greatness and Limitations of Freud's Thought*, x.
[98]Fromm: "Beyond Egotistical Religion" (lecture in 1957).
[99]ibid.

Fromm is right in claiming that authoritarian religion alienates man. He gave a description on great merit of how submission to God psychologically functions. But I can not agree with him in his claim that the only non-alienating and non-idolatrous way to believe in God is to reduce Him to a pure symbol. It is possible to be a theist, to believe that God is more than a symbol, and to make this belief into a source of vitality and strength. A theistically understood God can also be a liberating God. Kügler has argued that Fromm did not understand Christianity correctly. Christianity is not a theistic system that postulates that man is totally dependent on an outer force. The New Testament message is that God is with us here and now, he is our partner, not the partner of the parents, the state or the rulers. Understanding that God is our partner does not make us blind to reality or cling to illusions. On the contrary, it gives us courage to face the world in which we are living realistically.[100]

Despite this criticism, I regard Fromm's description of idolatry an excellent account of how religion can work as an alienating force. It is interesting to note that Irving Block, while rejecting Fromm's interpretation of the Bible, still writes: "Fromm's discussion of idolatry is the best and, I think, the finest description of the Jewish notion of idolatry in English."[101]

Before we leave the theme of idolatry, let us look at one more idea of Fromm, concerning Marx and religion. In Fromm's opinion, what Marx did was to fight not true religion but alienating religion. Marx's fight was not against God, but against the idol called God, thus showing a resemblance with mysticism and negative theology.[102] Therefore Fromm can state: "Marx war nicht antireligiös. Er war ein im tiefsten religiöser Mensch und gerade deshalb ein Feind der 'Religion'."[103]

---

[100]Kügler, SJ: "Humanistische Religion und christlicher Glaube" *SZ* 202 (1984), 555. For a similar defence of the Christian faith, see Forsyth-Beniskos: "Biblical Faith and Erich Fromm's Theory of Personality" *RUO* 40 (1970), 90f.

[101]Block: "Radical Humanism and the Bible" *Tradition* (Winter 1968), 137. similarly Ahren: "Im Kampf gegen Götzendienst. Nachruf auf den Psychoanalytiker Erich Fromm" *Berliner Allgemeine Jüdische Wochenzeitung* 28.3 1980. It is interesting to note that Fromm's concept of idolatry is to some extent similar to that of Luther's in his explanation of the first commandment. (Luther: *Werke 30*, 132-136)

[102]Fromm: *Marx's Concept of Man*, 63f.; Fromm: "Einige post-marxsche und post-freudsche Gedanken über Religion und Religiosität" *Concilium* 7 (1972), 472. In his claim that Marx fought against idols, not against God, Fromm refers to Karl Löwith (Fromm: *Marx's Concept of Man*, 44 n.1. See Löwith: *Sämmtliche Schriften 4*, 442)

[103]Fromm: "Religion und Gesellschaft". In: Funk: *Mut zum Menschen*, 360.

4.6.2. The messianic age

The other theme in the teaching of the prophets which Fromm considered to be of extraordinary importance was the concept of the messianic age. The vision of the messianic age was, in his opinion, perhaps the most important for world history of anyything the prophets said.[104] And although he so eagerly emphasized that the great world religions shared many basic concepts and ideas, he stated that "the utopia is the one element that is almost exclusively a product of the Western mind", starting with the messianic vision.[105]

Fromm not only claimed that the prophetic vision of the messianic age has been important for world history, he also declared its profound significance for himself. In old age he was asked about the difference between his faith and the faith of Isaiah, who talked about a day when there is no more war and weapons have been transformed into useful tools (Is. 2:4). Fromm answered that there is no difference, this is his deepest religious faith. "Deshalb ist für mich die messianische Idee, das Warten auf den Messias, von zentraler persönlichen Bedeutung."[106]

Fromm's interpretation of the messianic age is closely connected with his view of the "fall". The Bible depicts man's development towards freeedom and full realization of his capacity. This development started with man's disobedience in the Garden of Eden, and it will reach its culmination in the messianic age, when man "becomes what he potentially is, and he attains what the serpent - the symbol of wisdom and rebellion - promised, and what the patriarchal, jealous God of Adam did not wish: that man would become like God himself."[107] Between Paradise and the messianic age there is a "dialectic relationship". The two ages are both a state of harmony, but while the state of harmony in Paradise existed because man had not yet been born, the new state of harmony exists because man has been fully born, and has regained a home again - in the world.[108]

Fromm understands the messianic age thisworldly. It will be realized in this world and as a result of man's growing to total humanity. It will not be brought about by

---

[104]Fromm: "Die Aktualität der prophetischen Schriften" *GA VI*, 79. Cf. Fromm: *You shall be as gods*, 115.
[105]Fromm: "Foreword". In: Bellamy: *Looking Backward*, vii. Cf. Fromm: *Marx's Concept of Man*, 64.
[106]Fromm: "Interview with Alfred A. Häsler: Das Undenkbare denken und das Mögliche tun" *Ex libris* 22 (No.5 1977), 18.
[107]Fromm: *You shall be as gods*, 123.
[108]op.cit., 123f.

an act of grace or through divine intervention. In the apocalyptic literature starting with the Book of Daniel there is a shift; the coming of the messianic age is seen as the coming of a new world and the Messiah as a supernatural savior. Later Talmudic and rabbinic Judaism has preserved the prophetic concept of the messianic age as the fulfillment of history, the horizontal perspective, while the apocalyptic vertical view has influenced Christianity.[109]

Fromm's claim that the messianic harmony is not predetermined by God, that "it will not happen except through man's own effort", has been criticized by Maly, who writes that this may be Fromm's conviction but it is certainly not the Old Testament's. The prophets talked about Yahweh's intervention in history. One of the most forceful descriptions of the messianic age (Is. 9:1-7) concludes with the words: "The zeal of the Lord of hosts will do this!"[110] Maly is correct in the sense that the Old Testament prophets certainly expected the messianic age to be the result of divine intervention. But Fromm believed that the statement that "God has done this" was just a way of expressing that man had reached this level, as the biblical statement that God hardened Pharaoh's heart was a way of saying that Pharaoh hardened his heart. And Fromm is not alone. There is a long rabbinical tradition that says that the arrival of the Messiah will depend on the moral and spiritual progress of the people, a tradition that Fromm clearly points out.[111]

One's view of the Messiah is, of course, crucial for one's understanding of the messianic age. Fromm describes how differently the Messiah was understood by the prophetic books.[112] They all, and later Judaism, too, see the Messiah as a man of purely human origin. He is not a "savior" who transforms man and changes his substance. In Talmud there are two opposite ideas about the conditions for the coming of the Messiah. According to one, the Messiah will come when suffering and evil have reached such a degree that man will repent and thus be ready; according to the other, he will come as the result of man's own continuous improvement.[113] Both concepts are reflected in a saying in the Talmud that the Messiah will come in an age that is either fully pure or fully corrupt (Sanhedrin 98a).[114]

---

[109]op.cit., 133-138, Fromm: *The Revolution of Hope*, 18. Cf. Fromm: *The Sane Society*, 234f.; Fromm: "Foreword". In: Bellamy: *Looking Backward*, viii; Fromm: *On Being Human*, 18.
[110]Maly: "Review of Fromm: *You shall be as gods*" *CBQ* 29 (1967), 620.
[111]Fromm: *You shall be as gods*, 140-143.
[112]op.cit., 124f.
[113]op.cit., 138-143. Fromm also descibes the appearance of different false Messiah figures during Jewish history. (op.cit., 143-152)
[114]Fromm: *On Being Human*, 141. Maccoby reports that in the late 1960's Fromm asked what the difference is between Christianity and Judaism, and answered himself: "The only real

144

But Fromm goes one step further. For him it is not sufficient to say that the Messiah is not a divine figure, but "man, and nothing but man".[115] The Messiah is a symbol, as is God; the Messiah is "a symbol of a new *historical* period".[116] And because man is the maker of history and therefore the one who will realize the messianic vision, the Messiah "is a symbol of man's own achievements".[117]

The messianic age will be characterized by *peace*, and peace in the prophetic sense as something more than the absence of war and violence. Peace is harmony, as seen by the Hebrew word *shalom*, which Fromm translates as "completeness".[118] In the messianic age the curse that came over man as a result of the "fall" will be reversed. The curse (see 4.3) concerned man's relation to his neigbors but also to nature. Therefore harmony in the messianic age will characterize both the relation between man and man, and nature, as can be seen from Is. 11:6-9 and Hos. 2:18. Man's new harmony with nature signifies that nature will become the all-loving, nurturing mother (Is. 35:5-10, 43:19f.). The idea of harmony among men culminated in the famous prophetic vision of how weapons will be turned into useful tools (Micah 4:3f.).[119]

The messianic age, further, has a *universalistic* aspect. Man will overcome the experience of separateness between one nation and another; having become fully human, the stranger will cease to be a stranger, the illusion of the essential differences between nation and nation will disappear and there will no longer be any "chosen people". In the Bible there was always one favorite son, but in the messianic age all nations will be equally loved by God. Fromm sees the universalistic aspect of the messianic age in passages like Am. 9:7 and Is. 19:23-25.[120]

---

difference is the meaning of hope in the two religions. For the Christian, since the messiah already has come, hope lies in the life to come, immortality. Hope for the Jew is that the messiah will come and put the world in order. And that can happen at any time, if we are ready. (Maccoby: *The Role of Hope in Psychoanalysis: Erich Fromm's View of Psychoanalysis and Religion*, 5f.)

[115]Fromm: *You shall be as gods*, 138.
[116]op.cit., 138.
[117]Fromm: *The Dogma of Christ*, 144.
[118]Fromm: *The Dogma of Christ*, 145; Fromm: *You shall be as gods*, 126, 197; Fromm: *The Sane Society*, 235 n.1; Fromm: "Zur Theorie und Strategie des Friedens" *GA V*, 243; Fromm: *On Disobedience*, 133.
[119]Fromm: *The Dogma of Christ*, 144-147; Fromm: *You shall be as gods*, 125-128. Fromm used Micah 4:3f. as a motto - together with other sayings - for *The Sane Society*.
[120]Fromm: *The Dogma of Christ*, 147f.; Fromm: *You shall be as gods*, 129. Cf. Fromm: *On Disobedience*, 44; Fromm: *Beyond the Chains of Illusion*, 169; Fromm: *On Being Human*, 64.

While discussing the universalistic aspect of the messianic age Fromm makes a strange comment. According to him, the messianic age will be characterized by religious tolerance, no specific concept of God will be demanded. The evidence for this is Micah 4:5a, which says: "For all the peoples walk each in the name of its god." Fromm interprets this to be a prophecy about what will happen in the messianic age. "Religious fanaticism, the source of so much strife and destruction, will have disappeared. When peace and freedom from fear have been established, it will matter little which thought concepts mankind uses to give expression to its supreme goals and values."[121]

But Fromm makes things too easy. Micah 4:1-4 is a prophecy about how all nations will make a pilgrimage to Jerusalem, where they will be taught by Jahwe. The vision is universalistic, all nations are involved, but it is not an expression of religious tolerance, because they will listen to and learn from Yahwe. Verse 5 is thus normally interpreted to be an utterance about how it is today, as opposed to how it will be on the day of the pilgrimage of the nations. Today each people has its own god. This utterance is thus not seen as describing the messianic age to come - as Fromm sees it - but the present situation.[122]

Fromm also connects the messianic age with the *Sabbath*, which he sees as the anticipation of the messianic age. He considers the Sabbath to be "the most important of the biblical concepts", and the keeping of it gave the powerless and often despised Jews in the Diaspora pride and dignity.[123] He already emphasized in his dissertation the importance of the Sabbath as a means for man's freedom from the sorrows of this world. His next publication was a study of the Sabbath, in 1927.[124] This essay was written at a time when he was an orthodox Freudian, and the interpretationn of the Sabbath is indeed very Freudian. A critic of psychoanalysis has called the theory expressed in this essay "sheer nonsense" (baren Unsinn).[125] Fromm later disassociated himself from orthodox Freudianism, and the position he holds in this essay is not representative of his thought. We will therefore not analyze this essay in detail.

---

[121]Fromm: *You shall be as gods*, 128f. Cf. Fromm: *On Being Human*, 141 n.2. In a lecture in 1957 Fromm made the same point and this time quoted the King James Version, which suits his interpretation better, because it says: "For all people will walk every one in the name of his god." (Fromm: "Beyond Egotistical Religion" (lecture in 1957).) In *You shall be as gods* Fromm quoted the Revised Standard Version.

[122]See, e.g., Mays: *Micah*, 99; Rudolph: *Micha-Nahum-Habakuk-Zephanja*, 81: Wolff: *Dodekapropheton 4*, .

[123]Fromm: *To have or to be?*, 50. Cf. Fromm: *You shall be as gods*, 193f.

[124]Fromm: "Der Sabbath" *GA VI*, 1-9.

[125]Hardeck: *Vernunft und Liebe*, 133.

The mature Fromm interpreted the Sabbath as the expression of the central idea in Judaism, freedom. The Sabbath commandment was not only a socio-hygienical law of great blessing for all men, and as such possessing "the dignity of one of the great innovations in human evolution".[126] It can be understood only if we remember that the biblical idea of work and rest differs from our modern concept. "Work" in the Bible is any interference by man with the physical world, while "rest" is a state of peace, complete harmony between human beings and between humans and nature. Therefore man must, during the Sabbath, refrain from any interference in the natural process, thereby maintaining the man-nature equilibrium. By not working, man is freed from the chains of time, he ceases to be an animal whose main occupation is to fight for survival and to sustain his biological life. While keeping the Sabbath, man is fully man, with no other task than to be human.[127] "On the Shabbat one lives as if one *has* nothing, pursuing no aim except *being*, that is, expressing one's essential powers: praying, studying, eating, drinking, singing, making love."[128]

Thus understood, it is easy to see the connection between the Sabbath and the messianic age. The complete harmony between man and man, and between man and nature that is the *raison d'être* of the Sabbath will be realized in totality - not only for one day a week - when man reaches his ultimate goal: total freedom. Therefore the Sabbath is the anticipation of the messianic age, and the messianic age is "the time of the perpetual Sabbath". But it is not purely a symbolic anticipation of the messianic age, it is its real precursor. As the Talmud says: "If all of Israel observed two Sabbaths (consecutively) fully only once, the messiah would be here." (Shabbat 118a) The harmony between man and man, and between man and nature that the prophets so beautifully described in their messianic visions can be experienced here and now, by keeping the Sabbath through a form of practice which puts man in a real situation of harmony and peace.[129]

---

[126]Fromm: *To have or to be?*, 50.
[127]Fromm: *The Forgotten Language*, 241-248; Fromm: *You shall be as gods*, 194-198.
[128]Fromm: *To have or to be?*, 51. Shapira ("Fromm and Judaism". In: Eletti (Ed.): *Incontro con Erich Fromm*, 235) writes about Fromm's interpretation of the Sabbath: "Here we see Fromm in a different perspective, more as a child in his father's house - a monotheist rather than the atheist we have seen before - more of a humanist who understands the inner content and spirit of Halacha, its humanity and justice, and who wishes to be part of it."
[129]Fromm: *The Forgotten Language*, 246f.; Fromm: *You shall be as gods*, 197. Fromm further makes some historical comments on how the Babylonian holiday Shapatu was transformed into the biblical Sabbath (Fromm: *The Forgotten Language*, 248f.; Fromm: *You shall be as gods*, 198f. Cf. Fromm: *To have or to be?*, 51) Fromm also suggests how the principle of the Sabbath could be adopted by large numbers of people in modern society. "The Sabbath day, for them, would be a day of contemplation, reading, meaningful conversation, a day of rest and

The term "messianism" has been widely used as a designation of different kinds of movements with a utopian aim. Thus Fromm, as well, views the messianism of the prophets as the basis for later utopistic visions.[130] The Renaissance was, according to him, the time when the messianic-prophetic vision was transformed into the form of utopias, with the utopias of Thomas More, Tommasso Campanella and Johann Valentin Andreä as the most important. Marx was, in Fromm's opinion, also a utopist, although he himself rejected and warned against utopias.[131] He viewed the Marxist vision of a society without classes, exploitation and alienation as the most important modern variant of the messianic vision.[132] The dialogue between Marxists and Christians is, he writes, based on the common messianic heritage.[133] Marx's philosphy was a new and radical step forward in the tradition of prophetic messianism, but expressed in non-theistic language.[134] The messianic idea found its last and most complete expression in Marx's concept of socialism. Independent of how much the Old Testament ideas influenced Marx directly, he was well aware of the messianic idea through the philosophers of the Enlightenment and through Spinoza, Goethe, and Hegel.[135] Fromm also frequently referred to socialism in general - without specific mention of Marx - as a form of secular messianism.[136] He also made an interesting comparison between the deterministic attitude of some socialists, and the passive messianism that believed that we can only wait for the messianic age to come.[137]

---

joy, completely free from all practical and mundane concerns." (Fromm: *You shall be as gods*, 199n.

[130]See, e.g., Fromm: "Foreword", in: Bellamy: *Looking Backward*, vi-ix.

[131]Fromm: *On Being Human*, 19f.

[132]Ten days before his death Fromm said in an interview that the prophetic vision of the messianic age was "fast identisch" with Marx's concept of socialist society. (Fromm: Interview with Guido Ferrari 8.3 1980.

[133]Fromm: *The Revolution of Hope*, 19. In a footnote to this passage Fromm states that Ernst Bloch, in his work *Das Prinzip Hoffnung*, analyzed the prophetic principle of hope within Marxist thinking in greater depth than anyone else.

[134]Fromm: *Marx's Concept of Man*, 3,5; Fromm: "Einige post-marxsche und post-freudsche Gedanken über Religion und Religiosität" *Concilium* 7 (1972), 472; Fromm: *On Being Human*, 115, 133.

[135]Fromm: *Marx's Concept of Man*, 66. Fromm mentions that the connection between messianic prophetism and the socialism of Marx has been emphasized by several authors, and refers to Löwith, Tillich, Lukács, Schumpeter, and Alfred Weber. (op.cit., 69 n11) In another passage he mentions Cohen as one who has emphasized the connection between messianism and socialism. (Fromm: *On Being Human*, 143)

[136]Fromm: *On Disobedience*, 70; Fromm: "Foreword". In: Bellamy: *Looking Backward*, xix; Fromm: *You shall be as gods*, 115; Fromm: *Die Pathologie der Normalität*, 89, 91. In *On Being Human* there is a subchapter with the title "Humanism as Secular Messianism", but the subchapter deals exclusively with the humanism of Marx.

[137]Fromm: *Die Pathologie der Normalität*, 98f.

Fromm himself, of course, rejected both attitudes, but the point here is the comparison he made, which shows how close he thought socialism and messianism to be.

4.7. The Psalms

Although the most important part of the Old Testament for Fromm was the prophetic books, he also appreciated the Psalms. As noted above, he regarded the prophetic books, but also the Psalms as "an inexhaustible source of vitality".[138]

In his book on the Bible *You shall be as gods* Fromm included a chapter on the Psalms. He himself states that it might seem odd to do so, but the importance of psalms in the religious life of the Jews, especially in the Diaspora, is reason enough for doing so.[139]

According to Fromm the critical approach to the Book of Psalms was first concerned with issues like authorship and origin. The newer critical approach has been concentrating on the particular function of different psalms. Fromm's own approach is based on the psychic attitude, the subjective state of mind, the "mood", in which each psalm is written.[140]

While Gunkel reckoned with five different types or classes (Gattungen) of psalms and Oesterley with seven additional smaller ones, Fromm, from his own starting point, divides the psalms into four classes. The two main classes are the one-mood psalms and the dynamic psalms, the two minor classes are the hymnic psalms and the messianic psalms.[141]

The *one-mood psalm* - of which there are 66 (the figures are approximate only, since many psalms can be placed in several classes) - is written in one mood. It can be the mood of hope, fear, hate, contentment, whatever. The basic thing is that the poet remains in the same mood from beginning to end. Examples of one-mood psalms are Psalm 1 (the self-righteous mood), Psalm 23 and Psalm 121 (the mood of quiet confidence and inner peace), and Psalm 137 (the mood of merciless hate).[142]

---

[138]Fromm: *For the Love of Life*, 101.
[139]Fromm: *You shall be as gods*, 201.
[140]op.cit., 202f.
[141]ibid.
[142]op.cit., 204-207.

The *dynamic psalm* - of which there are 47 - is the opposite to the one-mood psalm. It is characterized by a change of mood within the poet, a change that is reflected in the psalm. Normally it is a change from despair and anxiety to hope and faith. The change is not simple and straightforward. The psalm starts in some despair, changes to some hope, then returns to deeper despair and reacts with more hope, arriving at the very deepest despair. Only then is the despair really overcome. The victory of hope over despair is realized only after the despair has been fully experienced.[143]

Fromm analyzes the change in mood in Psalm 6. The despair deepens in v. 1-7, and in v. 8 all of a sudden a decisive turn takes place. A miracle has happened - within man. The transformation is sudden and revelation-like. Psalm 8 and Psalm 90 are also dynamic psalms, but very different from Psalm 6. They are more philosophical psalms describing the change in mood soberly, without the despair of Psalm 6. Fromm finally analyzes Psalm 22, which he divides into 11 parts, each expressing one mood.[144]

The movement from sadness to joy characteristic of the dynamic psalms is also visible in the Psalter as a whole. It also characterized later Jewish tradition. It can be seen in the classical Kol Nidrei and has found "its most distinct and beautiful expression" in the songs of Hasidism.[145]

The *messianic* and the *hymnic psalms* - of which there are 24 and 13 respectively - are one-mood psalms, but Fromm classifies them separately because the mood in which they are written has a different quality from the other one-mood psalms. The messianic psalms - e.g. Psalm 96 - are written in the mood of faith in the salvation of mankind, and the hymnic psalms - e.g. Psalm 150 - in the mood of pure enthusiasm.[146]

If Fromm thought that his analysis of the different moods in which the psalms were written would influence biblical sholarship he was wrong. In no major commentary on the Psalms written after 1966 is his theory even mentioned. The classification of the psalms is still made in the footsteps of Gunkel, and no non-theologian is allowed to disturb that. Nobody can expect Fromm's classification to become the standard one or to replace Gunkel's, but as an additional theory one

---

[143]op.cit., 297f. Fromm compares this principle with the psychoanalytical method, where the making of the painful unconscious conscious is the condition for liberation.
[144]op.cit., 208-220. On Fromm's analysis of the New Testament use of Ps. 22, see 4.6.
[145]op.cit., 220f.
[146]op.cit., 221-223.

might expect it to be mentioned, discussed, and criticized. But the exegetical reaction was silence.

4.8. Comments on the New Testament

Fromm's knowledge of the New Testament seems to have been good, though not as wide as his knowledge of the Old Testament. Dellbrügge writes that Fromm was a man who knew the Jewish tradition much better than most Christians know their Bible, but that there were gaps in his understanding of the New Testament.[147] Very seldom does Fromm analyze a text or a theme from the New Testament in more detail. Usually he just quotes a suitable passage from the New Testament. For example, the saying of Jesus that "the truth shall make you free" (John 8:32b) is often used by him to express the essence of psychoanalysis.[148]

The notion sometimes held by Christians that the Old Testament is quite cruel, while the New Testament teaches the importance of love and forgiveness, is not shared by Fromm. He detested the stories of the cruelty of the Israelites, but he stressed the humanistic aspects of the Old Testament. He stated that it was regrettable that most Christians read the Old Testament with prejudice. They wrongly believe that the Old Testament expresses exclusively the principle of justice and revenge and is written in a spirit of narrow nationalism. Many even believe that the sentence, "Love your neighbor as yourself", is derived from the New and not the Old Testament.[149]

In writing on the history of the humanistic idea, Fromm mentions as an expression of humanism in the Old Testament the idea that mankind originates from one man, that man is created in the likeness of God, and the prophetic concept of messianism. As the only contribution to the humanistic idea from the New Testament he mentions the commandment to love one's enemies (Mt. 5:44). But he adds that the difference between this commandment and the Old Testament commandment to love the stranger is very small.[150]

---

[147]Dellbrügge: "Impressionen eines Theologen beim Lesen Erich Fromms". In: Evangelisches Studienzentrum Heilig Geist (Hrsg.): *Erich Fromm und der christliche Glaube*, 37.
[148]Fromm: *Psychoanalysis and Religion*, 6f., 79; Fromm: *Beyond the Chains of Illusion*, 13; Fromm: *The Art of Listening*, 47; Fromm: *Gesellschaft und Seele*, 113.
[149]Fromm: *You shall be as gods*, 4. Fromm once compared the Old Testament with Marx, in that "everybody talks about it but nobody has read it, or read more than a little bit of it." (Fromm: "Interview with Mike Wallace" *Survival and Freedom* 5 (1958), 13)
[150]Fromm: *On Being Human*, 64. Cf. Fromm: *On Disobedience*, 44f.; Fromm: *The Heart of Man*, 89.

151

In *To have or to be?* Fromm devotes a chapter to "Having and Being in the Old and New Testaments and in the Writings of Master Eckhart". Here he states that the New Testament protest agains the having structure of existence is even stronger than in the Old Testament. The reason for this is sociological. The first Christians were poor and socially despised and uncompromisingly denounced wealth and secular power.[150]

According to Fromm, the revolutionary spirit of the first Christians appears with special clarity in the oldest parts of the gospels, the so-called Q-source. Following the theory of Siegfried Schulz, he distinguishes between an older and a younger tradition in the Q-source.[151] In the older tradition we find the radical renunciation of one's own rights (Mt. 5:39-42, Lk. 6:29f.), the commandment to love one's enemies (Mt. 5:44-48, Lk. 6:27f., 32-36), the prohibition against judging others (Mt. 7:1-5, Lk. 6:37f., 41f.), and the harsh criticism of wealth (Mt. 6:19, 21, Lk. 12:33f.). This radicality was the result of the apocalyptic conviction that a dramatic change would soon take place and the powerful Roman Empire would soon collapse. "Realistically, to be sure, they were mistaken; as a result of the failure of Jesus' reappearance, Jesus' death and resurrection are interpreted in the gospels as constituting the beginning of the new eon, and after Constantine an attempt was made to shift the mediating role of Jesus to the papal church."[152]

From the younger tradition of the Q-source Fromm brings out the story of Jesus' temptation by Satan (Mt. 4:1-11, Lk. 4:1-13). In his interpretation Jesus and Satan here appear as representatives of two opposite principles. Satan is the representative of material consumption and of power over nature, while Jesus is the representative of being, and of the idea that non-having is the premise for being.[153]

Fromm sometimes added New Testament quotations to ideas developed from the Old Testament. To the idea that the messianic age means a regression to the state of the Paradise but with maturity, Fromm connects the New Testament saying that one has to become like a child to enter the Kingdom of God (Lk. 18:17). It means that we must be children again to be able to sense the world non-

---

[150]Fromm: *To have or to be?*, 53f.
[151]Schulz: *Q. Die Spruchquelle der Evangelisten*. Fromm erroneously writes Siegrid and not Siegfried as the first name of Schultz. Schultz' theory of two strata in the Q-source is not widely accepted, but only one among several theories of different layers in the Q-source. (See, e.g., Tuckett: "Q. (Gospel Source)". In: Freedman (Ed.): *The Anchor Bible Dictionary 5*, 568.)
[152]Fromm: *To have or to be?*, 56, see 54-56.
[153]op.cit., 56f.

alienatingly and creatively, but at the same time we are not children but adults. To this he adds 1 Cor. 13:12.[155]

According to Fromm ,the greatest statement about love is to be found in the New Testament. "When on the shore of Galilee Jesus asked Peter whether he loved Him and received an affirmative answer, His next words, repeated three times to fasten them forever in Peter's mind, were, 'Feed my sheep'. Love entails a disposition to labor for the wellbeing of the persons or things which are loved."[156]

The only New Testament text which Fromm analyzes in some detail - in an appendix to *You shall be as gods* - is Mt. 27:46, where it says that Jesus used the first words of Ps. 22, "My God, my God, why hast thou forsaken me?", on the cross. For Fromm it is impossible that Jesus should have died with words of utter despair. Most human martyrs, such as Rabbi Akiba, have died in full faith, showing no trace of despair. Fromm's answer to this question is that on the cross Jesus recited the whole of Psalm 22, i.e. a dynamic psalm beginning in despair but ending in an enthusiastic mood of faith and hope. It is a normal Jewish custom to cite the first words of a text while denoting the whole text, and the writer of the gospel was well aware of this custom. Further evidence for this theory is that there are many allusions to Psalm 22 in the gospel narrative of the crucifixion. The later gospels - Luke and John - could not accept that the last words of Jesus were words of despair, and therefore they added other sayings to the story. In John the last words of Jesus, "It is accomplished", are - in Fromm's opinion - a quotation (although not literal) of the end of Psalm 22 (verse 32b: "he has done it").[157]

The question of the last words of Jesus seems to have interested Fromm a lot. He mentions personal discussions with Father Jean Lefèbre and Professor James Luther Adams. Fromm was very surprised to find that most Christian theologians have accepted the idea that Jesus died with words of despair instead of recognizing that he died reciting Psalm 22. Fromm's explanation for this is simple: "The reason seems to lie simply in the fact that Christian scholars did not think of this small and rather unimportant Jewish custom of citing a book or a chapter by its first sentence."[158] Yet another reason for Christian theologians to study Judaism more.

---

[155]Fromm: "Psychoanalysis and Zen Buddhism". In: Suzuki - Fromm - de Martino: *Zen Buddhism and Psychoanalysis*, 129.
[156]Fromm: "Love in America". In: Smith (Ed.): *The Search for America*, 130.
[157]Fromm: *You shall be as gods*, 231-236.
[158]op.cit., 233.

Fromm's theory is not new. Many, from Justin Martyr in the second century onwards, have tried in different ways to connect the words of Jesus with Psalm 22 as a whole. Fromm mentions that according to information from "learned theologians, only C.H. Dodd in his *According to the Scriptures* (1952) clearly indicates that the first verse introduces the whole psalm."[159] This is not totally correct. Dodd just writes: "The psalm as a whole was clearly regarded as a source of testimonies to the passion of Christ, and His ultimate triumph, and probably from an early date, since it is woven into the texture of the Passion-narrative, and used in writings almost certainly independent of one another."[160] One scholar before Fromm who clearly stated that not only should the crucifixion passage be interpreted in the light of the whole Psalm 22, but that Jesus most probably recited the whole psalm, is Stauffer.[161] Today it is an *opinio communis* that the cry of Jesus must be interpreted in the context of the whole psalm.[162] Some commentators also claim that Jesus had the whole psalm in mind.[163] But very few seem to believe that Jesus actually recited the whole psalm. One reason for this is that according to the following verse in the gospel the people erroneously reacted to the cry of Jesus by claiming that he was crying for Elijah. This reaction must have been to the words "Eli, Eli" from the beginning of the psalm. If Jesus recited the whole psalm - in all 32 verses - nobody would have thought about Elijah after such a long recital.

That Jesus could have died with a cry of despair was unbelievable for Fromm, but not for one believing in the Christian concept of reconciliation. According to the traditional Christian interpretation, Jesus carried the sins of all mankind on the cross. And therefore, as a sinner, with the burden of the sin of all people, he was really abandoned by God, as his desperate cry indicates.[164]

4.10 Conclusions

As we have seen, Fromm did not present an overall systematic analysis of the Bible. He comments on some biblical passages and themes in many of his books. And in *You shall be as gods* he delivers a more thorough interpretation of the Old

---

[159]op.cit., 234.
[160]Dodd: *According to the Scriptures*, 98.
[161]"Jesus aber betet vermutlich den ganzen Psalm..." (Stauffer: *Jesus. Gestalt und Geschichte*, 106)
[162]See, e.g., Albright-Mann: *Matthew*, 353; Schnackenburg: *Matthäusevangelium II. Teil*, 280; Gnilka: *Das Matthäusevangelium*, 475.
[163]For references, see Blinzler: *Der Prozess Jesu* 4th ed., 373f. n.64.
[164]See, e.g., Lane: *The Gospel According to Mark*, 572f.

Testament and the Jewish tradition. It is this interpretation - presented earlier in this chapter - which we will now evaluate.

Fromm's interpretation of the Bible has been accused of being selective and eclectic,[165] and it is true that he did ignore many parts of the Old Testament. He himself stated that there are parts of the Bible he abhorred from early youth.[166] The point in the critique is not whether Fromm is selective - he undoubtedly is - but whether the selection he makes is justified.

Fromm clearly states that the Old Testament is a book of many colors, containing ideas of both primitive clannishness and humanistic universalism. He does not therefore overlookthe fact that there are authoritarian non-humanistic passages and notions in the Bible. The Bible was formed during a long historical period and the evolutionary process is reflected in its text. Therefore it is important "to select those elements that constitute *the* main stream, or at least *one* main stream in the evolutionary process; this means weighing certain facts, selecting some as being more and others less representative."[167] This is what Fromm is trying to do in *You shall be as gods*, although he seems to have wanted to anticipate the critique by stating: "It would require a work of much greater scope to offer proof that radical humanist thought is the one which makes the main stages of the evolution of the Jewish tradition, while the conservative-nationalistic pattern is the relatively unchanged relic of older times and never participated in the progressive evolution of Jewish thought in its contribution to universal human values."[168]

Fromm's aim is thus to present the humanist thought of the Old Testament or a humanist interpretation of biblical stories and themes. This is exactly where the severest critique has been delivered. Fromm is said to pick some passages that are "manipulated to support a preconceived hypothesis".[169] Or as Block puts it, since there is no direct evidence of radical humanism in the Bible, "Fromm must discover some slow kind of growth or development of ideas that can be seen clearly moving towards radical humanism."[170]

---

[165]E.g., Block: "Radical Humanism and the Bible" *Tradition* (Winter 1968), 133; Maly: "Review of Fromm: *You shall be as gods*" *CBQ* 29 (1967), 620; Y. Suzuki: *An Examination of the Doctrine of Man of Erich Fromm and Reinhold Niebuhr*, 46-49.
[166]Fromm: *Beyond the Chains of Illusion*, 5.
[167]Fromm: *You shall be as gods*, 11.
[168]op.cit., 12.
[169]Maly: "Review of Fromm: *You shall be as gods*" *CBQ* 29 (1967), 621.
[170]Block: "Radical Humanism and the Bible" *Tradition* (Winter 1968), 131.

Is this critique justified? Is Fromm manipulating certain biblical passages to make them preach a humanistic message? Is he artificially making biblical passages contain a seed of radical humanism?

The manipulation accusation may be refuted by saying that it is a propagandistic play with words based on the notion that when I use a biblical text it is an interpretation, but when somebody else does it it is a manipulation. The clearest evidence of humanism in the Old Testament can be found in the prophets, in their emphasis on social justice and in their messianic vision of universal peace. None of Fromm's critics have questioned this, only his claim that the messianic age will be the work of man. His interpretation of idolatry has not only been spared from criticism, it has even received praise from his opponents (see 4.6.1.).

The critique against Fromm concerns his interpretation of God and of man. The development of the concept of God which he depicts and his interpretation of the story of the "fall" are the main evidence for the alleged manipulation and artificiality of his exegesis. Let us take Gen. 3 as an example of the difference between the radical humanist Fromm on the one hand and the Catholic Maly and the orthodox Jew Block on the other.

Unlike many other biblical commentators, Fromm does not believe Adam and Eve eating the forbidden fruit to be a historical event. For him it is a mythical story. This means that there is no historical truth to reveal, "only" a myth to interpret. It also means that there is no true interpretation. Fromm's interpretation is not *the* true interpretation corresponding to what happened, because nothing happened in the literal sense. His is one interpretation focusing on some features in the text that correspond to human experience: the dialectical relation to nature (being part of it and at the same time transcending it), the feeling of separateness from other human beings, the feeling of estrangement that can be overcome only through love, the enmity between man and woman. This is not the one and only correct interpretation, but it is no less correct than any other. There is nothing to say that an interpretation is correct or better than another simply because it is the "traditional" interpretation.

A fundamentalist believes that God - though indirectly - is the author of the Bible. The correct interpretation is thus what God has intended with the text. For a non-theist this is, of course, not so. It can then be claimed that the correct interpretation is the one that corresponds to the original intention of the author, whoever he was. But if one regards the Bible as being the result of a long development, it is possible to interpret the earlier stages in the light of the later. This is exactly what Fromm is doing. He is looking for the seed of radical humanism in the Bible. "The seed becomes clearly recognizable only if one knows the flower; the earlier phase is often to be interpreted by the later phase, even though, genetically, the earlier phase precedes the later."[171]

Fromm's claim is that the utmost logical consequence of the development depicted in the Bible is the total freedom of man, including freedom from God. This final stage is not found in the Bible, because there are limits to how far a religion can go. "Hence, the Jewish religion could not take the last logical step, to give up 'God' and to establish a concept of man as a being who is alone in this world, but who can feel at home in it if he achieves union with his fellow man and with nature."[172] The point from which he studies the Bible - a position he calls radical humanism - is thus in Fromm's opinion the logical end station of the development towards freedom in the Bible, but it is not in itself described in the biblical text but transcends it.

It is evident that Fromm sometimes presses a biblical statement too much and that he sometimes misunderstands a text (e.g. Micah 4:5a, see 4.6.2.) in his search for the seeds of radical humanism. But his method is legitimate and his interpretation is often logic, coherent, and, especially, challenging and stimulating. And that is more than can be said of many exegetes.

Fromm's radical interpretation of the Bible has also received praise from both believing Christians and Jews. Harvey Cox wrote a very sympathetic review in which he stated: "Unless the trivialization of theology has gone further than even theology's severest critics think, the response to this book should be a lovely one."[173] N. Bar-Giora Bamberger has stated that *You shall be as gods* is - with the exception of some unimportant and partly unnecessary comments - a positive Jewish confession of faith.[174] And Rev. Frank A. Hall from the Universalist Church wrote that *You shall be as gods* "is the most readable, informative and exciting piece of literature I've seen on the Bible."[175]

My own opinion is that *You shall be as gods* is one of the few exegetical books that I have read with pleasure and without getting bored.

---

[171]Fromm: *You shall be as gods*, 14.
[172]op.cit., 226.
[173]Cox: "A Test of Faith" *NYTBR* 27.11 1966.
[174]N. B-G. Bamberger: "Erich Fromm" *Das Neue Israel* 33 (1981), 564f.
[175]Hall: "Letter to the Editor" *Sun Chronicle* 21.3 1980.

5. From idolatry to life

Although Erich Fromm is mentioned in practically every modern study on the critique of religion, he was a deeply religious man. Schwarzschild recalls how Fromm "once said to me so impressively that I wrote it down when I got back to the hotel: 'I can't use the word 'God' unless I am praying.' Rosenzweig once said about someone: one has to be extremely religious for such atheism."[1]

In this concluding chapter we will first sum up the conclusions of this study before debating whether Fromm is a threat to religion or not.

We have looked at Fromm's utterances about the whole spectrum of religion, and at what he thought about minor religious movements like Transcendental Meditation and Scientology. The three institutional religions to which he devoted most time were Buddhism, Christianity, and Judaism. Because he knew Buddhism only in its intellectual form, not as a religion for the broad masses, he was very uncritical and even enthusiastic about it. Had he lived in a Buddhist country he might have been more critical about contemporary Buddhism, and also about original Buddhism, which in one way or another laid the foundations for the later development.

Christianity was more familiar to Fromm. He criticized the "Christian" West for in reality being heathen, only professing Christian values in words. He picked up certain themes from the New Testament, like the critique of richness and the having orientation, and studied some phenomena from church history, like the Reformation. But he never presented any real interpretation of the personality and the message of Jesus. Jesus was praised as one of the great teachers of mankind, but some features connected with him - like viewing God as a heavenly Father - he declared as being childish naivety (but without mentioning Jesus in the context). His attitude to Jesus, and that also means his attitude to Christianity, seems to have been somewhat ambiguous.

In the case of Judaism Fromm's knowledge was, of course, much deeper. Not accepting the theism of Judaism, and being extremely critical of many features within world Jewry, Zionism for instance, he nevertheless identified closely with the Jewish tradition. As for so many other Jews - especially after Auschwitz - the God of Judaism was dead for Fromm, but the humanistic and universalistic spirit of Judaism was alive. The intricate question raised by the attitude of Fromm and

---

[1]Schwarzschild: "Remembering Erich Fromm" *The Jewish Spectator* (Fall 1980), 31.

many other Jews is how long the spiritual tradition of Judaism can live if the people cease to believe in God.

Are the ideas of Fromm a threat to religion? To answer this question we have to distinguish between institutionalized religion and religiosity.

Fromm's attitude to religion was identical to that of Marx, or - to put it more exactly - to that of Marx according to Fromm's interpretation of Marx. He was a religious atheist,for whom living religiously was the important thing. Institutionalized religions had no value in themselves, only insofar as they were able to promote real religiosity. "His [Fromm's] opposition is not to religion as such, as any fair reading of his works must make obvious. He rightly opposes any religion that oppresses valid human freedoms and restricts authentic human growth - as do most institutionalized religions in one way or another."[2]

Despite this fact - very well expressed by the Catholic priest Helminiak - Fromm has been seen as a threat to religion. It is totally legitimate to criticize Fromm, and some of his ideas about religion deserve to be criticized. But to see his whole thought and effort as a threat to religion is an expression of a - perhaps unconscious - fear that the religion oneself is professing is an authoritarian, oppressing one. And in that case Fromm is, of course, a real danger.

Let us listen to two totally different valuations of Fromm's religious thought delivered by two Christian theologians. Mark C. Ebersole writes: "Fromm's god is man himself, his messiah is the scientific method, and his gospel is one of self-reliance."[3] Rev. Frank A. Hall writes: "His [Fromm's] nontheistic approach to religion was sensitive and inoffensive, leaving room for the conservative as well as the liberal approach to religion."[4]

How can two judgements from a Christian perspective be so totally different? Maybe the answer lies in one's basic attitude to views that challenge one's own belief. If one is very eager to maintain dogmatic orthodoxy, if one strives to be in accordance with tradition in dealing with conceptualizations, if one is - to speak with the Zen Buddhists - occupied with the finger, then one must combat that which challenges one's own position. But if, on the contrary, one is aware of the fact that one's own theology is just *one* conceptualization, one effort to express the truth, but not *the* truth, then one can be open and receptive to other aspects

[2]Helminiak: "Spiritual Concerns in Erich Fromm" *JPT* 16 (No.3, 1988), 229.
[3]Ebersole: *Christian's Faith and Man's Religion, 47.*
[4]Hall: "Letter to the editor" *Sun Chronicle* 21.3 1980.

and approaches. As one far-sighted Christian wrote after the death of Fromm, the prophets outside the church (Fremdpropheten) perhaps see from a distance more than the Christians on home ground.[5]

Reading Fromm's statements about religion challenges us to look closer at religion in the present-day world. The question is: what is more important, the shell or the content, the institution or the message, the system or the experience? Fromm's insistence that a religious bureaucracy runs the risk of damaging the religious life that it alleges to promote is a healthy warning that should lead to self-awareness. For Fromm this notion led to sympathy for the most anti-institutionalized form of religiosity, mysticism.

Fromm himself did not consider his teaching to be a threat to religion. That it was sometimes seen as such was because of the unfortunate tendency to center the religious discussion on God. Religion is for Fromm about man, "the problem of religion is not the problem of God but the problem of man; religious formulations and religious symbols are attempts to give expression to certain kinds of human experience."[6]

When asked if what he demanded from man was Christianity without God, Fromm answered in the affirmative, Christianity without God or prophetism without God.[7] But his point is that we should concentrate on that on which we agree, and not on that on which we disagree, i.e. belief in God. With a truly believing person Fromm stated that he had no problem, unless that person was a fanatic.[8] Fromm's message to those who profess a belief in God is not to get caught iup n Fromm's denial of God, but to work together on all the things they have in common, especially the fight against idols. For Fromm God is a poetic word that symbolizes all that man is striving for. "If for somebody else it is more than a symbol but a reality I have no quarrel with it. I certainly would not argue. All I can say, I cannot do anything with it because I cannot experience it as a reality, but I claim that what matters is not a thought. If we could agree on a

---

[5]Modehn: "Die Kunst des Liebeslernens" *Berliner Sonntagsblatt. Die Kirche* 23.3 1980. Another Christian has stated with reference to Fromm that the heretical tradition is to some extent much more fruitful than the sterile clerical dogmatism. (Dellbrügge: "Impressionen eines Theologen beim Lesen Erich Fromms". In: Evangelischer Studienzentrum Heilig Geist (Hrsg.): *Erich Fromm und der christliche Glaube*, 37) And further: "Die Stimmen E. Fromms, A. Schweitzers und B. Russells sind für mich von grösseren ethischer und religiöser Deutlichkeit und Relevanz als die Stellungnahmen der grossen Kirchen." (ibid.)
[6]Fromm: *Psychoanalysis and Religion*, 113.
[7]Fromm: Interview with Heiner Gautschy in 1979.
[8]ibid.

certain human reality, on a certain way of acting and feeling, then I think we would not quarrel anymore at all whether one of us has this or that thought-concept or the other one has the other, because we would not confuse the finger with the moon."[9]

Jesus once said that those who shall enter the Kingdom of God are not those who say, 'Lord, Lord', but those who do God's will. (Matth. 7:21) Fromm once wrote: "I am happy to do what God commands, without the support of the belief that God exists."[10] In his opinion centering the religious discussion on the acceptance or denial of the symbol God is a mistake. Totally in accordance with the saying of Jesus quoted above, he claims that the crucial thing is how you live. "It is easy to see that many who profess the belief in God are in their human attitude idol worshipers or men without faith, while some of the most ardent 'atheists', devoting their lives to the betterment of mankind, to deeds of brotherliness and love, have exhibited faith and a profoundly religious attitude."[11] It is easy to include Fromm in the latter group.

Erich Fromm was a real *homo humanisticus*[12] whose aim was the liberation of man from all fetters. He understood perfectly well that man needs a frame of orientation and an object of devotion. He saw the catastrophic consequences when this need was filled with idolatry. He vividly opposed the notion that the choice is between theistic religion and soulless, idolatric materialism. There is another alternative, a frame of reference common to the theist and the non-theist person, where "the goal of life is the fullest development of human powers, specifically those of reason and of love, including the transcending of the narrowness of one's ego and of the development of the capacity to give oneself as well as full affirmation of life and all that is alive as against the worship of the mechanical and dead."[13] This cannot be a threat to true religion, unless we have totally lost sight of what is central in the Judaeo-Christian tradition.

Erich Fromm was an extraordinary man. Those who knew him speak of his extreme aliveness and warmth. "Erich Fromm was the most fully alive and awake man I have ever met or can imagine."[14] Not having ever met him, but having

---

[9]Fromm: "Beyond Egotistical Religion" (lecture in 1957).
[10]Letter Fromm - Schwarzschild 9.1 1970. Quoted from Schwarzschild: "Remembering Erich Fromm" *The Jewish Spectator* (Fall 1980), 31.
[11]Fromm: *Psychoanalysis and Religion*, 113.
[12]Aramoni: "Fromm, el amigo, el terapeuta, el hombre universal". In: Millán - Gojman de Millán (Eds.): *Erich Fromm y el psicoanálisis humanista*, 19f.
[13]Fromm: *On Being Human*, 56.
[14]Schechter: "Tribute to Erich Fromm" *Cont Psycha* 17 (No.4, 1981),, 445.

come very close to him through his writings, I can feel the same aliveness. Erich Fromm was indeed "a man whose words are ways and whose ways are reason, love and faith in man's possibilities."[15]

---

[15]Landis - Tauber: "On Erich Fromm". In: Landis - Tauber (Eds.): *In the Name of Life*, 11.

Abbreviations

ASR	American Sociological Review
BBC	Brittish Broadcasting Company
CBQ	Catholic Biblical Quarterly
Cont Psycha	Contemporary Psychoanalysis
EvK	Evangelische Kommentare
GA	Erich Fromm: Gesamtausgabe
HUC	Hebrew Union College
JCS	Journal of Church and State
JIR	Jewish Institute of Religion
JPT	Journal of Psychology and Theology
MEW	Marx-Engels: Werke
NYT	New York Times
NYTBR	The New York Times Book Review
NZSThR	Neue Zeitschrift für systematische Theologie und Religionsphilosophie
Past Psych	Pastoral Psychology
RUO	Revue de l'Université Ottawa
SA	Scientific American
SSI	Social Science Information
SZ	Stimmen der Zeit
ThWAT	Theologisches Wörterbuch zum Alten Testament
TRE	Theologische Realenzyklopädie
WuD	Wort und Dienst
ZSF	Zeitschrift für Sozialforschung

Bibliography

Works by Fromm

Unpublished (All at the Erich Fromm Archives in Tübingen. If nothing else is stated the language of the unpublished works is English)

Appeal for Cooperation between Jews and Arabs (different versions) 1948 (manuscripts, German translation in Fromm: *Ethik und Politik*, 228-235)

Letter to Ernst Strauss 13.4 1948

"Mental Health in Contemporary Society" Lecture held 6.1 1953 at Hebrew Union College - Jewish Institute of Religion, Cincinnate (cassette tape)

Letter to D.T. Suzuki 18.10 1956

"Beyond Egotistical Religion" Lecture in 1957 sponsored by the First Unitarian Church, Philadelphia (transcript)

Letter to Dean James A. Pike 13.6 1957

Letter to Ernst Simon 24.6 1957

Letter to Norman Thomas 18.7 1957

Letter to Dean James A. Pike 23.10 1957

Letter to Thomas Merton 3.11 1960

Letter to Thomas Merton 9.10 1961

Letter to Thomas Merton 30.1 1962

Letter to Thomas Merton 10.9 1963

Letter to D.T. Suzuki 14.12 1963

Letter to T.E. Rabinkow-Rothbard 9.7 1964 (German)

Letter to Thomas Merton 7.2 1966

"The Renaissance of Humanist Socialism" Lecture held in 1966 (transcript)

"Responsibility, Duty and Independence" Lecture held 17.5 1966 (transcript)

"Doubts and Certainties" Oliver Hunkin talks to Dr. Erich Fromm. TV-Interview by BBC. Sent 29.8 1968 (video tape)

"The Myth of the Paradise" Lecture held in New York City in 1970 (tape)

Letter to Leo Jung 7.10 1970

Letter to Nyanaponika Mahathera 8.9 1972

Letter to Leo Jung 18.10 1972

Letter to Nyanaponika Mahathera 4.12 1972

Letter to Ernst Simon 21.7 1973

Letter to Karl D. Darmstadter 9.10 1973

Letter to Ernst Simon 9.10 1973

Letter to Dietmar Mieth 27.6 1974

Letter to Steven S. Schwarzschild 11.10 1974

Letter to Karl D. Darmstadter 16.12 1974

Letter to Ernst Simon 23.12 1974

Letter to Karl D. Darmstadter 27.1 1975

Antwort auf das Referat von Prof. Dr. Auer zum Thema: "Gibt es eine Ethik ohne Religiosität?" May 1975 (transcript, German)

Letter to Karl D. Darmstadter 7.6 1975

Letter to Nyanaponika Mahathera 1.12 1975

"Buddhism" (manuscript from the mid-1970's)

Letter to James Luther Adams 1.10 1976

Letter to Ernst Simon 7.1 1977

Letter to Ernst Simon 28.2 1977

Letter to James Luther Adams 2.5 1977

Interview with Micaela Lämmle and Jürgen Lodemann. Südwestfunk 26.6 1977 (transcript, German)

Letter to Ernst Simon 24.10 1977

Interview with Heiner Gautschy. Sent on Swiss TV 7.9 1979 (transcript, German)

Interview with Gerard Khoury in 1979 (transcript)

Interview with Guido Ferrari 8.3 1980 (transcript, German)

Published

"V.J.St. Achduth, Frankfurt a.M." *Der Jüdische Student. Zeitschrift des Kartells Jüdischer Verbindungen* XIV Jahrgang. Heft 3 (Mai 1919), 107

"Rabbiner Nobel als Führer der Jugend" *Neue Jüdische Presse* 2.2 1922, 3

- Fritz Goithein - Leo Löwenthal - Ernst Simon - Erich Michaelis: "Ein prinzipielles Wort zur Erziehungsfrage" *Juedische Rundschau* No. 103/104 23.12 1922

"Der Sabbath" (1927) *Gesamtausgabe VI*, 1-9

"Die männliche Schöpfung" (1933). In: Erich Fromm: *Liebe, Sexualität, Matriarkat. Beiträge zur Geschlechterfrage* Hrsg. von Rainer Funk. München 1994, 68-94

"Die sozialpsychologische Bedeutung der Mutterrechtstheorie" (1934) *Gesamtausgabe I*, 85-109

Review of "Sandford Fleming: *Children and Puritanism*" *Zeitschrift für Sozialforschung* III (1934), 277

Letter to Max Horkheimer 17.7 1935, in: Max Horkheimer: *Gesammelte Schriften. Band 15: Briefwechsel 1913-36.* Hrsg. von Gunzelin Schmid Noerr. Frankfurt am Main, 371-374

"Selfishness and Self-Love" *Psychiatry. Journal for the Study of Interpersonal Process* 2 (1939), 507-523

Escape from Freedom. New York 1941

"Faith as a Character Trait" *Psychiatry. Journal for the Study of Interpersonal Process* 5 (1942), 307-319

"Individual and Social Origins of Neurosis" *American Sociological Review* 9 (1944), 380-384

Man for Himself. An Inquiry into the Psychology of Ethics New York 1947

"The Nature of Dreams" *Scientific American* 180 (No.5, May 1949), 44-47

Psychoanalysis and Religion New Haven 1950

"For Seekers of Prefabricated Happiness. Review of L. Ron Hubbard: *Dianetics*" *New York Herald Tribune* 3.9 1950, 7 (Reprinted in Wissenschaft vom Menschen/Science of Man. Jahrbuch der International Erich Fromm-Gesellschaft Vol.3 (1992), 155-157)

The Forgotten Language. An Introduction to the Understanding of Dreams, Fairy Tales and Myths New York 1951

"Man - Woman". In: M.M. Hughes (Ed.): *The People in Your Life; Psychiatry and Personal Relations* New York 1951, 3-27

The Sane Society New York 1955

"Psychoanalysis". In: J.R. Newman (Ed.): *What is Science? Twelve Eminent Scientists and Philosophers Explain Their Various Fields to the Layman* New York 1955, 362-380

The Art of Loving. An Inquiry into the Nature of Love. World Perspective. Vol 9. Planned and edited by Ruth Nanda Anshen. New York 1956

"Interview with Mike Wallace" *Survival and Freedom* 5 (1958), 1-16

Sigmund Freud's Mission. An Analysis of his Personality and Influence. World Perspectives. Vol. 21. Planned and edited by Ruth Nanda Anshen. New York 1959

"Values, Psychology, and Human Existence". In: Abraham H. Maslow (Ed.): *New Knowledge in Human Values* New York 1959, 151-164

"Love in America". In: Huston Smith (Ed.): *The Search for America* Englewood Cliffs 1959, 123-131

"Freedom in the Work Situation". In: Michael Harrington and P. Jacobs (Eds.): *Labor in a Free Society* Los Angeles 1959, 1-16

"Psychoanalysis and Zen Buddhism". In: D.T. Suzuki - Erich Fromm - Richard de Martino: *Zen Buddhism and Psychoanalysis* New York 1960, 77-141

"Foreword". In: Edward Bellamy: *Looking Backward (2000-1887)* New York 1960, v-xx

"Interview with Huston Smith: Man's Needs" *Science and Human Rersponsibility* St. Louis 1960, 10-13

May Man Prevail? An Inquiry into the Facts and Fictions of Foreign Policy New York 1961

Marx's Concept of Man. With a Translation of Marx's Economic and Philosophical Manuscript by T.B. Bottomore. New York 1961

Beyond the Chains of Illusion. My Encounter with Marx and Freud Credo Perspectives. Planned and edited by Ruth Nanda Anshen. New York 1962

"The Philosophy Basic to Freud's Psychoanalysis" *Pastoral Psychology* 13 (1962), 26-32

The Dogma of Christ and Other Essays on Religion, Psychology and Culture New York 1963

"C.G. Jung: Prophet of the Unconscious. A Discussion of 'Memories, Dreams, Reflections' by C.G. Jung" *Scientific American* 209 (No.3, Sept. 1963), 283-290

"Humanism and Psychoanalysis" *Contemporary Psychoanalysis* 1 (1964), 69-79 (Translated from the Spanish by Erich Fromm)

War Within Man. A Psychological Inquiry into the Roots of Destructiveness. A Study and Commentars Philadelphia 1963

"Religious Humanism and Politics. To the editor of *Judaism*" *Judaism. A Quarterly Journal* 12 (Spring 1963), 223f.

The Heart of Man. Its Genius for Good and Evil. Religious Perspectives. Vol. 12. Planned and edited by Ruth Nanda Anshen. New York 1964

"Foreword". In: Karl Marx: *Selected Writings in Sociology and Social Philosophy*. Edited by T.B. Bottomore and M. Rubel. New York 1964, xii-xviii

"Introduction". In: Erich Fromm (Ed.): *Socialist Humanism. An International Symposium*. New York 1965, vii-xii

"Preface". In: A. Reza Arasteh: *Rumi the Persian: Rebirth in Creativity and Love* Lahore 1965, vii-x

"Interview with Richard Heffner" *McCalls* 92 (Oct. 1965), 132f. and 213-219

You shall be as gods. A radical interpretation of the Old Testament and its tradition New York 1966

"Is Germany on the March Again?" *War/Peace Report* 6 (March 1966), 3f.

"Memories of Dr. D.T. Suzuki" *The Eastern Buddhist* New Series II (August 1967), 88f.

"Foreword II". In: Erich Fromm: *Psychoanalysis and Religion*. Eighteenth printing. New Haven 1967, vi-viii

The Revolution of Hope. Toward a Humanized Technology. World Perspectives. Vol. 38. Planned and edited by Ruth Nanda Anshen. New York 1968

and Ramón Xirau (Eds.): *The Nature of Man.* Readings selected, edited and furnished with an introduction by Erich Fromm and Ramón Xirau. New York 1968

"The Condition of the American Spirit. Are We Fully Alive?" *Newsday* 13.1 1968[1]

and Ramón Xirau: "Introduction". In: Erich Fromm - Ramón Xirau (Eds.): *The Nature of Man.* Readings selected, edited and furnished with an introduction by Erich Fromm and Ramón Xirau. New York 1968, 3-24

"Marx's Contribution to the Knowledge of Man" *Social Science Information* 7 (1968), 7-17

The Crisis of Psychoanalysis. Essays on Freud, Marx and Social Psychology New York 1970

and Michael Maccoby: *Social Character in a Mexican Village. A Socio-psychoanalytic Study* Englewood Cliffs 1970

"Essay". In: *Summerhill: For and Against* New York 1970, 251-263

"Die psychologischen und geistigen Probleme des Überflusses" (1970) *GA V*, 317-328

"Introduction". In: Ivan Illich: *Celebration of Awareness. A Call for Institutional Revolution* New York 1970, 7-10

Letter to Martin Jay 14.5 1971. In: Michael Kessler - Rainer Funk (Hrsg.): *Erich Fromm und die Frankfurter Schule.* Akten der internationalen, interdisziplinären Symposions Stuttgart - Hohenheim vom 31.5 bis 2.6 1991. Tübingen 1992, 249-256

---

[1]This is the fact about this article that is given by Funk in *GA X*, 440. At the Erich Fromm Archives in Tübingen this article is preserved only as a manuscript.

"Einige post-marxsche und post-freudsche Gedanken über Religion und Religiosität" *Concilium. Internationale Zeitschrift* 8 (1972), 472-476

Letter to Brian R. Betz 14.10 1972. In: Brian R. Betz: *An Analysis of the Prophetic Character of the Dialectical Rhetoric of Erich Fromm.* Northwestern University Dissertation 1974

The Anatomy of Human Destructiveness New York 1973

"Einführung in H.J. Schultz *Psychologie für Nichtpsychologen*" (1974) *Gesamtasugabe VIII*, 71-90

"Die Zwiespältigkeit des Fortschritts. Zum 100. Geburtstag von Albert Schweitzer" *Evangelische Kommentare* 8 (1975), 757f.

"Die Aktualität der prophetischen Schriften" (1975) *Gesamtasugabe VI*, 77-81

To have or to be? World Perspectives. Vol. 50. Planned and edited by Ruth Nanda Anshen. New York 1976

"Die Bedeutung der Ehrwürdigen Nyanaponika Mahathera für die westliche Welt" (1976) *Gesamtausgabe VI*, 359-361

"Interview with Alfred A. Häsler: Das Undenkbare denken und das Mögliche tun" *Ex libris* 22 (No.5, 1977), 13-19

"Religion und Gesellschaft". In: Rainer Funk: *Mut zum Menschen. Erich Fromms Denken und Werk, seine humanistische Religion und Ethik.* Mit einem Nachwort von Erich Fromm. Stuttgart 1978, 359f.

Letter to Karola Bloch. In: Karola Bloch - Adelbert Reif (Hrsg.): *"Denken heisst überschreiten". In memoriam Ernst Bloch 1885-1977* Köln - Frankfurt 1978, 317

Greatness and Limitations of Freud's Thought New York 1980[2]

"Konsumreligion" *Neues Forum* 302/302 (Jänner/Februar 1979), 12f.

"Interview with Heinrich Jänecke: Ich habe die Hoffnung, dass die Menschen ihr Leiden erkennen: den Mangel an Liebe" *Der Stern* 14 (27.3 1980), 306-309

---

[2]Although written in English this book was first published in German translation in 1979.

On Disobedience and Other Essays New York 1981

For the Love of Life. Edited by Hans Jürgen Schultz. Translated from the German by Robert and Rita Kimber. New York 1986

"Reminiscences of Shlomo Barukh Rabinkow". In: Leo Jung (Ed.): *Sages and Saints.* The Jewish Library: Volume X. Hoboken, N.J. 1987, 99-105

Gesamtausgabe. Band I-X. Hrsg. von Rainer Funk. München 1989

The Art of Being. London 1993[3]

Das jüdische Gesetz. Zur Soziologie des Diaspora-Judentums. Dissertation von 1922. Herausgegeben und bearbeitet von Rainer Funk und Bernd Sahler. Schriften aus dem Nachlass. Band 2. Weinheim - Basel 1989

The Revision of Psychoanalysis. Edited by Rainer Funk. Boulder - San Fransisco - Oxford 1992[4]

Ethik und Politik. Antworten auf aktuelle politische Fragen. Herausgegeben von Rainer Funk. Schriften aus dem Nachlass. Band 4. Weinheim - Basel 1990

The Art of Listening. London 1994[5]

Die Pathologie der Normalität. Zur Wissenschaft vom Menschen. Herausgegeben von Rainer Funk. Schriften aus dem Nachlass. Band 6. Weinheim - Basel 1991

Gesellschaft und Seele. Sozialpsychologie und psychoanalytische Praxis. Herausgegeben von Rainer Funk. Schriften aus dem Nachlass. Band 7. Weinhiem - Basel 1992.

On Being Human. New York 1994[6]

---

[3]German version as volume 1 of *Schriften aus dem Nachlass* in 1989.
[4]German version as volume 3 of *Schriften aus dem Nachlass* in 1990.
[5]German version as volume 5 of *Schriften aus dem Nachlass* in 1990.
[6]German version as volume 8 of *Schriften aus dem Nachlass* in 1992.

Fragments on Meister Eckhart. In: Volker Frederking: *Durchbruch vom Haben zum Sein. Erich Fromm und die Mystik Meister Eckharts*. Paderborn - München - Wien - Zürich 1994, 423-457

Other works

Unpublished (all at the Erich Fromm Archives in Tübingen. The letters are in English if nothing else is stated)

Darmstadter, Karl D.: Letter to Erich Fromm 9.10 1967

Fromm-Reichmann, Frieda: Autobiographical Tapes (circa 1954) (transcript)

Funk, Rainer: "Die jüdische Wurzeln des humanistischen Denken von Erich Fromm". In: *Erich Fromm. Zu Leben und Werke*. Referate des Symposium der Internationalen Erich-Fromm-Gesellschaft 1988 in Locarno (manuscript)

Merton, Thomas: Letter to Erich Fromm 2.10 1954

- Letter to Erich Fromm 12.11 1955

- Letter to Erich Fromm 13.10 1966

Nyanaponika Mahathera: Letter to Erich Fromm 31.12 1972

Sahler, Bernd: "Die Dissertation Erich Fromms über das jüdische gesetz aus dem Jahr 1922. Darstellung des Inhalts". In: *Erich Fromm. Zu Leben und Werk*. Referat des Symposions der Internationalen Erich-Fromm-Gesellschaft 1988 in Locarno. Tübingen 1988 (manuscript)

Salzberger, Georg: "Erinnerungen von Rabbiner Dr. Georg Salzberger an die 20er Jahren" (transcript of a radio programme, sent 4.8 1974)

Simon, Ernst: Letter to Erich Fromm 13.8 1973 (German)

- Letter to Erich Fromm 26.12 1976 (German)

Steinberg, Catharine: *Hasidic Elements in the Writings of Erich Fromm.* Thesis. Los Angeles 1963

Thomassen, Beroald: *Erich Fromm's 'Entwicklung des Christusdogmas' ist darzustellen und historisch und dogmatisch zu beurteilen.* Wissenschaftliche Hausarbeit zum Ersten Theologischen Examen bei der Evangelischen Kirche in Rheinland 1985

Published

Ahren, Yizhak: "Im Kampf gegen Götzendienst. Nachruf auf den Psychoanalytiker Erich Fromm" *Berliner Allgemeine Jüdische Wochenzeitung* 28.3 1980

Albright, W.F. - Mann, C.S.: *Matthew.* The Anchor Bible 26. Garden City, New York 1971

Appel, Werner: "Erich Fromms Dialog mit dem Buddhismus". In: Lutz von Werder (Hrsg.): *Der unbekannte Fromm. Biographische Studien. Forschungen zu Erich Fromm.* Band 2. Frankfurt 1987

Aramoni, Aniceto: "Erich Fromm, el amigo, el terapeuta, el hombre universal". In: Salvador Millán - Sonia Gojman de Millán (Eds.): *Erich Fromm y el psicoanálisis humanista* México 1981, 15-26

Aregger-Moros, Urs: *Das Konzept der Entfremdung im geschichts-philosophischen Denken von Erich Fromm.* Dissertation Philosophisch-Historische Fakultät der Universität Basel. Bern 1989

Bamberger, I. Nathan: "A Note on Erich Fromm's Rabbinic Roots" *Tradition-A Journal of Orthodox Thought* 29 (Spring 1995), 52-54

Bamberger, N. Bar-Giora: "Erich Fromm" *Das Neue Israel* 33 (1981), 564-565

Banks, Robert: "A Neo-Freudian Critique of Religion: Erich Fromm on the Judaeo-Christian Tradition". *Religion. A Journal of Religion and Religions 5 (1975), 117-135*

Beit-Hallahmi, Benjamin: "Religiously based differences in approach to the psychology of religion: Freud, Fromm, Allport and Zilboorg". In: L.B. Brown (ed.): *Advances in the Psychology of Religion*. International Series in Experimential Social Psychology. Volume 11. Oxford - New York - Toronto - Sydney - Paris - Frankfurt 1985

Bentley, J.: "Three German Marxists Look at Christianity" *Journal of Church and State* 22 (1980), 505-517

Benz, Ernst: *ZEN in westlicher Sicht. Zen-Buddhismus - Zen-Snobbismus.* Weilheim/Oberbayern 1962

Betz, Brian R.: *An Analysis of the Prophetic Character of the Dialectical Rhetoric of Erich Fromm.* Northwestern University Dissertation 1974

- *Erich Fromm - Prophet in the Name of Life.* Paper presented at the Gull Lake Communication Ethics Conference. May 15-18, 1994 at Oswego, New York.

Blinzler, Josef: *Der Prozess Jesu.* Vierte, erneut revidierte Auflage. Regensburg 1969

Bloch, Ernst: *Atheismus in Christenthum. Zur Religion des Exodus und des Reiches.* Frankfurt a. M. 1968

- *Das Prinzip Hoffnung.* Gesamtausgabe in 16 Bänden. Band 5. Frankfurt a.M. 1977

- *Zwischenwelten in der Philosophiegeschichte. Aus Leipziger Vorlesungen.* Gesamtausgabe in 16 Bänden. Band 12. Frankfurt a.M. 1977

Block, Irvin: "Radical Humanism in the Bible" *Tradition. A Journal of Orthodox Thought* (Winter 1968), 131-137

Boisen, Anton T.: "Review of Erich Fromm: *Escape from Freedom*" *Psychiatry. Journal of the Biology and the Pathology of Interpersonal Relations* 5 (1942), 113-117

Browning, Don S.: *Generative Man: Psychoanalytic Perspectives.* Philadelphia 1973

Buber, Martin: *Werke. Zweiter Band. Schriften zur Bibel.* München - Heidelberg 1964

Burnstein, Alexander J.: "Niebuhr, Scripture, and Normative Judaism". In: Charles W. Kegley - Robert W. Bretall (Eds.): *Reinhold Niebuhr. His Religious, Social, and Political Thought.* The Library of Living Theology. Volume II. New York 1956, 411-428

Burston, Daniel: *The Legacy of Erich Fromm.* Cambridge, Mass. - London 1991

- "A Profile of Erich Fromm" *Social Science and Modern Society* 28 (No. 4, 1991), 84-89

Bühler, Michael: *Erziehung zur Tradition - Erziehung zum Widerstand. Ernst Simon und die jüdische Erwachsenenbildung in Deutschland.* Studien zu jüdischem Volk und christlicher Gemeinde. Band 8. Berlin 1986

Chrzanowski, Gerard: "Das psychoanalytische Werk von Karen Horney, Harry Stack Sullivan und Erich Fromm". In: Dieter Eicke (Hrsg.): *Tiefenpsychologie. Band 3: Die Nachfolger Freuds.* Kindleys "Psychologie des 20. Jahrhunderts". Weinheim - Basel 1982

Cohen, Hermann: *Die Religion der Vernunft aus den Quellen des Judentums.* Schriften herausgegeben von der Gesellschaft zur Forderung der Wissenschaft des Judentums. Leipzig 1919

- *Jüdische Schriften. Zweiter Band. Zur jüdischen Zeitgeschichte.* Hrsg. von Bruno Strauss. Veröffentlichungen der Akademie für die Wissenschaft des Judentums. Berlin 1924

- *Jüdische Schriften. Dritter Band. Zur jüdischen Religionsphilosophie und ihrer Geschichte.* Mit einer Einleitung von Franz Rosenzweig herausgegeben von Bruno Strauss. Veröffentlichungen der Akademie für die Wissenschaft des Judentums. Berlin 1924

Coser, Lewis A.: *Refugee Scholars in America. Their Impact and Their Experiences.* New Haven and London 1984

Cox, Harvey: "A Test of Faith" *The New York Times Book Review* 27.11 1966, 10 and 12

- "Fromm's Eclecticism" *New York Times* 7.5 1980

Croatto, J. Severino: *Biblical Hermeneutics. Toward a Theory of Reading as the Production of Meaning.* Translated from the Spanish by Robert R. Barr. Maryknoll 1987

"A Decade of Non-Conformity. The Jewish Newsletter". Advertisement in *The New York Times Book Review* 27.10 1957

Dellbrügge, Georg-Hermann: "Impressionen eines Theologen beim Lesen Erich Fromms". In: Evangelisches Studienzentrum Heilig Geist (Hrsg.): *Erich Fromm und der christliche Glaube*, 35-96

Dodd, C.H.: *According to the Scriptures. The Sub-Structure of New Testament Theology.* New York 1953

Dumoulin, Heinrich: *Zen. Geschichte und Gestalt.* Bern 1959

Dunn, James D.G.: *Christology in the Making. An Inquiry into the Origins of the Doctrine of the Incarnation.* London 1980

Ebersole, Mark C.: *Christian's Faith and Man's Religion. E. Fromm, D. Bonhoeffer, F. Schleiermacher, K. Barth, R. Niebuhr. A Study in Modern Thought* New York 1961

Erikson, Erik H.: *Young Man Luther. A Study in Psychoanalysis and History.* Norton Library Edition. New York 1962

Feldman, Seymour: "Spinoza". In: Daniel H. Frank - Oliver Leaman (Eds.): *History of Jewish Philosophy.* Routledge History of World Philosophies. Volume 2. London - New York 1997, 612-635

Flückiger, Felix: "Funktion und Wesen der Religion nach Erich Fromm" *Theologische Beiträge. Zweimonatsschrift der Pfarrer-Gebet-Bruderschaft* 16 (No.5, 1985), 201-223

Forsyth, James J. - Beniskos, J.M.: "Biblical Faith and Erich Fromm's Theory of personality" *Revue de l'Université Ottawa* 40 (1970), 69-91

Frederking, Volker: *Durchbruch vom Haben zum Sein. Erich Fromm und die Mystik Meister Eckharts.* Paderborn - München - Wien - Zürich 1994

Friedman, Maurice: *To Deny our Nothingness. Contemporary Images of Man.* London 1967

Friedman, Menachem: "Habad as Massianic Fundamentalism: From Local Particularism to Universal Jewish Mission". In: Martin E. Marty - R. Scott Appleby (Eds.): *Accounting for Fundamentalisms. The Dynamic Character of Movements.* The Fundamentalism Project. Volume 4. Chicago - London 1994

Funk, Rainer: *Mut zum Menschen. Erich Fromms Denken und Werk, seine humanistische Religion und Ethik.* Mit einem Nachwort von Erich Fromm. Stuttgart 1978

- *Erich Fromm. Mit Selbstzeugnissen und Bilddokumenten.* Rowohlts Monographien 322. Reinbek bei Hamburg 1983

- "Biophilia and Fromm's Criticism of Religion". In: Pier Lorenzo Eletti (Ed.): *Incontro con Erich Fromm. Atti del Simposio Internazionale su Erich Fromm: "Dalla necrofilia lla biofilia: linee per una psicoanalisi umanistica"* Firenze 1986, 215-222

- "Der Humanismus in Leben und Werk von Erich Fromm. Laudatio zum 90. Geburtstag". In: Wissenschaft vom Menschen/Science of Man. Jahrbuch der Internationalen Erich-Fromm-Gesellschaft. Vol. 3. Münster 1992, 133-152

- *Bibliography of the Literature about Erich Fromm - Bibliographie der Literatur über Erich Fromm.* Tübingen 1996

Glen, J. Stanley: *Erich Fromm: A Protestant Critique* Philadelphia 1966

Gnilka, Joachim: *Das Matthäusevangelium. II. Teil.* Herders Theologischer Kommentar zum Neuen Testament, Freiburg - Basel - Wien 1988

Goldmann, Nahum: "Reminiscences of Shlomo Barukh Rabinkow". In: Leo Jung (Ed.): *Sages and Saints.* The Jewish Library: Volume X. Hoboken, N.J. 1987, 105-107

Gordon, Cyrus H.: *Introduction to Old Testament Times.* Ventnor, N.J. 1953

Gottwald, Norman K. (Ed.): *The Bible and Liberation. Political and Social Hermeneutics.* Third Printing. Maryknoll 1989

Greinacher, Norbert: "Erich Fromm" in: Wilhelm Schmidt (Hrsg.): *Die Religion der Religionskritik*. München 1972, 28-37

Hall, Frank A.: "Letter to the Editor" *Sun Chronicle* 21.3 1980

Hammond, Guy B.: *Man in Estrangement. A Comparison of the Thought of Paul Tillich and Erich Fromm*. Nashville 1965

- "Patriarchy and the Protestant Conscience: A Critique" *Journal of Religion and Ethics* 9 (1981), 84-102

- "The Conscience-less Society and Beyond: Perspectives from Erich Fromm and Paul Tillich." *Neue Zeitschrift für systematische Theologie und Religionsphilosophie* 25 (1983), 20-32

Hardeck, Jürgen: *Vernunft und Liebe. Religion im Werk von Erich Fromm*. Frankfurt/M - Berlin 1992

Hausdorff, Don: *Erich Fromm*. Twayne's United States Authors Series, Vol. 203. New York 1972

Helminiak, Daniel A.: "Spiritual Concerns in Eric Fromm" *Journal of Psychology and Theology* 16 (1988), 222-232

Hertzberg, Arthur: *The Zionist Idea. A Historical Analysis and Reader*. Fifteenth Printing. New York 1984

Heschel, Abraham I.: "A Hebrew Evaluation of Reinhold Niebuhr". In: Charles W. Kegley - Robert W. Bretall (Eds.): *Reinhold Niebuhr. His Religious, Social, and Political Thought*. The Library of Living Theology. Volume II. New York 1956, 391-410

Honigmann, Peter: "Der Talmudistenkreis um Salman Baruch Rabinkow". In: Norbert Giovannini - Jo-Hannes Bauer - Hans-Martin Mumm (Hrsg.): *Jüdische Leben in Heidelberg. Studien zur einer unterbrochenen Geschichte*. Heidelberg 1992, 265-272

Huxley, Julian: *Religion without Revelation*. New and Revised Edition. London 1957

Isaac, Erich: "Review of Fromm: *You shall be as gods. A Radical Interpretation of the Old Testament and Its Tradition.*" *Commentary* 43 (May 1967), 99

Israel, Joachim: *Alienation: från Marx till modern sociologi. En makrosociologisk studie.* Andra omarbetade och utökade upplagan. Stockholm 1971

Jeremias, Jörg: *Die Theorie der Projektion im religionskritischen Denken Sigmund Freuds und Erich Fromms.* Dissertation Universität Oldenburg 1983

Kantzenbach, Friedrich Wilhelm: *Albert Schweitzer. Wirklichkeit und Legende.* Persönlichkeit und Geschichte, Band 50. Göttingen - Zürich - Frankfurt 1969

Kaufmann, Walter: *Critique of Religion and Philosophy.* Garden City, New York 1961

Knapp, Gerhard P.: *The Art of Living. Erich Fromm's Life and Works.* American University Studies: Series VIII, Psychology; Vol. 13. New York 1989

Knox, John: *The Humanity and Divinity of Christ. A study of Patterns in Christology.* Cambridge 1967

Kügler SJ, Herrmann: "Humanistische Religion und christlicher Glaube. Anfragen der humanistischen Psychologie Erich Fromms an christlicher Theologie und Pastoralpsychologie" *Stimmen der Zeit* 202 (1984), 546-556

- "Religiöse Erfahrung - humanistisch und christlich. Die humanistische Religion Erich Fromms und die christliche Glaubenserfahrung." *Stimmen der Zeit* 203 (1985), 125-136

Landis, Bernard - Tauber, Edward S.: "On Erich Fromm". In: Bernard Landis - Edward S. Tauber (Eds.): *In the Name of Life. Essays in Honour of Erich Fromm* New York 1971, 1-11

Lane, William L.: *The Gospel According to Mark.* The New International Commentary on the New Testament 2. Grand Rapids, Michigan 1974

Lee, Lester C.: *An Investigation of Erich Fromm's Theory of Authoritarianism.* Claremont Graduate School Dissertation 1963

Luther, Martin: *Werke. Kritische Gesamtausgabe. 30. Band* Weimar 1910

Löwith, Karl: *Sämtliche Schriften 4. Von Hegel zu Nietsche.* Stuttgart 1988

Maccoby, Michael: *The Role of Hope in Psychoanalysis: Erich Fromm's View of Psychoanalysis and Religion.* Paper presented to the William Alanson White Institute, New York, February 7, 1996

Maimonides, Moses: *The Guide of the Perplexed.* Translated with an Introduction and Notes by Shlomo Pines. With an Introductory Essay by Leo Strauss. Chicago - London 1963

Maly, Eugen H.: "Review of Fromm: *You shall be as gods. A Radical Interpretation of the Old Testament and Its Tradition*" *Catholic Biblical Quarterly* 29 (1967), 619-621

Marx, Karl - Engels, Friedrich: *Werke.* Band 1. 7. Auflage. Berlin 1970

- *Werke.* Band 4. 4. Auflage. Berlin 1969

Mays, James Luther: *Micah. A Commentary.* Old Testament Library. London 1976

Modehn, Christian: "Die Kunst des Liebeslernens" *Berliner Sonntagsblatt. Die Kirche* 23.2 1980

Moltmann, Jürgen: "The Impossible Dream?" *Critic* (Febr./March 1969), 80-82

Paulsen, Henning: "Jakobusbrief" *Theologische Realenzyklopädie. Band 16,* 488-495. Berlin - New York 1987

Picht, Werner: *Albert Schweitzer. Wesen und Bedeutung.* Hamburg 1960

Poliakov, Léon: *The History of Anti-Semitism. Volume I. From Roman times to the Court Jews.* Translated from the French by Richard Howard. The Littman Library of Jewish Civilization. London 1974

- *The History of Anti-Semitism. Volume III. From Voltaire to Wagner.* Translated from the French by Miriam Kochan. The Littman Library of Jewish Civilization. London 1975

Pollard, T.E.: *Johannine Christology and the Early Church.* Society for New Testament Studies. Monograph Series 13. Cambridge 1970

Pröpper, Thomas: *Der Jesus der Philosophen und der Jesus des Glaubens. Ein theologisches Gespräch mit Jaspers, Bloch, Kolakowski, Gardavsky, Machovec, Fromm, Ben-Chorin.* Mainz 1976

Pöhlmann, Horst-Georg: *Der Atheismus oder der Streit um Gott.* Gütersloh 1977

Rabinkow, Salman Baruch: "Individuum und Gemeinschaft im Judentum". In: Th. Brugsch - F.H. Lewy (Hrsg.): *Die Biologie der Person. Ein Handbuch der allgemeinen und speziellen Konstitutionslehre. Band IV: Soziologie der Person.* Berlin - Wien 1929, 799-824

Robinson, John A.T.: *Twelve New Testament Studies.* Studies in Biblical Theology. No. 34. London 1962

Rosenberg, Göran: *Det förlorade landet. En personlig historia.* Falun 1996

Rubins, Jack L.: *Karen Horney. Gentle Rebel of Psychoanalysis* New York 1978

Rudolph, Wilhelm: *Micha - Nahum - Habakuk - Zephanja.* Mit einer Zeittafel von Alfred Jepsen. Kommentar zum Alten Testament XIII 3. Gütersloh 1975

Rössler, Andreas: "Zwei Pole in Gott. Über Paul Tillich und Erich Fromm." *Evangelische Kommentare* 15 (1982), 259-262

Saavedra, Victor: *La promesa incumplida de Erich Fromm.* México 1994

Schaar, John H.: *Escape from Authority. The Perspectives of Erich Fromm.* New York 1961

Schacter, Jacob J. (Ed.): "Reminiscences of Shlomo Barukh Rabinkow". In: Leo Jung (Ed.): *Sages and Saints.* The Jewish Library: Volume X. Hoboken, N.J. 1987, 93-132

Schechter, David E.: "Tribute to Erich Fromm" *Contemporary Psychoanalysis* 17 (No.4, 1981), 445-447

Schnackenburg, Rudolf: *Matthäusevangelium*. Die Neue Echter Bibel. Kommentar zum Neuen Testament mit der Einheitsübersetzung. Band 1. Würzburg 1987

Schneider-Flume, Gunda: "Fromm". In: Karl-Heinz Weger (Hrsg.): *Religionskritik von der Aufklärung bis zur Gegenwart*. Freiburg 1979, 117-122

Scholem, Gershom: *Major Trends in Jewish Mysticism*. New York 1961

- *Walter Benjamin - die Geschichte einer Freundschaft*. Frankfurt am Main 1975

- *Von Berlin nach Jerusalem. Jugenderinnerungen* Frankfurt 1977

Schopenhauer, Arthur: *Aus Arthur Schopenhauer's handschriftlichem Nachlass. Abhandlungen, Anmerkungen, Aphorismen und Fragmente*. Herausgegeben von Julius Frauenstädt. Leipzig 1864

- *Sämmtliche Werke. Dritter Band. Die Welt als Wille und Vorstellung II*. Nach d. 1., von Julius Frauenstädt besorgten Gesamtausg. neu bearb. u. hrsg. von Arthur Hübscher. Mannheim 1988

Schultz, Hans Jürgen: "Humanist ohne Illusionen. Zu Werk und Person von Erich Fromm" *Evangelische Kommentare* 9 (1976), 36-38

Schulz, Siegfried: *Q. Die Spruchquelle der Evangelisten*. Zürich 1972

Schwarzschild, Steven S.: "Remembering Erich Fromm" *The Jewish Spectator* (Fall 1980), 29-33

Seeskin, Kenneth: "Jewish Neo-Kantianism: Hermann Cohen". In: Daniel H. Frank - Oliver Leaman (Eds.): *History of Jewish Philosophy*. Routledge History of World Philosophies. Volume 2. London - New York 1997, 786-798

Sesterhenn, Raimund (Hrsg.): *Das Freie Jüdische Lehrhaus - eine andere Frankfurter Schule*. Schriftenreihe der Katholischen Akademie der Erzdiözese Freiburg. München & Zürich 1987

Shapira, Jochach: "Fromm and Judaism". In: Pier Lorenzo Eletti (Ed.): *Incontro con Erich Fromm. Atti del Simposio Internazionale su Erich Fromm: "Dalla necrofilia lla biofilia: linee per una psicoanalisi umanistica"* Firenze 1986, 223-235

Simon, Ernst: "Reminiscences of Shlomo Barukh Rabinkow". In: Leo Jung (Ed.): *Sages and Saints*. The Jewish Library: Volume X. Hoboken, N.J. 1987, 119-120

Stauffer, Ethelbert: *Jesus. Gestalt und Geschichte*. Bern 1957

Stählin, Traugott: "Die Kunst des Liebens und der christliche Glaube. Gespräch und Auseinandersetzung mit Erich Fromm" *Wort und Dienst* 18 (1985), 253-265

Suzuki, Yugo: *An Examination of the Doctrine of Man of Erich Fromm and Reinhold Niebuhr*. University of Virgina Dissertation 1971

Sölle, Dorothee: *Die Hinreise. Zur religiösen Erfahrung. Texte und Überlegungen*. Stuttgart 1975

Tamaret, Aaron Samuel: "Politics and Passion: An Inquiry into the Evils of Our Time". Translated from the Hebrew and with an Introduction by Everett E. Gendler. *Judaism* 12 (Winter 1963), 36-56

Tarr, Zoltan - Marcus, Judith: "Erich Fromm und das Judentum". In: Michael Kessler - Rainer Funk (Hrsg.): *Erich Fromm und die Frankfurter Schule*. Akten des internationalen, interdisziplinären Symposions Stuttgart - Hohenheim vom 31.5 bis 2.6 1991. Tübingen 1992, 211-220

Theissen, Gerd: *Soziologie der Jesusbewegung. Ein Beitrag zur Entstehungsgeschichte des Urchristenthums*. Theologische Existenz Heute. Nr. 194. Hrsg. von Trutz Rendtorff und Karl Gerhard Steck. 2. Auflage. München 1978

- *Psychologische Aspekte paulinischer Theologie*. Forschungen zur Religion und Literatur des Alten und Neuen Testaments. Hrsg. von Wolfgang Schrage und Rudolf Smend. 131. Heft der ganzen Reihe. Göttingen 1983

Thomas, Hugh: *The Spanish Civil War*. New York 1961

Tillich, Paul: "Review of Erich Fromm: *Psychoanalysis and Religion*" *Pastoral Psychology* 2 (1951), 62-66

- "Erich Fromm's *The Sane Society*" *Pastoral Psychology* 6 (1955), 13-16

- *Das religiöse Fundament des moralischen Handelns. Schriften zur Ethik und zum Menschenbild.* Gesammelte Werke III. Stuttgart 1965

Torres, Mauro: *El irracionalismo en Erich Fromm. La posición científica del psicoanálisis.* Monogafias Psicoanaliticas, Vol. 6. México 1960

Tuckett, C.M.: "Q (Gospel Source)". In: David Noel Freedman (Ed.): *The Anchor Bible Dictionary. Volume 5.* New York - London - Toronto - Sydney - Auckland 1992, 567-572

Waschke, Ernst-Joachim: "tehom". In: Heinz-Josef Fabry - Helmer Ringgren (Hrsg.): *Theologisches Wörterbuch zum Alten Testament VIII* Stuttgart 1995, 563-571

Weinrich, Michael: "Priester der Liebe. Fragen eines Theologen an die Religionspsychologie von Erich Fromm und Hanna Wolff" *Einwürfe* 1 (1983), 90-175

Wolff, Hans Walter: *Dodekapropheton 4. Micha.* Biblischer Kommentar Altes Testaments XIV/4. Neukirchen-Vluyn 1982

Index of names

Klaus Engel

Meditation

Vol. I

History and Present Time

Frankfurt/M., Berlin, Bern, New York, Paris, Wien, 1997. 243 pp., num. fig.
ISBN 3-631-31600-3 · hardback DM 75.–*
US-ISBN 0-8204-3273-3

Meditation can be viewed as a path along which spiritual change and perfection can be achieved. The historical review gives an account of the development of meditation both in the Orient – India, Tibet, China und Japan – and in the Western World – Christianity, Judaism and Islam. The development of meditation in modern times is illustrated in the biographies of prominent representatives from both the Eastern and the Western World. The section of the book that deals with the systematics of meditation describes the practical procedures of individual meditative paths. Volume I provides the historical background for Volume II, a treatise on Empirical Research and Theory.

Contents: Historical roots of meditation · The lives of prominent figures in meditation of the present · Meditative paths and accounts of experience depicting what meditation strives to achieve

Frankfurt/M · Berlin · Bern · New York · Paris · Wien
Distribution: Verlag Peter Lang AG
Jupiterstr. 15, CH-3000 Bern 15
Fax (004131) 9402131
*includes value added tax
Our prices are subject to change without notice